INSIGHT GUIDE

CYPRUS

APA PUBLICATIONS
Part of the Langenscheidt Publishing Group

ABOUT THIS BOOK

Editorial
Project Editor
Julia Roles
Managing Editor
Emily Hatchwell
Editorial Director
Brian Bell

Distribution
UK & Ireland
GeoCenter International Ltd
The Viables Centre
Harrow Way
Basingstoke
Hants RG22 4BJ
Fax: (44) 1256-817988

United States
Langenscheidt Publishers, Inc.
46–35 54th Road
Maspeth, NY 11378
Fax: (718) 784-0640

Worldwide
APA Publications GmbH & Co.
Verlag KG (Singapore branch)
38 Joo Koon Road
Singapore 628990
Tel: (65) 865-1600
Fax: (65) 861-6438

Printing
Insight Print Services (Pte) Ltd
38 Joo Koon Road
Singapore 628990
Tel: (65) 865-1600
Fax: (65) 861-6438

© 1998 APA Publications GmbH & Co.
Verlag KG (Singapore branch)
All Rights Reserved
First Edition 1991
Third Edition 1998

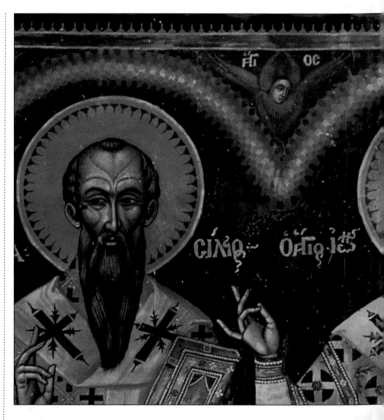

Like all Insight Guides, this book is the work of many hands, involving a team of writers and photographers – all either residents of Cyprus or experts on particular aspects of the island, from the buzzing coastal resorts to the magnificent wild flowers and the fascinating archaeological sites.

How to use this book
The book is carefully structured both to convey an understanding of the island and its cul-tures and to guide you through its attractions:

◆ To understand Cyprus today you need to know something of its past. The **History** section explains the complex story from its mythical beginnings to the modern events that have left the island scarred and divided, while the **Features** section introduces the reader to the land and its peo-ple, with topics rang-ing from the geology of the island to the Cypriots' culture and customs.

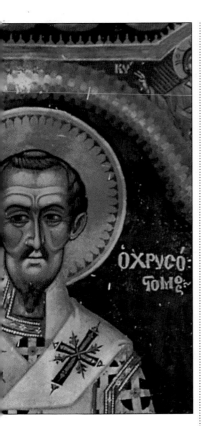

Paintings in Agios Irakleidios

◆ The main **Places** section provides a run-down of all the places worth seeing. Places of major interest are cross-referenced by numbers or letters to specially commissioned full-colour maps. Icons at the top of right-hand pages indicate where to find the relevant maps.
◆ The listings in the **Travel Tips** section give easy-to-find information on such things as transport, hotels, restaurants, shops and outdoor activities. Information may be located quickly by using the index printed on the back cover flap, which can also serve as a bookmark.
◆ The book is illustrated with **photographs** selected to convey both the beauty of the island and the character of the people.
◆ Four special **pictorial spreads** provide insight into particularly photogenic areas of interest.

The contributors
This new edition was edited by **Julia Roles**, an experienced travel guide editor and past visitor to Cyprus, who built on the original edition produced by **Hansjörg Brey** and **Claudia Müller**.

George McDonald, a tried-and-tested Insight writer and researcher, who regards Cyprus as his second home, updated most of the text, injecting new life into sections written by **Klaus Hillenbrand, Joachim Willeitner, Alexander Laudien, Günter Weiss** and **Angelika Lintzmeyer**. George McDonald also wrote several new features as well as the pictorial spreads on *Hellenic and Roman Sites, Byzantine Landmarks* and the *Akamas Peninsula.* Northern Cyprus was covered by **Marc Dubin**, while botanist **Lance Chilton** described the diversity of Cyprus's plant life in the *Island of Flowers* pictorial spread.

Bill Wassman, George Taylor and several other photographers favoured by Insight for their flair and expertise, made an indispensable contribution.

Thanks go to **Penny Phenix** for proofreading and indexing the book, and to **Sue Platt** for editing Travel Tips in order.

Map Legend

- - -	Buffer Zone
- - - -	District Boundary
- • -	National Park/Reserve
✈ ✈	Airport: International/Regional
🚌	Bus Station
P	Parking
❶	Tourist Information
✉	Post Office
⛪ † ⛪	Church/Ruins
†	Monastery
☾	Mosque
✡	Synagogue
🏰 🏯	Castle/Ruins
∴	Archaeological Site
∩	Cave
𝟙	Statue/Monument
★	Place of Interest

The main places of interest in the Places section are coordinated by number with a full-colour map (e.g. ❶), and a symbol at the top of every right-hand page tells you where to find the map.

CONTENTS

A map of Cyprus is on the inside front cover.

Routes of walking trails in the Troodos Mountains and Akamas Peninsula are shown on the inside back cover

A young boy
herds his
goats through
the arid fields
behind Agia
Napa

Insight on ...

Information panels

Travel Tips

Places

BETWEEN THE LINES

History has shaped Cyprus and, as the divided island
debates its future, the past is still a potent force

Sunshine, blue sky and beaches are the criteria that determine many people's choice of holiday destination, and in the summer months Cyprus scores a hat-trick. But the island is not only a paradise for indolent sun-seekers: archaeological finds dating back to 7,000 BC, medieval castles, remote mountain villages, and inviting cedar forests, orange groves and vineyards attract more adventurous travellers, too.

Although Cyprus, the easternmost island of the Mediterranean, is engirdled by the Near East, the pervading Eastern culture is matched by a large dose of European influences. The ancient Greeks, Rome and Byzantium, the crusaders and the Venetians, the Turks and the British have all left traces. The English writer Robert Byron, in *The Road to Oxiana* (1937), said of Cyprus: "History in this island is almost too profuse. It gives one a sort of mental indigestion." But Lawrence Durrell had a heartier appetite for history. In *Bitter Lemons*, his impressionistic account of his life on Cyprus between 1953 and 1956, he rejoiced in "the confluence of different destinies which touched and illumined the history of one small island in the eastern basin of the Levant, giving it significance and depth of focus."

Compared with the surrounding countries of Syria, Lebanon and Turkey, Cyprus is prosperous. Evidence of new industry and development is everywhere, although it is not always agreeable to the eye.

But the thin veneer of prosperity hides deep cuts. The war of 1974, which resulted in Turkey occupying almost 40 percent of the island and one in three Cypriots becoming refugees in their own country, is still fresh in local minds. As for visitors, they often face the stark choice of exploring either the north or the south, as freedom of movement across the border is almost impossible.

So Cyprus is much more than sunshine, blue sky and beaches. This Insight Guide will acquaint you with the many different aspects of the island, both positive and negative, and provide you with a true insight into the nature of the place and its people. ❏

PRECEDING PAGES: writing on the wall, Kolossi; inside Limassol's castle; the church of Agia Paraskevi in Geroskipou; sunset over the Rock of Aphrodite near Pafos.
LEFT: door in Alsancak.

Decisive Dates

7000–3000 BC: Neolithic Period. First traces of settlement on Cyprus at Choirokoitia.

4500–3500 BC: Traces of Neolithic settlement in Sotira. Ceramic production begins.

3500–2300 BC: Chalcolithic Period. Areas of settlement spread towards the west. Copper is used for making tools and jewellery. Red-on-white ceramics predominate.

2300–1050 BC: The Bronze Age. Copper production increases. First immigrants arrive from Anatolia. Trade with Syria and Egypt. Red polished ware predominates.

1900–1625 BC: First fortifications. Ceramic art developed further (white and red-on-black ware, ceramics with black rim).

1625–1050 BC: Egkomi becomes the centre of metalworking and the export trade.

1500 BC ONWARDS: Cypro-Minoan syllabic script used.

1400–1200 BC: Economic prosperity.

1200 BC ONWARDS: Large Aphrodite cult in Palea Pafos.

1200 BC: Destruction of Egkomi and Kition by "Peoples of the Sea".

1050 BC: Egkomi destroyed again, along with most Late Bronze-Age settlements. Salamis is re-founded.

1050–750 BC: The Iron Age. Phoenicians settle the island. Temple of Astarte in Kition. Royal Tombs at Salamis.

750–475 BC: The Archaic Period.

700 BC: Assyrian king Sargon II subjugates the city-kingdoms of Cyprus.

650 BC: The Royal Tombs at Tamassos are built.

560–540 BC: Egyptian rule by Ahmose II.

540 BC: Persian rule begins.

498 BC: Every kingdom on Cyprus except Amathus joins the Ionian Revolt. It fails. The Persians tighten their grip on the island.

480 BC: At the Battle of Salamis, Cyprus joins the Persians against Athens.

475–325 BC: The Classical Period. Cyprus remains a Persian naval base.

411–374 BC: King Evagoras I of Salamis. Evagoras unites the island, despite Phoenician resistance.

333 BC: Alexander the Great, with Cypriot kings' support, defeats the Persians at Issos.

325–250 BC: The Hellenistic Period. Cyprus becomes a Hellenistic cultural province, most notably under the rule of Evagoras I.

323 BC: After the death of Alexander Cyprus becomes embroiled in the various fights to succeed him.

312 BC: Zeno of Kition founds Stoicism in Athens.

310 BC: Nicocreon, King of Salamis, commits suicide. In 294 BC, Ptolemy I assumes control of the island. Cyprus becomes an Egyptian province.

294–258 BC: Ptolemaic rule. Pafos becomes the capital. Tombs of the Kings at Pafos built. Economic and cultural upswing.

58 BC: Cyprus becomes a province of Roman Empire.

AD 45: Apostles Paul and Barnabas arrive as missionaries. Temples to Apollo Hylates in Salamis, Soli and Kourion are built.

AD 115–116: Major Jewish uprising culminates in the expulsion of all Jews.

313: Christianity becomes the official religion of the Roman Empire.

3rd–4th CENTURIES: Mosaics at Pafos.

332 and 342: Pafos and Salamis destroyed by earthquakes. Reconstruction of Salamis, which, called Constantia, becomes the island's capital.

395–647: Early Byzantine Period.

5th CENTURY: The island becomes autocephalous – that is, independent of the Patriarchate of Antioch.

5th–6th CENTURIES: High point in the construction of Early Christian basilicas.

648: Arabs occupy the island.

688: Cyprus is forced to pay tribute to both the Byzantine Empire and the Caliphate.

730: Iconoclastic Controversy over the use of religious images.

787: The Council of Nicaea condemns iconoclasm and restores the iconodule doctrine, but not before a great deal of the Early Byzantine art is destroyed.

843: End of Iconoclastic Controversy.

965: Cyprus is regained for Byzantium by the emperor Nicephorus II Phocas.

965–1185: Middle Byzantine Period. Cyprus flourishes. Towns founded include Kiti, Episkopi, Lapithos.

1094: Kykkos monastery founded. Churches with several cupolae at Geroskipou, Kiti and Peristerona.

11th–12th CENTURIES: The foundation of Machairas and Neofytos monasteries, castles at Hilarion, Kantara and Buffavento.

1184: Reign of terror by Isaac Comnenos.

1191: Cyprus is taken by Richard the Lionheart.

1192: The island is sold to the Knights Templar, who then sell it to the French Crusader, Guy de Lusignan.

1192–1489: Lusignan (Frankish) rule.

13th–14th CENTURIES: St Sophia in Nicosia and St Nicholas in Famagusta, and the abbey of Bellapais are built.

1372: War between Genoa and Cyprus.

1374–1464: Genoese occupy Famagusta.

1426: Island is overrun by a marauding expedition from Egypt, and is forced to pay tribute to Cairo.

1427: Peasant uprisings.

1460–1473: Reign of Lusignan King James II.

1472: King James II marries the Venetian Caterina Cornaro, who becomes queen following the premature death of her husband.

1489: Caterina Cornaro cedes Cyprus to the Venetian Republic.

1489–1571: Venetian rule. Byzantine painting flourishes around the turn of the century.

1517: Egypt conquered by Ottoman Turks, to whom Cyprus is forced to pay tribute.

1562: Rebellion against Venetian rule.

1570: Ottoman troops invade Cyprus.

1571: Famagusta capitulates.

1571–1878: Ottoman rule, based on the millet system, which tolerates religious and ethnic diversity. Christian and Muslim uprisings among the population.

1660: The Sublime Porte bestows the right of independent representation upon bishops.

1774: The archbishop is recognised as the representative of the Christian population.

1804: The Turkish population rebels against dragoman Georgakis Kornesios, who is executed in 1808.

1816: Hala Sultan Tekkesi built near Larnaka.

1821: Mainland Greece's war of liberation against Ottoman rule results in bloody massacres, and there

is looting, directed at the Greek population of Cyprus.

1878: Cyprus is leased to England.

1914: Britain annexes Cyprus.

1930s: Economic boom. Attempts to unify Cyprus with Greece (enosis) and to liberate the island from Britain.

1955: Terrorist activities by the right-wing EOKA under the command of General Grivas in order to secure union with Greece.

1959: Archbishop Makarios III becomes president.

1960: Republic of Cyprus formed. Guarantor powers are Britain, Turkey and Greece.

1963: Fighting between Greek and Turkish Cypriots, who begin to form enclaves.

1964: United Nations peace-keeping force is sta-

tioned in Cyprus.

1967: Military junta takes over in Athens.

1974: Coup carried out against Makarios by the Cyprus National Guard, under orders of the Greek military authorities.

JULY 1974: Turkish troops invade the north of the island. Exchange of sections of the population according to their respective ethnic groups. De facto partition of Cyprus.

1977: Archbishop Makarios dies.

1983: The north unilaterally declares itself the "Turkish Republic of Northern Cyprus". Only Turkey recognises it.

1997: Cyprus is to be considered for membership of the European Union – but without the support of the Turkish Cypriots. ❑

PRECEDING PAGES: prehistoric remains at Choirokoitia.
LEFT: the goddess Aphrodite.
RIGHT: Hala Sultan Tekkesi near Larnaka.

MYTHICAL BEGINNINGS

Shrouded in myths and the mists of time, the earliest known settlements in
Cyprus are thought to date back to the Neolithic Period

A history of Cyprus usually begins with the description of the island by the Greek historian and geographer Strabo of Amasia. Although his text dates from around AD 19, he quotes several earlier sources (for example, Eratosthenes, from the 3rd century BC) and gives a detailed account of the original state of this fertile, densely-forested island.

In the following extract, he mentions its important mineral resources and agricultural products, as well as the changes brought about by civilisation: "As a fertile island, Cyprus is unsurpassed, for it produces good wine, good oil and also enough corn for its own use. In Tamassos there are, moreover, a large number of copper mines, containing copper sulphates as well as copper oxide, which is suitable for medical purposes. Eratosthenes tells us that in ancient times the plains used to be covered with dense forest and, as a result, could not be cultivated, but the mines remedied the situation, for the in-habitants chopped down trees in order to smelt copper and silver. Eratosthenes also says that ship-building was a further reason for deforestation, for the sea was a traffic route, sometimes for whole merchant fleets. Since the islanders were unable, in spite of this, to master the sheer extent of forest on the island, they allowed anyone who was willing and able to fell trees to adopt the land thus won as their own property, without having to pay any taxes." (*Strabo 14.6.5*)

Earliest history

Strabo's account does not go back as far as the Neolithic Period (7000–3000 BC), to which the earliest known settlements of Cyprus are thought to belong. Archaeologists have discovered finds linking Cyprus with Asia Minor, Syria and Palestine all over the island, many of them in fertile river-valley regions such as Choirokoitia (Khirokitia), Petra tou Limniti,

Troulli and Kalavasos. It is evident that the people lived from hunting and fishing, but the existence of primitive forms of agriculture and animal husbandry (sheep and pigs) has also been determined. From roughly 4800 BC onwards, rough brown pottery was manufactured. The houses, made of rubble, wood and

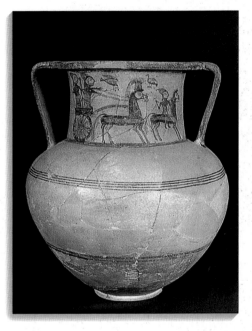

mud-brick, were elliptical in shape, and some were built underground. Religious life featured primitive forms of the Near Eastern "great mother goddess" or *magna mater*, influencing later concepts of God.

From around 3000 to 2300 BC, during the Chalcolithic (literally, "copper-stone") Period, copper played an increasingly important role, as Strabo stresses, and the metal that proved so plentiful probably gave the island its name. The word "copper" cannot be traced back to Indo-Germanic or Semitic roots (the theory that the island derived its name from the Greek word for the henna-bush or cypress tree has been rejected). One of the first copper implements, a

LEFT: a smile from former times.
RIGHT: amphora decorated with chariots and riders, from Marion (850–700 BC).

simple chisel discovered in Erimi, is thought to have been imported by immigrants from Asia Minor or southern Palestine.

Soon, however, around 2000 BC, from the Early Bronze Age onwards, Cyprus was exporting its own copper. It was tempered by a complicated process, and then reduced to metal over a charcoal fire. Tamassos (Politiko), mentioned by Strabo, was the centre of copper production on Cyprus from the Middle Bronze Age (2000–1600 BC) onwards. The only evidence of settlements from this period are tombs, but it is thought that the island must have been densely populated and prosperous.

the hands of the Hyksos Kingdom (c. 1650–1550 BC), although current evidence suggests that Cyprus was not subjected to any large-scale raids.

In the Late Bronze Age (1600–1050 BC), Cyprus received a major influx of immigrants, initially merchants and craftsmen and then, by the end of the 13th century BC, refugees: the Greek Achaeans, bearing the Mycenaean culture. Integration with the indigenous population, the so-called "Eteo-Cypriots", or "True Cypriots" (traces of whose non-Greek and also non-Semitic language survived in Cypro-Minoan syllabic script until the 4th century AD,

It was in close contact with the rest of the eastern Mediterranean. The earlier advanced civilisations of Mesopotamia, for instance, were developing fast, and the pyramids were being built in Egypt. In particular, it kept in touch with the coast of Syria and Palestine, and with Minoan Crete.

Cyprus retained its political independence and its unique culture based on the production of weapons and other high-quality metal artefacts and ceramics featuring red-on-black paintings of men and animals. Various fortifications (e.g. in Krini, Agios Sozomenos and Nitovikla) were built during this period, a sign of the harassment the island was receiving at

especially in the kingdom of Amathus), resulted in the birth of a Near-Eastern/Aegean/Greek culture unique in the Mediterranean.

Vases portraying chariots, ships, bulls, birds and human figures, as well as high-quality ivory carvings and seals, all bear magnificent witness to this period.

Archaic cults and myths

Later records (in particular those of Herodotus) and archaeological finds give us only a vague idea of the sheer profusion of temples and cults on Cyprus, but it seems that many were ecstatic as well as mystic: for example, Temple IV at Kition (Citium) contained an opium pipe for religious use. The cult of Aphrodite (symbol of the island for medieval religious travellers and pilgrims) at Pafos is typical of the island's mixed religious culture, a characteristic which has its roots far back in the Bronze Age. In Salamis a male deity was worshipped who was subsequently put on an equal footing with Zeus. The Semitic god Resheph, with his two horns, became the mighty Apollo.

According to legend, Cinyras was priest-king of Old Pafos before being driven from power

SANCTUARIES

There are few places in the Mediterranean that had so many sanctuaries in such a confined area. The goddess Aphrodite alone was worshipped at 12 different sites on the island.

written evidence identifying Cyprus with craftsmanship (*Il. II, 19-23*).

The legend of Agapenor and Cinyras reflects the generally peaceful colonisation by the Greek Achaeans of areas that had often already been settled.

The "Achaean Coast" – the name given to the northern tip of the island – the Mycenae-like fortifications at Egkomi, Palaeokastro, Maa and Kition, ceramics, and traces of the Arcadian-Aeolic languages in Greek-Cypriot names and inscrip-

by Agapenor, king of Tegea and leader of the Arcadian troops at Troy.

Agapenor's ship was driven off course after the city had fallen, and he ended up at Pafos. Pindar, who died in 445 BC, refers to Cinyras as "the darling of Apollo, the gentle priest of Aphrodite" (*Pyth. Ode 2.15*), and his forefathers are supposed to have come from Ashur. Agapenor built a new temple of Aphrodite.

Homer's *Iliad* tells us that Agamemnon, the Greek leader at Troy, received a coat of mail from Cinyras as a present. This is the earliest

LEFT: one of the many fertility symbols.
RIGHT: embossed gold plaques (700 BC).

tions all provide conclusive proof of Achaean colonisation.

Cyprus, known as *Alashiya* or *Alasia* in Ugaritic and Egyptian records because of its capital of Alashiya (Egkomi) of that time, and as *Kittim* to the Hebrews (cf. *Jes. 23,1 and 12*), retained its political independence right up to the end of the Late Bronze Age – even when Rameses III (1192–1160 BC) claimed sovereignty over the island.

The Early Iron Age

When many Late Bronze Age settlements were destroyed by earthquakes around 1050 BC (such as Egkomi and Kition), and while colonisation

Aphrodite

Aphrodite, known as Venus to the Romans, was worshipped by several cultures in the ancient world, and was also associated with Ishtar and Astarte. She originally arrived from the east, as the *magna mater*, or great mother, and was worshipped as the goddess of war as well as the goddess of the sea. Her reputation for valour did not last, however. She was disarmed by the ancient Greeks and thus reduced to the erotic functions and attributes associated with her today

In the *Iliad*, Homer thus had Zeus, the father of the

gods, say: "Fighting, my child, is not for you. You are in charge of wedlock and the tender passions."

In the 12th century BC, long before Homer wrote the *Iliad*, the first sanctuary to Aphrodite was built at Palaia (Old) Pafos. Its high priest was Pafos's founder-king, Cinyras. As Herodotus mentions, the cult in Palaia Pafos (Kouklia) included temple prostitution, whereby young women sacrificed their virginity, ostensibly to the goddess though, in fact, to whomever happened to be passing the temple at the time. The usual procedure was for the virgins to go to the temple, hang around until chosen by a man, and then submit to a night of unbridled passion. The proceeds earned from such sacrifice were dedicated to the goddess. In spring, the temple's festival of Aphrodite and her lover

Adonis drew pilgrims from all over the ancient world.

Surviving artefacts from the cult include a statue of a phallus with salt, symbolising the birth of Aphrodite from the sea-foam; this is a myth famously illustrated by Botticelli's *The Birth of Venus*, in which the goddess rises from the waves on a vast cockle shell. According to the legend related by Hesiod, Aphrodite was born from the white foam produced from the severed genitals of Uranus (Heaven) when he was castrated by the Titans. (According to some versions of the legend, she originally rose from the waves off the island of Kythera in the Peloponnese but, finding the land there too rocky, sped away on her shell to Cyprus.) The claim that Aphrodite was descended from a man is usually seen as an attempt to integrate the eastern goddess of fertility into the patriarchal pantheon of Greek gods. She was worshipped as Aphroditos, a bearded man, in many Cypriot towns, particularly at Amathus.

As patroness of love and desire, and as an embodiment of feminine beauty, Aphrodite features in - numerous Greek myths, including the legend of Atalanta, also associated with Cyprus, in which the eponymous heroine is left to perish at birth by her father and must fend for herself in the forests. She grows into a beautiful woman, and offers to marry anyone who can outrun her – but vows to spear those whom she overtakes. Among the suitors is Hippomenes, a great-grandson of the sea-god Poseidon. Just before the contest begins, Eros, son of Aphrodite, shoots one of his famous arrows at Atalanta. Overcome with love for Hippomenes and fearful of his fate, she implores him not to enter the race. Distraught at her inability to change the rules of the contest, which she herself has devised, Atalanta thinks of a trick: she plucks three golden apples from a tree on Cyprus and tells Hippomenes to drop them as he runs. When he drops them, she stops to pick them up, and thus loses the race to Hippomenes, who consequently wins happiness for them both.

Aphrodite's legendary birthplace, the rock known as Petra tou Romiou to the south of Pafos, is bewitching, and especially romantic at sunset.

If you have come to Cyprus in the hope of finding something of the Aphrodite spirit, or have brought somebody who might benefit from her influence, it might also help to take a quick swig from the Fontana Amorosa. The waters of this spring, found at the northwestern point of the Akamas peninsula, not far from the Baths of Aphrodite, are said to enamour anyone who drinks them. ❑

LEFT: the Baths of Aphrodite in the Akamas peninsula.

continued elsewhere (for example in Palaia Pafos, today's Kouklia), the so-called Dark Age descended on Cyprus and Greece. The island became insignificant and poverty-stricken. The only archaeological evidence there is about this period comes from finds in family tombs.

But the Early Iron Age (1050–750 BC) did see the arrival on Cyprus of Phoenicians from Tyre. They were experienced merchants and sailors, and introduced their highly sophisticated Semitic-Syrian culture to the island.

At first only trading posts were founded on Cyprus, but later on – perhaps as early as the 10th century BC – Kition had become a full-

The Archaic Period

During the so-called "Archaic Period" of Assyrian domination (*circa* 750–470 BC), seven Cypriot kings were overthrown, as a stele erected at Kition by the Assyrian king Sargon II (721–705 BC) makes clear. The cities were not destroyed, however; indeed, Assyrian influence was probably rather nominal.

It is at this stage that the seven kings of Cyprus (or possibly 10 of them: Assyrian documents are not quite clear on this) play a more distinct role. Their city-kingdoms were hereditary, and were probably sacred in character too, especially the one at Pafos. In some cities, such

blown colony, independent of the rest of the country, with its own king.

After 850 BC, Phoenician temples to Astarte and Melqart were built above the remains of older temples that had probably been destroyed by earthquakes.

The magnificent Royal Tombs of Salamis, which date from the end of the Early Iron Age, bear witness to the prosperity of the upper social classes during this era. Ceramics dating from this period developed the ideas and designs of the Late Bronze Age, and have been traced to Eteo-Cypriot influences.

ABOVE: gold jewellery dating from 750–600 BC.

as Amathus and Kition, the dynasties were of Phoenician descent, while others were ruled by Greek dynasties, such as the Teucrid dynasty in Salamis and the Cinyras dynasty in Pafos.

Egyptian domination

After the break-up of the Assyrian Empire, there came a brief period of Egyptian domination of Cyprus, under Pharaoh Ahmose II (569–525 BC); politically this period was peaceful and not particularly significant, but the influence of Egyptian culture was very evident on the island. Human figures acquired a rigidity, similar to that of the Kouroi style of Ancient Greece, and scarabs were copied.

Cyprus under Persian rule

In 545 BC the Cypriot kings transferred their allegiance to the initially very relaxed rule of the mighty Achaemenid (Persian) kingdom, and deferred to a culturally superior power structure that was also open to Greek influence. In fact, this was the greatest structure of its kind to have arisen in the Near East before Alexander the Great. Cyprus thus became embroiled in the tensions between Greece and Persia, and in 498 BC it joined the Ionian Revolt in western Asia Minor.

> **THE HELLENISTIC ERA**
>
> While Cyprus still retained Near-Eastern characteristics, the cultural influence in the island was predominantly Hellenistic.

Herodotus doesn't relate why they decided to do this, and makes no mention of any Greek nationalist sentiment on Cyprus.

Onesilos, the younger brother of the king of Salamis, persuaded all of Cyprus's major cities to join the Greek side. Only Amathus, with its strong Eteo-Cypriot and Phoenician influence, demurred. Once the ignominious revolt had ended, its inhabitants impaled the head of Onesilos above their city gates. At the famous and decisive battle against the Persians near Salamis, the king of Kourion, Stasenor, deserted his allies, and the Salaminians followed suit. It was only in Soli that the Persians encountered tougher resistance. Rulers friendly to Persia were installed in power, and supplied with Persian troops for protection.

At the Battle of Salamis in 480 BC, a Cypriot contingent of 150 ships fought on the side of the Persians, alongside Egyptians, Cilicians and Pamphylians. "A bunch of good-for-nothings", pronounced Queen Artemisia of Caria (*Herodotus VIII, 68*).

Greeks against Persians

During this period (470–325 BC) Cyprus continued to be affected by the political tensions between Greece and Persia. Nevertheless, neither Athens nor Sparta succeeded in establishing a firm foothold on Cyprus for any length of time. By now the island had become a highly desirable naval base, as well as a valuable source of wood for shipbuilding, and Cyprus remained Persia's most important Mediterranean naval base; the Persian fleet which put paid to Spartan naval domination near Knidos in 394 BC set sail from Cyprus.

At this time, Cypriot art came under strong Attic influence, as discoveries in the handsome palace of Vouni reveal. Greek sculpture and vase-painting was widely imitated, but the traditional Cypriot forms held their own against the new trends and influences.

King Evagoras I of Salamis (411–374 BC) became a symbol of Attic influence. He was an adept politician, who had wrested control of Salamis from a Tyrian called Abdemon, under the successful pretext of being descended from the city's ancient kings. He capitalised on the tensions between Persia and Athens, and despite resistance from the Phoenician-based dynasties of Kition, Amathus, Golgoi and Soli, he succeeded, albeit by force, in uniting the island politically for the first time. According to his eulogist, Isocrates, "[Evagoras] assumed control of the government [of Salamis], which as a result of Phoenician domination was run by barbarians; the city despised the Greeks, showed no interest in the arts and had neither a market place nor a harbour; Evagoras remedied all these deficiencies and increased the city's territory still further, surrounding it with new walls and providing it with triremes..." ❑

LEFT: limestone head of a general or king.
RIGHT: statue of Aphrodite in the Pafos museum.

HELLENES AND ROMANS

The importance of the Hellenes and Romans in the history of Cyprus is evident from the profusion of their cultural remains throughout the island

The history of Cyprus is in many ways quite different from the histories of other Mediterranean regions: the island had experienced a special kind of "Hellenism". There was an interplay of Greek and Near Eastern influence in its political, cultural and religious life long before the mighty campaigns o f the great was a strategic base, and as a supplier of copper, silver, grain and wood (for use in shipbuilding), it acquired vital economic importance. Politically, however, its kingdoms were divided into two camps: Salamis, Pafos, Soli and Amathus lined up strongly on the side of the Ptolemies; while Kition, Lapithos,

Macedonian general Alexander the Great. So when a Cypriot fleet, with soldiers and technicians, fought alongside Alexander's army in his campaign to conquer the east, the island's integration into his enormous empire (356–323 BC), which stretched to India, was inevitable.

Power struggles

The power struggles that ensued between Alexander the Great's successors – Ptolemy, governor of Egypt; King Antigonus, the governor of Phrygia, whose power base was Macedonia and Greece; and the Seleucid Empire, based in Asia Minor, Syria and Persia – proved politically disastrous for Cyprus. The island

Keryneia and Marion took the side of Antigonus (the rulers of Kition and Lapithos were of Phoenician descent, but spoke Greek).

In 318 BC Ptolemy set out to subdue the cities. Only Nicocles of Pafos tried to oppose him. The consequences were tragic: King Nicocles fell on his sword, together with his wife and family. Inscriptions inform us that he was closely connected with the Hellenism of Argos, Delos and Delphi, and the luxury and splendour of his court were embellished into legends.

By the beginning of the 2nd century BC an astoundingly diverse assortment of peoples were living on Cyprus, including a Jewish community.

The Ptolemaic Kings

For the next two centuries (294–58 BC) Cyprus was a province of Ptolemaic Egypt, ruled by a governor-general, or *strategus*. These *strategoi* resided in Nea Pafos, and were often related to the Ptolemaic royal family. The *strategus* of Cyprus was also in full command of the entire Egyptian navy. The local dialect on Cyprus was replaced by the common idiom of Hellenistic Greek, and the island's coins started to bear the heads of the ruling Ptolemies. The cities on the island were ruled by tough garrisons of foreign mercenaries under the command of Greek officers (most of whom were not Cypriots), and

rulers of the island. The cities all joined forces to form a new cultural organisation which was known as the *Koinon Kyprion.*

Egyptian cultural and religious influence, in particular that of Alexandria, the centre of Hellenistic city culture, increased on the island. Serapis, Isis, Osiris, Zeus and the Libyan god Ammon were just a few of the deities worshipped, and the market-places and gymnasia were decorated with sculptures and carvings influenced by Alexandrian craftsmen. The "Tombs of the Kings" at Nea Pafos (Kato Pafos) near Ktima are the most important archaeological find dating from the Hellenistic

by local Phoenician families (such as the Lapithos and Kitions). Local Greek Cypriots started filling important political posts only at the beginning of the 1st century BC.

It was in the realms of culture, arts and religion that the flourishing cities, with their magnificent market-places, gymnasia and theatres, enjoyed most independence. New towns were founded, three of which were called Arsinoë in tribute to the sister of Philadephus, one of the Ptolemaic

period on Cyprus and are based on Egyptian designs. Cypriot literature was written exclusively in Greek, and the island produced a modicum of literary talent, such as Stasinos with his epic *Kypria*, and Sopatros, who wrote comedies.

The philosopher Zeno of Kition (334–262 BC) occupies a central place in the history of European thought. The son of a merchant named Mnaseas – the Greek version of the Phoenician name Manasse or Menahem – he frequented as a young man the philosophy schools of Crates, Stilpon and Xenocrates in Athens. In 308 BC he founded his own Athens school: the Stoic School. His ideas were heavily influenced by Greek tradition.

PRECEDING PAGES: the Battle of Salamis against the Athenians.
LEFT: mosaic from the Cyprus Museum, Nicosia.
RIGHT: Aphrodite and Apollo, most favoured deities.

Roman rule

A rather suspect testament legitimised the Senate's decision to take control of Cyprus on a "provisional basis". Although Egypt managed to regain the island twice during the civil wars of the Republic, the Romans held on to Cyprus for good once the Empire was established. The puritanical Marcus Portius Cato tried to persuade the last of the Ptolemaic rulers to relinquish all claim to Cyprus in return for the office of high priest of the Aphrodite cult at Pafos (the unfortunate ruler

ROMAN CONTROL

The transfer of control of Cyprus to the Roman Empire in 58 BC completed Roman domination of the Mediterranean and left Egypt politically isolated.

Romani) dating from this period can still be seen in the area around Salamis, which gradually decreased in importance as Pafos grew. Two well-preserved Roman theatres can be seen at Soli and Kourion.

The splendid mosaics at the 3rd-century, 70-room House of Dionysos at Nea Pafos – as well as the fine mosaics discovered in Kourion – illustrate the smoothness of the cultural transition. An oath of allegiance to the emperor Tiberius, dating from AD 14, demonstrates Cyprus's loyalty to Rome:

preferred to commit suicide instead). The orator Cicero was one of the island's first proconsuls, but even he, staunch opposer of corruption and injustice, was noticeably passive in his attitude towards the various civil servants who bled the island dry with extortionate "loans".

The Romans adopted the original strict administrative structure of the Ptolemies. Cyprus was now ruled by a proconsul, and his officials, from Pafos. The road network on the island was improved, but there were few changes which affected the native population. The Roman contingent on Cyprus numbered only 2,000 men. Ruins of some of the spacious public buildings (*ager publicus populi*

"By our Aphrodite of the mountains, by our mistress, by our Apollo Hylates, by our Apollo of Kyrenia… by all the gods of Cyprus together with the council, the gods and goddesses of our fathers who belong to this island, the birthplace of Aphrodite, by Caesar Augustus who is our god, by eternal Rome and by all other gods and goddesses, we and our children do hereby solemnly swear… to remain loyal to Tiberius Caesar and to honour him… to accord holy honours to Rome and to Tiberius Caesar Augustus… and only to the sons of his blood." (*Rise and Fall of the Roman World* by T.B. Mitford.) ❐

LEFT: hedonistic pursuits.

Zeno: The original indifferent Stoic

Stoic indifference is an attitude which visitors often need in Cyprus, especially at those times when their wishes are not answered as quickly or as efficiently as they might be in another country. It is fitting, therefore, that the philosophy of Stoicism dates back to the Cypriot philosopher Zeno, born in 336 BC in Kition (Latin *Citium*), north of today's Larnaka. In the words of the Cyprus expert F. G. Maier, Cyprus's most famous Stoic made "a unique and inestimable contribution to the history of European thought".

Impressed from an early age by the Greek philosophers, and by Socrates in particular, Zeno left Cyprus around 312 BC to go to Athens where he could devote himself to the study of philosophy. He visited various philosophy schools in the city, including that of the famous Cynic, Crates. In contrast to today's definition of this term, the Cynics of ancient times were not bitter and vicious fault-finders but thinkers whose philosophy stressed the benefits of returning to a more "natural" life, free of social conventions.

Around the year 300 BC, Zeno decided to found his own school. Since he did not have the capital to buy a building of his own, and possibly because of his cynical attitude to property, he gave his lectures in the agora in Athens, in the colonnade know as the *stoa poikile*. It was this venue which gave Stoicism its name.

The Stoic school was less formally organised than some of its competitors, such as the Epicurean or Peripatetic school. Zeno was the only philosopher in Athens at that time to run a school of philosophy from a public building.

Zeno practised what he preached: his lifestyle was austere. He said that man's highest aim in life should be to live in harmony with nature, and he maintained that the conscious abstinence from passion and the active cultivation of apathy allowed man to develop enough insensitivity to face the fortunes and ills of his life with indifference.

Against the laws of nature, he also maintained, the joys and sorrows of the individual were of no significance. If man lived a life according to rationally established values, one that was in harmony with his own inner being, he would then become insensitive to such things as pain, suffering, love and even death.

RIGHT: the philosopher Zeno.

This philosophy was accompanied by a belief in the divine corporeality of all things.

To begin with, enthusiasm for Zeno's teachings was slow, though his short work, the *Politea*, attracted more attention and abuse than any other work by a Stoic (by the mid-2nd century onwards Stoics were trying to minimise the importance attributed to this work). After Zeno's death, his successor, Ariston of Chios, diverged from Zeno's teachings and brought the Stoic school to the verge of insignificance.

It was only under Chrysippus of Soli (281–208 BC) that the school flourished again: Chrysippus adhered strictly to Zeno's original teachings, but bolstered them with tenets of his own, thereby laying the foun-

ZENO FLORVIT OLIMP. 130
Exigua prudens arctatur zeno tabella'
Immensum cuius mentis acumen erat.

dations for Stoicism as understood today. In the words of Diogenes Laertius, in *The Lives and Opinions of the Philosophers*, "Without Chrysippus there would have been no Stoa."

Zeno's teachings were particularly popular in the Roman Empire, especially since they gave man the possibility of securing a personal happiness quite independent of external circumstances and social conditions. The Roman emperor Marcus Aurelius (AD 121–180), a supporter of Stoicism, illustrated what he called the "trivial nature of life" with the slogan "a drop of sperm today, a handful of ashes tomorrow!" Zeno died at the age of 72 when he committed suicide. What, one wonders, could have robbed him of his famous indifference? ❑

SITES TO BEHOLD – OF HELLENES AND ROMANS

Cyprus has a wealth of remains of the Greek and Roman civilisations – in the ground, dotting the landscape and filling the shelves in museums

From 325 BC, when Cyprus joined the empire of Alexander the Great, through the Roman era and up to the 7th century, when the island came under fire from the Arabs, Cyprus enjoyed almost 1,000 years of peace. The Greeks and Romans put their lengthy period of leisure to good use.

Greek culture reigned supreme under the Hellenistic rulers. Cypriot cities were graced with fine market-places and temples, and many of today's top archaeological sites were begun at this time. During six centuries of the Pax Romana, only the occasional earthquake troubled the otherwise prosperous cities. Pafos, the seat of the Roman governor, was endowed with magnificent villas and mosaics and is now a designated UNESCO World Cultural Heritage Site.

Pafos remains the single biggest complex of ancient ruins, even though much of the site has recently disappeared beneath a car park. This, and other impressive ancient sites, such as the hillside Theatre at Kourion, and the city of Salamis in northern Cyprus, can stand comparison with all but the very best of the Mediterranean's Greek and Roman heritage.

Ancient sites appear in the most unlikely places, including incorporated into resort hotels. It is often the least-visited sites which offer the most memorable experience. The windy tranquility of the Greco-Persian palace at Vouni in the north and the underwater ruins of the harbour at Amathous, to mention just a couple, may offer the best chance for those who want time and space to hear the ghostly voices of ancient times.

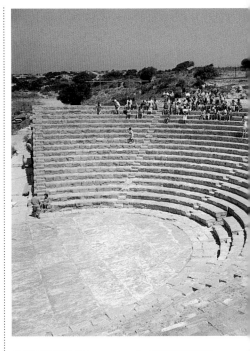

▽ **WOODLAND GOD**
The Greek god Apollo was worshipped at Kourion in the guise of Apollo Hylates, god of the forests. Partially restored, his sanctuary conjures up a vivid image of the ancient scene.

▷ **PICTURE SHOW**
The Roman-era mosaics at Pafos are among the most dazzling and best-preserved in the Mediterranean. This mosaic is from the House of Theseus, probably the Roman governor's palace.

▽ **MARKET FORCES**
The *agora* (market-place) of ancient Amathous stands beside the busy coast road east of Limassol. More of the ancient city, including its Phoenician-era harbour, lies in the sea just off the rocky shore.

◁ **NAKED TRUTH**
This bronze statue of the Roman Emperor Septimus Severus (ruled AD 193–211) was found at the village of Voni in northern Cyprus and is now a prized exhibit at the Cyprus Museum in Nicosia.

◁ THEATRICAL SCENE
The spectacularly sited odeon at Kourion was built by the Greeks, used by the Romans as a blood sports arena and, today, is again a venue for classical drama.

△ CRAZY PAVING
Mosaics were a widespread art form in Cyprus in the classical period, and the technique was revived much later, for use in Early Christian and Byzantine churches.

EMBARRASSMENT OF RICHES

It is almost impossible to plough anywhere in Cyprus without turning up evidence of the cultures which have left their imprint on the land. In the narrow Kalavasos Valley (near Limassol) alone, several hundred historic sites have been identified.

For the inevitably under-resourced and overworked Department of Antiquities, rescue archaeology is a top priority; when one of Cyprus's many development schemes hits ancient remains, researchers rush in to pick up the pieces before it is too late.

Foreign missions play an important role in excavations. Pictured above is the site at Fabrica Hill (Nea Pafos), where Australian excavators have brought to light an 8,000-seat Greek Theatre. The effective international cultural boycott of northern Cyprus means that little excavation work goes on there; indeed some partially excavated sites, including Salamis and Soloi, seem to be in danger of neglect.

Periods closer to our own also demand attention. One Cypriot archaeologist reckons that much of her career will be spent among the ruins of a Venetian sugar factory at Kolossi.

△ LAST RESORT
The Tombs of the Kings are located beside the sea at Pafos. No kings were buried here but it was the last resting place of Pafos's high and mighty.

▽ ROMANCING THE STONE
An indelible air of romance wafts around the Rock of Aphrodite outside Pafos, where the Greek goddess of love was borne ashore from the sea foam.

THE RISE OF THE CHURCH

A few Cypriots became Christians as early as AD 40 and their numbers
increased rapidly after the conversion of Emperor Constantine

The simple decision of the Roman emperor Constantine (*circa* AD 247–337) to give preferential treatment to Christianity as opposed to the many other forms of religion in the Roman Empire led to far-reaching religious, cultural and political changes across the whole Mediterranean region. The Christians, until then widely persecuted, now became the merciless persecutors of their pagan rivals. A politically and economically powerful ecclesiastical hierarchy arose, a kind of "state within a state". The effects this had on Cyprus, with its strong pagan traditions, were immense.

The spread of Christianity

From quite early on, perhaps even as early as AD 40, a number of Cypriots had been followers of St Stephen in Jerusalem. Some also became missionaries in Syrian Antioch, and on Cyprus itself (see *Apostles 11,19 f.*). A few years later, the converted Cypriot Jew Joseph Barnabas (see *Apostles 13,14 f.*) began his own missionary work, initially with the Apostle Paul. Travelling from Salamis to Pafos, they came across several Jewish communities.

The conversion of Roman proconsul Sergius Paulus (*circa* AD 46–48) is undisputed, but the story relating to the appointment of bishops in Soli and Tamassos at about the same time belongs to the realms of legend rather than historical fact.

Unlike Asia Minor, Cyprus bears few traces of Christianity before Constantine's time. After the conversion of Constantine, however, there was a swift increase in the number of bishoprics (there were 12 in AD 344 and 15 by AD 400), reflecting the island's intensive Christianisation. The emperor's mother, St Helena, is said to have brought several reliquaries of the Cross to Cyprus on her return from Jerusalem (some of them still survive in the island's monasteries, for example at Stavrovouni).

PRECEDING PAGES: Christ between the Apostles in the church of Agios Neofytos, near Pafos.
LEFT: Virgin and Child, Agios Lazaros, Larnaka.
RIGHT: St John with toothache, in Panagia Kiti.

Early Christian basilica construction reached its zenith in the 5th and 6th centuries. Two particularly impressive examples are the remains of a three-aisled basilica with mosaic decoration at Kourion, and the extensive church complex (four basilicas with hot springs) at Cape Drepanum. Very little, however, remains of the former seven-aisled basilica

at Salamis, a building which broke new architectural ground.

It was in the 5th century that the Church of Cyprus succeeded in becoming autocephalous, in other words, independent of other patriarchates, particularly that of Antioch – thus giving the archbishop of Cyprus a great deal of political power right up to the present day. It came about when Archbishop Anthemius of Constantia (Salamis), prompted by a vision, found the Gospel of St Mark in the tomb of St Barnabas. He sent it to the emperor Zeno in AD 488, who forthwith granted the archbishop of Cyprus the special imperial privileges of carrying a sceptre rather than a crozier, wearing a purple cloak, and writing his signature in red ink. Special status was confirmed at a council held in AD 692, the so-called Trullanum.

The Byzantine Empire

As a province belonging to the Diocese of the Orient, and governed by a consul based in Salamis (which became known as Constantia after AD 342), Cyprus was subject to the Eastern or Byzantine Empire at Constantinople. In the 6th century the island became an independent administrative unit, known as *quaestura*

<table>
<tr><td>ROMAN RICHES</td></tr>
<tr><td>In the second half of the 4th century, the Roman historian Festus Rufius commented that the island of Cyprus was "famed for its riches".</td></tr>
</table>

and the use of unleavened bread for the Sacrament were major bones of contention, and divided believers when they came up against representatives of Western Christianity – the so-called "Latins" – in the 13th century. Orthodoxy remained firm, however, and exerts a strong influence on the people of Cyprus to this day.

Taking traditional Roman administration as its model, the Byzantine Empire developed its own system of officials. They were well known for their ruthlessness

exercitus – a sign of its growing importance. It was thus a part of the Byzantine Empire, and as such gradually dissolved its political and cultural links with the West, and with the capital city of Rome. It was to survive the decline of the western half of the Empire by more than 1,000 years.

Several new church movements developed under the tough conditions of the Eastern or Byzantine Empire which was now taking shape. Among them was the Orthodox Church, which comprised primarily Greek-speaking Christians and possessed its own dogma and special liturgical and institutional forms. The marriage of priests, the lack of a papal primate

and the islanders frequently suffered at their hands. Nevertheless, up until the Arab raids of the 7th century – apart from a few attacks by pirates from the mainland around AD 404, and a brief uprising led by a governor – the island enjoyed 300 years of peace, just as it had during pagan Roman times. However, a period of severe drought at the beginning of the 4th century greatly reduced the island's population, and two earthquakes in AD 332 and 342 destroyed Pafos and Salamis (Constantia). Only Salamis – the seat of the consul – was rebuilt.

Cyprus was the first place to be attacked by the Arabs in their astonishingly swift rampage through the Mediterranean in the 7th century.

The first Arabian Mediterranean fleet was built in Syria in AD 648, and Cyprus was conquered just one year later in AD 649. The next three centuries, up until the final recapture of the island by Byzantine emperor Nicephorus II Phocas in the year 965, were among the darkest in the entire history of Cyprus: in 688 it was obliged to pay tribute to both the Byzantine Empire and the Islamic Caliphate. This unusual state of joint-owned neutrality, unique in the Mediterranean, did not stop either side from pillaging the island's cities, taking punitive action and forcing large sections of the population off the island altogether.

transferred to the island in the second half of the 6th century to help guard it) mingled with the militarily weak Cypriots, producing a population described by the Byzantine patriarch Nikolaos Mystikos at the beginning of the 10th century as not raising its hand against either the Byzantine Empire or the Caliphate, and made up of loyal vassals who were "more loyal to the Arabs than to the Byzantines".

Many Cypriots were forced to withdraw to remote areas in the mountains; their cities lay in ruins. Between 911 and 912 the island was pillaged for a full four months by a pirate, Damianus of Tarsus.

Between 692 and 698, following a new resettlement programme instigated by the Byzantine emperor and yet another Arab invasion, Cyprus became almost completely depopulated. Its inhabitants were later allowed to return from Syria and Asia Minor. No evidence remains as to whether the population underwent Islamisation at the hands of the Arabs, nor whether any Islamic families settled on Cyprus on a permanent basis. An Armenian element (over 3,000 Armenians had been

LEFT: fresco in St John's cathedral, Nicosia.
ABOVE: the legends of the saints provide endless inspiration for icon painters.

The Early Middle Ages

From 965 and 1192 the island was ruled by a Katepano and his officials, and was subject solely to the Byzantine Empire. This was a period of economic and cultural prosperity for the ecclesiastical élite, who busied themselves building monasteries and churches, while the officials, despite the church's protests, drained the rural population dry. The law tied most country people to the land; even though some had the status of peasant proprietors or free tenants, they were still subject to ferocious taxation. In a dialogue, part of which is reprinted here, written at the end of the 11th century, Nikolaos Muzalon, the archbishop of Cyprus, uses such unflattering terms as "Prince of the Evil Spirits" and "Beelzebub" to describe his chief official, and refers to his tax-collectors as "out-and-out robbers":

Questioner: *Does the land (on Cyprus) produce anything?*
Muzalon: *All kinds of fruit grow there.*
Questioner: *Gratifying indeed!*
Muzalon: *It only results in more complaints.*
Questioner: *How do you mean?*
Muzalon: *The tax-collectors devour whatever the farmers produce.*
Questioner: *A tragedy!*
Muzalon: *And they demand even more besides.*
Questioner: *Oh dear!*
Muzalon: *They maltreat those who have no property of their own...*

A class made up of merchants and business-men was responsible for the foundation of several new towns, including Kiti, Lapithos and Episkopi. As elsewhere in Byzantium they were all built at a respectful distance from the coast. It was also at this point that the island's most magnificent monasteries were built, with their wealth of splendid paintings and frescoes: Kykkos, under the patronage of Emperor Alexius Comnenos, with its famous icon of the Virgin Mary, and later the Machairas and Neofytos monasteries.

The arrival of the crusaders, the proximity of the Christian kingdom of Little Armenia in Asia Minor and the increasing activity of the Italian seafaring towns eventually put Cyprus back on the Mediterranean map. In 1148 Venice obtained numerous and far-reaching trading privileges on the island.

Historically, there seem to be no traces at all of any Cypriot regional or national feeling. The short-lived and bloodily suppressed attempts at independence on behalf of individual Byzantine governors that took place in 1042 and 1092 were probably inspired by demands for a cut in the level of taxation rather than strong nationalist feelings. And when the brutal despot Isaac Comnenos – a relative of the imperial family in Constantinople – finally succeeded in freeing himself from central control in 1184, it was a rebellion from above rather than below, and it had no popular support. ❑

RIGHT: a relic containing fibres from the hemp ropes said to have bound Christ to the cross is kept in the Omodos monastery, in the Troodos Mountains.

CRUSADERS, LUSIGNANS AND VENETIANS

Between 1191 and 1571 Cyprus was first won by Richard I of England and then ruled by the Knights Templar, the Lusignans and lastly the Venetians

The 900-years of East Roman-Byzantine imperial rule came to an end almost accidentally. What ensued was almost half a millennium of Latin rule in the Eastern Mediterranean, a period that even outlasted the crusader states of Palestine. The catalyst in this power shift was King Richard I of England.

Seized by the English

Richard the Lionheart's journey to Palestine in May 1192 was a difficult one: some of his ships sank, and the one carrying his bride, Berengaria, met with only slightly less danger when it limped into port near Limassol and was received by the Byzantine usurper Isaac Comnenos, mentioned earlier. Comnenos hated Latins, and held the lady and her entourage as prisoners, even depriving them of water.

When Richard arrived on the island several days later, he swore revenge and immediately requested reinforcements from Palestine. In the battle which followed Comnenos, underestimating Richard's strength, suffered a quick defeat, and went down in history as the last Byzantine ruler.

In general, the Cypriot population, mostly Greek Orthodox and Armenian, watched the collapse of Byzantine rule impassively, though some positively welcomed it. But the Cypriots were soon forced to realise the drawbacks of Crusader rule: the population was allowed no say in government, they were obliged to part with 50 percent of their capital, all the island's castles were occupied by Crusaders, and the men were made to shave off their beards as a sign of subjugation. In a letter written shortly after the arrival of the Crusaders, the Greek

monk Neofytos, said: "Our country is now no better than a sea whipped up by storm winds." The population was still subject to Byzantine law, however, and for the time being, ecclesiastical and religious matters were left alone.

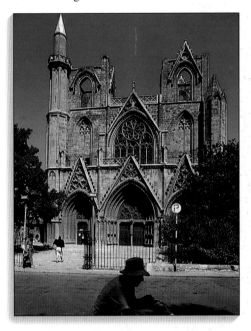

The Knights Templar

As far as Richard was concerned, the island was a bonus: Comnenos had been an exceedingly greedy despot, and had left considerable riches. Richard tried to trade the island for half of Flanders but, unsuccessful in his scheme, he sold it to the crusading order of the Knights Templar in return for 40,000 dinars and the pledge of a further 60,000 from its future income. (In fact, the Knights Templar never managed to make a profit out of the island.)

At the end of 1191 an uprising by the Armenians and the Greeks was brutally suppressed, and in the spring of 1192 the tyranny of the Knights Templar urged the local population of

---

PRECEDING PAGES: crusaders at the siege of Antioch.
LEFT: St Hilarion (now Agios Ilarion) in northern Cyprus, seized by the crusading Richard the Lionheart.
RIGHT: the cathedral of St Nicholas (now Lala Mustafa Paşa mosque) in Famagusta, which was built by the Lusignans.

Lefkosia (which soon became known as Nicosia) to a renewed attempt at resistance. An appalling blood bath ensued. The rebellion was one of the most important uprisings against a foreign oppressor in the entire history of the island. (A guerrilla war flared up once again in 1194, under the leadership of a certain Kanakis, but then the Cypriot population sank into centuries of passive and gloomy resignation, broken only by sporadic and fruitless guerrilla uprisings.)

The Knights Templar, preoccupied with their

ADAPTABLE CHRONICLER

Only a small number of Greek Cypriots, among them the 15th-century chronicler Leontius Machaira, were able to adapt to the crusaders' culture.

desirous of fiefs and land should come to him, and he would provide them with it. Thus they came, from the Kingdom of Jerusalem, from Tripoli, from Antioch and Armenia. They were then enfeoffed, and provided with land, and he gave the towns civil rights; many of the new arrivals were from the lower classes, and some were non-Cypriot Greeks."

The small governing class in Lusignan's feudal state was almost exclusively comprised of Latins, from the west and from the crusader states. The Greek property-owners and

battles against the Saracens, immediately sold the island for 40,000 dinars – the sum they themselves had paid – to one of Richard's henchmen, Guy de Lusignan, the dispossessed king of Jerusalem, thus introducing the 300-year rule of the Lusignan dynasty. The measures Guy had to take during his two years as king of Cyprus reveal what dire straits the island was in:

"When he took the island as his own - property, he sent out messages in order to win back the trust of the inhabitants, and he - populated the cities and castles anew; and he sent forth tidings to all the surrounding countries that all the knights, nobles and citizens

nobles on the island had been largely wiped out during the brutal reign of the Knights Templar.

The Greeks were hardly represented at all in the administration, nor in the ranks of the Italian, southern French and Catalan merchants, who had settled into relatively isolated enclaves in the coastal cities. A deep gulf separated the ruling Latins from the Greek Cypriot population. Indeed, the social status of the Cypriot population had worsened considerably since the Byzantine era: the peasant proprietors, who on top of paying tax had to provide their overlords with one-third of their income and two days' work a week, had lost most of their rights and were constantly in fear of their rulers, who punished them as they found fit – including mutilating and executing them.

Latin versus Orthodox

Conflict between the Roman Catholic and the Greek Orthodox churches became more critical during this period. Inflexible papal policies and fanatical monks increased the tension. The *Constitutio Cypria* (also known as the *Bulla Cypria*) of Pope Alexander IV in 1260, which was officially meant to end the ecclesiastical controversy, reduced the number of Greek bishoprics on the island to four, and these in remote villages. They had to swear an oath of loyalty munities of Augustinians, Dominicans and Premonstratensians – maintained its dominant role right up to the Ottoman era: its power was symbolised by the impressive French Gothic structure of the 13th-century cathedral of St Sophia (today the Selimiye mosque); the coronation church of the Lusignans in Nicosia; the cathedral of St Nicholas in Famagusta: and the mighty Belapais abbey, the "white abbey" of the Premonstratensian order, near Keryneia.

The nobility flourishes

The abject poverty of the Cypriot population stood in stark contrast to the late medieval

and according to a remark made in a letter by the Latin archbishop Raphael in 1280, their presence on the island was merely "tolerated".

When 13 Greek monks were condemned to death at the stake by a Dominican padre in 1231, Greek resentment escalated. Luckily, this was the only example of the Inquisition on Cyprus. The remains of the unfortunate monks were mixed with those of animals in order to prevent the possibility of any reliquary cult. The Latin church – its ranks swelled by com-

LEFT: the coronation of Richard the Lionheart in 1189.
ABOVE: the castle of Kantara, the comfortable base of the Lusignans.

pomp at the court of the Lusignans and in the castles of the wealthy ruling class. The pilgrim Ludolf von Suchen, from Westphalia in Germany, travelled through Cyprus between 1336 and 1341, during the reign of the Lusignan king Hugo IV (1324–59). It was a period of economic prosperity, especially as far as the two great trading rivals, Genoa and Venice, were concerned, and Ludolf remarks on the wealthy merchants living in Nicosia (he also mentions the cult of Aphrodite in Pafos, in particular its temple prostitution, a source of interest to many pilgrims):

"For the princes, the nobles, the barons and the knights of Cyprus are the wealthiest in the world. Anyone with an income of 3,000 florins treats it as if it were no more than an income of 3 marks. When it comes to hunting, however, no amount is too high to spend. I know a certain Count of Jaffa; he owns over 500 hounds, and one servant for every two of them, to protect them, bathe them and rub them with ointment; that is how well dogs are treated here. Another nobleman has 10 or 11 falconers, and gives them special wages and special rights. There are certain knights and noblemen upon Cyprus who pay less to keep and feed 200 armed men than they do their hunters and falconers... Thou shouldst know that all the princes, noblemen,

barons and knights on Cyprus are the wealthiest and most noble in all the world. They once lived in the land of Syria, in the wealthy city of Acre, but when that land and that city were lost to them, they fled to Cyprus and have stayed here ever since."

The history of Cyprus during this period is full of political intrigue. There were enough rivalries in the royal household of the Lusignans and among the island's powerful barons to outdo any play by Shakespeare. Peter I (1359–69) was the last of the fanatical crusaders. He even succeeded in conquering Alexandria in 1365, albeit only briefly and with appalling loss of life. He was brutally murdered

in his mistress's bedchamber by the mightiest barons on the island, after revenging himself for the alleged infidelity of his wife Eleonore.

It was not only the barons within who kept the power of the Lusignan kings in check: Genoa and Venice, the increasingly powerful Italian trading powers, formed independent, rival states within the Lusignan kingdom. Peter II's coronation in the cathedral in Nicosia in 1372 turned out very differently from the happy occasion expected when a fleet of seven Genoese warships arrived; a year of war followed, with heavy pillaging.

The end-result was the 90-year-long (1374–1464) occupation and exploitation of Famagusta and its surrounding area by the Genoese. The extortionate sum of 40,000 florins had to be paid annually to secure the return of the other areas that had been taken.

Life under the Venetians

Venice wanted Cyprus for its trade connections and as an advanced base against the Ottoman Turks. It prepared the ground by helping King James II to send the Genoese packing and got its reward when he married a Venetian noblewoman, Caterina Cornaro. James did not long survive the nuptials, dying in 1473. When his son and successor, James III, the last of the Lusignan line, died the following year it began to look mighty convenient for Venice. Caterina Cornaro tried to hold onto the throne, but she was leaned on by the Most Serene Republic and handed Cyprus over to the Venetians, a situation that was made "legal" in 1489.

Cyprus was a strategically important base for Venice in its war against Turkey, but was difficult to defend. In 1507 only one-quarter of Nicosia was inhabited, and the city walls were weak; in 1567, a team of master builders spent 10 months trying to improve them. Smaller fortified sites, such as the castles at St Hilarion (Agios Ilarion), Pafos and Kantara, were dismantled. All the island's defences were concentrated in Famagusta, where the city's four bastions, and the walls and towers connecting them, had undergone regular inspection and renovation since 1492. Its force of 800 soldiers was far too small, and typically there was not a Greek among them; this force, whose task was to guard the city and its various nationalities, was changed every few years.

The social stratification remained just as it

had under the Lusignans. In order to obtain money and soldiers, the *signori* tried to persuade the peasant proprietors to buy their freedom. The Venetians also had to recover enough money from the population of the island (estimated to be only 100,000 to 200,000) to pay tribute to the Turks.

The island's natural wealth was mined extensively. Venice sought to increase trading in traditional products such as wine, flax, hemp, cotton, wax, honey, sugar, indigo, oil and saffron. The saltworks at Larnaka, too, were important, and grain exports were under strict controls.

leaders executed. Thousands of peasants, gathered in readiness in Nicosia, dispersed.

The Ottoman invasion

In July 1570, after several warnings, 350 Turkish ships landed at Larnaka and the island fell to the Turks. The battle for Nicosia was a catastrophe for the Cypriots: they waited fruitlessly for relief to arrive, and their defence was completely uncoordinated. When the Turks, who brought in reinforcements unhindered from the mainland, sent in an attack force of 16,000 men, the city's resistance crumbled. Another bloodbath ensued. The Greeks fought bravely

The most important uprising on Cyprus since the beginning of the Lusignan kingdom broke out in the year 1562. Significantly, the head of a Greek cavalry unit, the *Megadukas*, was involved (proving, perhaps, that the Venetians' distrust of Greek Cypriot soldiers was justified). Frankish noblemen, led by Jacobus, known as Didaskalus, a teacher in Nicosia, also joined the uprising. The Venetians were informed of the rebellion and had the ring-

LEFT: ruins of the castle of St Hilarion (Agios Ilarion), built on the site of a Byzantine monastery.
RIGHT: St Neofytos, a hermit and stern critic of Richard the Lionheart.

on the side of their Latin rulers and incidents of open siding with the Turks among the rural population were rare.

The 10-month-long battle for Famagusta raged from 23 September 1570 until 1 August 1571. Seven major offensives were warded off; the Turks allegedly lost 80,000 soldiers out of some 200,000–250,000, while the defenders had only 3,000–4,000 infantrymen, 200–300 cavalrymen and 4,000 Greeks. When the gun-powder finally ran out, the white flag of surrender was hoisted. In flagrant defiance of the terms of capitulation, the Venetian commander-in-chief Bragadino was taken prisoner; his nose and ears were cut off, and he was flayed alive. ❏

بِسْمِ اللّٰهِ الرَّحْمٰنِ الرَّحِيمِ

الم ۚ ذٰلِكَ الْكِتَابُ لَا رَيْبَ ۛ فِيهِ ۛ هُدًى لِّلْمُتَّقِينَ ۙ الَّذِينَ يُؤْمِنُونَ بِالْغَيْبِ وَيُقِيمُونَ الصَّلَاةَ وَمِمَّا رَزَقْنَاهُمْ يُنفِقُونَ ۙ وَالَّذِينَ يُؤْمِنُونَ بِمَا أُنزِلَ إِلَيْكَ وَمَا أُنزِلَ مِن قَبْلِكَ وَبِالْآخِرَةِ هُمْ يُوقِنُونَ

سورة فاتحة الكتاب

بسم الله الرحمن الرحيم

الحمد لله رب العالمين ۞ الرحمن الرحيم

مالك يوم الدين ۞ إياك نعبد وإياك نستعين

اهدنا الصراط المستقيم صراط الذين أنعمت

عليهم غير المغضوب عليهم ولا الضالين

مكية وهي سبع آيات

THE OTTOMANS

During the rule of the Ottomans, the Christian population of Cyprus
mingled remarkably little with their conquerors

The violent battles and subsequent emigration of the Latin-Frankish inhabitants (conversion to Islam was a precondition of remaining) resulted in a catastrophic drop in the population. Of the 200,000 or so recorded in 1570, only 120,000 were left by the year 1600; the figure continued to plummet, and in 1740, after bouts of further emigration and a series of natural disasters, it reached an all-time low of 95,000. The island had now become a poverty-stricken province of the Ottoman Empire.

In the early days of Ottoman rule, relatively few Turks occupied the large and soon-to-be-rebuilt fortresses at Nicosia, Famagusta, Pafos, Limassol and Keryneia: there were only 1,500 to 2,000 cavalrymen (*sipahi*) and the same number of infantrymen (*janissaries*). In 1590 a contemporary observer (Memmo) estimated the total number of Turkish troops on Cyprus at around 4,800. Six *firmans* (Sultan's decrees) ordered the forcible immigration of workers from Anatolia, including some Greeks. "Islamising" or "Turkifying" the island was not the express intention of these *firmans*.

By 1600 the Turkish section of the population had increased to 22,000, though this growth stagnated during the course of the next two centuries. According to a census taken in 1841, the Turks formed only 31 percent of the island's population. At the beginning of the British Protectorate, there were 45,458 Turks on the island out of a total of 185,630 people.

Christians and Muslims

Though the Muslims were on a higher level, both administratively and socially, than the "infidels" (*rayas*), who were the only ones to pay a special, three-tiered tax (*kharadsh*) and sacrifice their most promising sons for the élite troops of the *yeniceri* (janissaries), the Christians enjoyed a certain degree of self-government. In the middle of the 19th century the traveller-historian Mas Latrie counted 705 Christian and mixed villages, and 130 villages with a Turkish majority. He estimated the population of Nicosia at roughly 11,950; 8,000 were Turks, 3,700 were Greeks and 250 were Armenians or Maronites (a Christian community that had emigrated to

CHANGE FOR THE BETTER

Archbishop Kyprianos, who wrote an extensive, if very one-sided, chronicle of Cyprus in 1788, was forced to admit that the Greeks were pleased with the change from Venetian to Ottoman rule. The Orthodox Church had regained the status it had enjoyed at the end of the Byzantine period. The slave-like status of the peasant proprietors was abolished, and although the payments they had to make remained, they were much reduced: people were forced to work only one day a week (rather than two), taxes were reduced and market duties were abolished. Christians and Moslems lived in the same villages and towns, although in separate areas.

PRECEDING PAGES: Cyprus culture opens up to Islam.
LEFT: Ottoman-style salon, House of the Dragoman Georgakis Kornesios, Nicosia.
RIGHT: Gothic cathedrals were turned into mosques.

Cyprus, predominantly from Lebanon). Larnaka, the main port on the island, was an important European colony, and, according to Mas Latrie, the city of Famagusta, much of which lay in ruins, was inhabited only by Turks (the Greeks lived in the suburbs). The main concern of the Turkish administration was to keep the "infidels" as far away as possible from the centres of fortification in the major cities.

The administrative system

In theory, it was the declared duty of the Sublime Porte to avoid tyranny and suppression, to achieve peaceful coexistence between popu-

justice: all the problems of this land have been caused either by a failure to observe these laws, or by their improper application."

Both Christians and Muslims suffered equally from the pressure of high taxation and its arbitrary nature. Famine, droughts, swarms of locusts, attacks by pirates, and the plague (1641) all contributed to the aforementioned drop in the number of inhabitants, which reached its lowest point at the end of the 17th century. Thus it was that the uprisings, which had been occurring on a regular basis since 1572, were directed at overly high taxation rather than against population groups with dif-

lation groups and secure a just system of administration in order to revive the island's natural riches. At least, this was the substance of the various *firmans* that were issued, and of the various administrative reforms.

In reality the island was suffering from the same old disease it had inherited from Byzantium: its officials could not be controlled and corruption was rife. As the English captain Savile noted at the beginning of British rule: "What needs to be reformed is not so much the law itself as the application of the law. The Ottoman government is famous for its numerous *firmans*, laws and regulations, which can hardly be bettered for their comprehensiveness or their

ferent religious beliefs. Both the Greeks and the Turks complained about the *dragoman* Markoulles (1669–73). Turks and Christians also showed solidarity in their rebellions against the unscrupulous governor Chil Osman Agha in 1764 as well as against the illegal rule of the adventurer Hadj Baki (1771–83). Nonetheless it was during this period that the incipient tensions which were later to split the two peoples asunder developed.

The Greek clergy

The power of the Orthodox Church was at its height during this period, exerting crucial influence on both the economy and administration: as early as 1660, the Sultan had recognised the Orthodox archbishop and the three other bishops as spokesmen of the Orthodox population, and they were granted the right to send their petitions directly to the Porte in Constantinople, and even to go there in person. In 1754 a *firman* bestowed the title of "ethnarch" – head of the autocephalous Church of Cyprus and leader of the Greek Cypriot nation – on the archbishop of Cyprus.

The Church was thus drawn into the corrupt Turkish administration, and as an English diplomat noted in 1792, it was soon practically running the island. The unpleasant task of col-

is allowed to employ every method of exploitation. The Turks would thus be subjected to the same wretched conditions as the Christians, had the latter – in addition to the demands made on them by the government – not been forced to lend their support to a number of lazy and greedy monks. Every matter concerning the Greeks is presided over by the archbishop and the dragoman of Cyprus (one of the officials appointed by the Porte), who is responsible to the non-Orthodox community for levies, taxes, and the like."

The most fertile and also the most pleasant areas of the island were the regions of Cerina

lecting taxes remained the responsibility of the *dragoman*, or "interpreter" to the Porte, who was very influential and often of Greek descent. In 1814, John Macdonald Kinneir, a "captain in the service of the East India Company", described the wretched conditions on the island, and the role of the Church in perpetuating them:

"The drastic effects of the Turkish system of government are nowhere more evident than on Cyprus, where the governor, appointed annually by the island's official owner, Capudan Paşa,

(Keryneia) and Baffo (Old Paphos) where, according to Tacitus, Aphrodite rose from the waves. Here, there were forests of oak, beech and pine, as well as olive and sycamore trees. Cyprus was justly famed for the quality of its fruit, wine, oil and silk; its oranges tasted as sweet as those from Tripoli, and its wines – both red and white – were shipped to the Levant, where they were adapted to suit the tastes of the English market. The island produced two different kinds of silk, yellow and white, but the former was preferred. The corn grown on the island was of excellent quality, and rice was grown in regions where the producers could amass enough capital to prepare

LEFT: the minarets of Nicosia.
ABOVE: wood block engraving illustrating the weaving industry during the Ottoman period.

the soil. However, the Greek rural population, who constituted the only labouring class on the island, had been under the thumb of Turks, monks and bishops for too long and were now reduced to extreme poverty; many emigrated the moment they got the chance.

Growing dissatisfaction

The governor and the archbishop engaged in extensive grain trading, indeed more so than the rest of the population put together; they often decided to confiscate the entire grain out-put for one year and then export it, or withhold it at a higher price. Tensions began to mount

between the island's Christians and Turks, who, as a French observer, L. Lacroix, put it, "were reluctant simply to stand by and watch those whom they had vanquished lord it over them now." In 1804 the Turks in Nicosia and in the surrounding villages rose against their governor, who had been a willing tool of the Greek clergy. The fact that two paşas with Otto-man troops from Asia Minor had to quell a revolt by their own people only served to increase the tensions between the two segments of the population.

As Lacroix makes clear, 1804 was a dress-rehearsal for the bloody events of 1821 when the Greek nationalist revolution against -

Ottoman rule on mainland Greece erupted. The strong-willed and highly-educated Archbishop Kyprianos, founder of the famous *Pankyprian Gymnasium* in Nicosia, kept himself aloof from the solicitations of the *Philike Hetaireia* or "Greek Revolutionary Union". As Lacroix observed, the Greek population wanted to be left in peace.

However, Governor Kucuk Mehmed had Kyprianos, the high clergy and every educated Greek on the island arrested on charges of alleged conspiracy. A total of 470 people were put to death in Nicosia alone – and Archbishop Kyprianos was one of the first. The Greeks' houses were looted, there were massacres, and property was confiscated. For six months the Greek population lived in terror. Greek nota-bles who succeeded in escaping the massacres fled to European consulates.

Thus, the so-called "rule of the bishops" came to an end in 1821. Tensions remained, however, because of Turkish envy at the prosperity of the Greek population. The educa-tion gap between the Greeks and the Turks began to widen, too, as new schools were founded, and the island's educated classes came into contact with the intellectual trends devel-oping in Europe, where nationalist ideas were playing an increasingly important role. Con-temporary observers also noted a lower level of education among the Turkish community.

But it was neither nationalist ideas nor internal tensions that ended Ottoman domination of the island: instead, it was a country which at that time was the most important power in the east-ern Mediterranean – Great Britain. Her Maj-esty's diplomats were becoming increasingly interested in the internal affairs of Cyprus, and the Levant Company had become the leading trading company.

The political weakness of Turkey in relation to Russia, tension with the second great power in the Mediterranean, France, and the secure pas-sage afforded by the opening of the Suez Canal in 1869 finally led the Porte to hand Cyprus over to Britain, without requesting any payment in return (though the Sultan was to remain in the island's official sovereign just as before). On 12 July 1878, British troops arrived on Cyprus. ❑

LEFT: worshippers look towards Mecca in the Turkish quarter of Nicosia.
RIGHT: dawn beckons the faithful to prayer.

NA

WANTED MEN
IN CYPRUS

This booklet must be looked after.
It was expensive to produce and
will not be replaced. It should
be issued ... on signature. A
few bl... s have been left
fo... be pasted in.

Nov. 1956.

CHIVAN GEORGE THEODHOROU
...RST. NICOSIA. 5'6½"

...TSIS KYRIAKOS CHRISTOFOROU ...
...KHORI, FORMERLY MITSERO.

GEORGHADJIS POLYKARPOS COST'N
...I PALEKHORI. 5'...

...EMAS STYLIANOS CHRISTOFI, 1952
... NICOSIA. 5'5"

...VLOU PAVLOS GEORGHIOU ...
...YLAKIS 1931 VAROSHA 5'...

SPANOS NICOS SAVVA 1934
...DEA 5'5"

SYMEONIDES PHIDIAS MIKHAEL 1...
LAS... from AY. OMOLOTITADHE...

...OFOCLEOU NEOPHYTOS 1936
...PEYIA 5'6

...GEORGHIOU NICOS 1919
...KHORI, formerly NICOSIA 5'7

MICHAELIDES ALEXANDROS NICOLA ...
... KOUNRAS, 1937, AMIANDOS. 5'...

ΜΕΛΗ ΤΗΣ Ε.

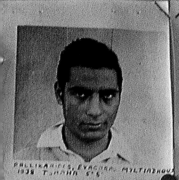

PALLIKARIDES, EVAGORAS, MILTIADHOUS
1938 TJHARA E'E

PERI CHRISTOFOROU, ANDREAS

CHRISTODOULOU, DEMETRAKIS
1936 DHEKELIA E'E

PAPADOPOULOS H TONIS KONSTANTINOU
VAROSHA E'E

CHRISTOFOROU, KTEIRKOS
KYPEROUNDA

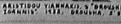

ARISTIDOU YIANNAKIS, O "DROUSKIO
IOANNIS" 1932, DROUSHA, E'E

PHILIPPIDES, ANDREAS CHRISTOU, 1932
ANDROSHAS, AN KTIMA E'E

EPAMINONDA, YIANNAKIS 1932
PEDHOULAS, NICOSIA E'E

PAPAVASILIOU, GEORKIOS
PANO ARHODES, KARP

A BRITISH COLONY

*With the British occupation, the centuries-long isolation of Cyprus
from the rest of Europe came to an end*

The Roman ruins of Curium (Kourion) lie on the road that leads from the harbour city of Limassol to Pafos in western Cyprus. The view from the rectangular stadium, stretching all the way to the Troodos mountains, is marred by several tall radio masts. A few miles further on, a series of British-looking terraced houses are grouped together not far from the roadside; barbed wire separates them from the main road. To the left, in the distance, one can sometimes make out a military aircraft taking off or landing. Down in the valley, there is a well-tended football pitch, its grass every bit as green as the playing fields of London. Welcome to the British Sovereign Base of Akrotiri.

Akrotiri, along with Dekelia and a military radar station at the highest point of the Troodos mountains, Mount Olympus, is one of the remnants of British rule in Cyprus. Inside these autonomous enclaves of Her Majesty, British law applies. The Union Flag, lowered for the last time in Nicosia in 1960, continues to flutter here. When Cyprus became independent, Britain secured 99 square miles (260 sq km) of the island for military purposes, and these bases have remained, the final vestiges of the former Crown Colony.

British rule on Cyprus began on Saturday, 13 July 1878. "In the name of Her Majesty Queen Victoria, I hereby take possession of this island," proclaimed Admiral Lord John Hay before a gathering of the island's notables in Nicosia. "Long live the Queen!" shouted the crowd. British troops had landed near Larnaka on the previous day.

Sir Garnet Wolseley was appointed High Commissioner, but at this stage Cyprus had only been leased to Britain by the Ottoman Empire, in payment for British help in wars against the tsars of Russia, and wasn't officially

British at all. Britain collected the annual "ground rent" it had to pay Istanbul from its Cypriot subjects.

Schools and hospitals

The British began modernising the administration and accurate statistics for the island were

obtained for the first time. A total of 186,173 people were living in Cyprus in the year 1881, including 140,793 Greek and 42,638 Turkish Cypriots. A modern education system was introduced, with separate schools for Christians and Muslims. The island's first ever hospitals were also built, and the malaria-infected swamps near Larnaka were drained.

As far as politics were concerned, the British introduced the Legislative Council, a committee (half-Cypriot, half-British) for making joint decisions. This new and – compared with conditions under Ottoman rule – liberal system of government meant that political clubs could be founded. The first newspapers appeared. Trade

PRECEDING PAGES: heroes of Cypriot resistance, Omodos Museum in the Troodos Mountains.
LEFT: newspapers first appeared in Cyprus when the British took over.
RIGHT: hoisting the British flag in 1878.

with Europe increased, and a Cypriot upper class evolved, comprising craftsmen and merchants. This programme of modernisation had a marked influence in the cities, but in the villages, where the great majority of Cypriots lived, conditions barely changed.

However, even in the cities disenchantment with the British soon set in. The hoped-for economic and technological developments were much slower than many had at first assumed, and people continued to labour under heavy taxation (many had hoped, rather naively, that all taxation would be abolished under British rule). Britain invested very little in the island: a

onwards the British had Alexandria at their disposal, and, since it enjoyed an even better position for these purposes, the military importance of Cyprus declined. At times the island was manned by as little as a single company, numbering between 200 and 300 men.

Even World War I did little to change things. In fact, the only thing that did alter as far as the Cypriots were concerned was a legal technicality: when Turkey joined the war on the side of Germany in 1914, Britain formally annexed the island. In 1923, under the terms of the Treaty of Lausanne, Turkey officially confirmed Cyprus as a British possession. In 1925,

few roads were rebuilt, a small railway was constructed and the harbour at Famagusta was dredged. The only jobs to be found were in the asbestos and copper mines, where workers slogged away for 10–12 hours a day under hideous conditions, receiving very little pay. Most smallholders were hopelessly in debt, and were living on the verge of starvation.

This lack of investment in the island was simply a reflection of British interests: Cyprus was important to the empire only from a strategic point of view. It was from here that sea traffic to India via the Suez Canal could be controlled, and any Russian intervention in the Mediterranean checked. But from 1882

the island was elevated to the status of a Crown Colony – a mere formality, which did nothing to alter conditions there.

It was only during the 1930s that the Cypriots began to see improvements in their economy. With the introduction of farmers' cooperatives, agricultural production could be stepped up. Craft and trade flourished. With the onset of World War II the island's military importance grew rapidly. More and more troops were dispatched to Cyprus, and the war gave the island's economy a huge boost. When Crete fell under German occupation and Rommel landed in Africa, the entire Near East seemed to be directly under threat. Cyprus was now an important military outpost along with Egypt, Palestine and Lebanon. Around 25,000 Cypriots volunteered to fight, many of them hoping to liberate the Greek "motherland" from the Germans. They made up an entire contingent in the British army. Fortunately, no fighting took place on Cyprus itself during the war. Indeed, former British soldiers posted to the island remember feeling extremely bored.

COLD WAR

The military importance of the island rose dramatically with the onset of the Cold War.

In 1945, just after the war had ended, the tourist guide *Romantic Cyprus* went into its second edition. Hotels, in particular those in summer spas in the Troodos mountains that benefited. At the time beach holidays were unfashionable.

In the realm of politics, increased efforts were made by Greek Cypriots for *enosis*, union with Greece. Britain's reaction to this was cool: "It has always been clear that certain parts of the Commonwealth, because of special conditions, can never expect to be granted full independence," was the message sent to Cyprus by the British secretary of state for colonial affairs in 1954.

The Quay, Lanarca, Cyprus

the mountains, advertised in the hope of attracting tourists. The guide's publisher, Kevork Keshishian, wrote: "The precise nature of post-war transport routes cannot be predicted, but one thing is fairly certain: Cyprus, because of its geographical situation and the excellent opportunities it offers, will play an important role in the forthcoming age of the aeroplane."

Sure enough, there was a slight increase in tourism in the years that followed. Unlike today, though, it was almost exclusively the

LEFT: the British influence extends to ships saluting the Duke of Edinburgh's birthday, Larnaka harbour.
RIGHT: the quay at Larnaka during the British heyday.

Struggle for Greek union

The British began by using military force to stop the guerrilla struggle for *enosis*, which began in 1955. This failed, however, and fighting developed into a civil war between the island's Greek and Turkish populations. This endangered the NATO alliance, still in its infancy, and Britain was thus compelled to negotiate. The military planners in London were satisfied with the result: Cyprus was given its independence in return for allowing two British sovereign bases to remain there. On 16 August 1960 British colonial rule ended, and the last governor handed over his official duties to the government of the Republic of Cyprus. ❏

THE CIVIL WAR

Following a bomb explosion in June 1958 in the Turkish press office in Nicosia, the island of Aphrodite became a battlefield

Even during the very first year of the British occupation of Cyprus the Cypriots were urging their new rulers to leave. Kyprianos, bishop of Kition, begged the first crown governor in 1878 to allow Cyprus to be "reunited with the Greek motherland".

The island's leading clergymen felt closer to Greece and it was not long before Greek Orthodox craftsmen and merchants joined the movement. The few educated Greek-speaking Cypriots saw Greece as the source of their culture, their linguistic and religious brother and their best chance for the long-hoped-for economic upswing. Britain was investing little in the island, and the Cypriots were impoverished and starving. The call for *enosis* (union with Greece) was the equivalent of social protest.

As far as the Muslim Cypriots were concerned, *enosis* was something to be sceptical about. The minority feared that marginalisation would occur if union with Greece took place. Since there was a disproportionately high number of Turkish-speaking Cypriots working for the administration, and far fewer in trade and crafts, the Muslim Cypriots were in favour of prolonging the island's colonial status, or returning it to Istanbul.

The conflict had no effect on daily life. Christian and Muslim Cypriots still lived in harmony with one another. In the mixed villages they sold agricultural produce side by side, and all Cypriots participated in the island's festivals, regardless of their ethnic background.

Emergent Greek Cypriots

Economic development and nationalism were the catalysts that changed the island's Greek Orthodox inhabitants into Greek Cypriots. Turkish Cypriots emerged a lot later, for it was only after Turkey was founded in 1920 that

Turkish nationalist feeling began to develop in Cyprus (though in 1923, Turkey relinquished all claims on the island). But, in spite of their more clearly defined aims, the Greek Cypriots were continually thwarted. Instead of *enosis*, Cyprus was developing closer ties with Britain, creating a swelling core of ill-feeling

fuelled by the British failure to develop the institutions of self-government.

In 1931 underlying social tensions erupted in a rebellion. Originally planned as a protest against increased taxes and customs duties, it grew into an all-out nationalist demonstration against Britain. A prominent Greek Orthodox priest hoisted the Greek flag, and declared that the revolution had begun. The governor's house was set on fire. Although most rebels were unarmed, the British were forced to send troops to Cyprus.

More than 2,000 Greek Cypriots were arrested as a result, all political parties were outlawed and censorship of the press was introduced.

PRECEDING PAGES: Turkish and Greek Cypriot unity, late 19th century.
LEFT: Odos Lidras, dubbed "murder mile", in Nicosia.
RIGHT: EOKA men crowned by laurel wreaths in Rhodes.

After World War II the calls for *enosis* became insistent. In 1950 the young bishop of Kition, Makarios, soon to become archbishop, organised a plebiscite which produced a 96 percent majority in favour of *enosis*. But Britain had no intention of letting the island go to Greece – Cyprus, its "unsinkable aircraft-carrier" in the Mediterranean, had by then become far too important militarily. From 1954 onwards, Greece took the side of Cyprus, and in 1956 Turkey maintained that Cyprus was an extension of the Turkish mainland. Tensions thus developed into an international conflict, and the notorious "Cyprus question" was born.

ENOSIS BY FORCE

A crucial factor in the development of events was the decision of Archbishop Makarios III and General Georgios Grivas, to use violence to achieve *enosis*. On 1 April 1955, Nicosia was rocked by a series of bomb explosions perpetrated by the National Organisation of Cypriot Struggle (EOKA). This conservative guerrilla movement wanted to achieve *enosis* by force, by "executing" British army officers and by murdering any of their fellow Greeks suspected of leftist sympathies. The British could not gain the upper hand over the partisan movement. The only effect of the mass arrests, was increased interest in the EOKA by the Greek Cypriots.

The British decided to form an anti-terror unit, recruiting members from the ranks of the Turkish Cypriots. Helped by Ankara, Turkish Cypriot nationalists formed their own terror unit to fight for Turkish interests, which were against *enosis*, and in favour of *taksim*, or partition of the island. The bloodshed was a foregone conclusion, and military confrontations between partisans and the British army led to conflicts between the island's ethnic groups.

Civil war

On 7 June 1958, a bomb exploded in the Turkish press office in Nicosia. It sparked a civil war. Cypriot fought against Cypriot; churches were set ablaze, houses and apartments looted. Members of racially mixed communities were forced to leave their homes, a migration that turned several city areas into ethnic enclaves.

At an international level, NATO partners Greece and Turkey were threatening to go to war over Cyprus, and fearful states sought a compromise. The US put pressure on Athens and Ankara to abandon their main claims and find a diplomatic solution.

Makarios declared forthwith that he would not insist on *enosis*, and after meetings between Greece, Turkey and Britain the so-called "London and Zurich Treaties" were signed: Cyprus was to become an independent state, but the Cypriots were not allowed to have any say in the drawing-up of their own constitution.

The treaties set the official seal on the division of the two ethnic groups: the island's Greeks and Turks were each given their own presidents, vice-presidents and ministers, as well as separate representation in parliament. Votes were taken separately. To prevent any minority discrimination, the Turkish Cypriots were granted the right of veto as well as over-proportional representation in the administration, the police and the army. The development of a single Cypriot nationality was thus effectively blocked; now the island was populated by Greeks and by Turks.

Greece, Turkey and Britain declared themselves "guarantor powers", with power to intervene should the Cypriots decide to change their constitution. On 16 August 1960, the foreign powers granted Cyprus its independence. ❑

LEFT: General Grivas, leader of EOKA.
RIGHT: statue of Archbishop Makarios.

INDEPENDENCE – AND PARTITION

*Only 14 years elapsed between Independence and the division of the island
into two autonomous communities separated by an impenetrable barrier*

On 16 August 1960 the last governor of Her Majesty's Crown Colony, Sir Hugh Foot, handed over his official duties to Makarios III, who was henceforth President of the Republic of Cyprus. An archbishop was now head of state. The tradition of a religious leader exercising both spiritual and secular

power, which had originated in Ottoman times, was thus continued in the newly-formed state. Makarios was the ethnarch and the undisputed leader of the Greek Cypriots.

At Makarios's side stood Vice-President Fazil Küçük, elected unanimously by the Turkish Cypriot minority. After a bloody civil war, during which one side had fought for union with Greece and the other for partition of the island, their task was to build a combined republic. In theory, the political activity would no longer centre on the separate interests of the island's Greeks and Turks, but on the concept of a unified state and one people – Cyprus and the Cypriots. Relations between the two ethnic

groups returned to normal in daily life, and in most cases good neighbourliness was re-established. Inhabitants who had fled now returned to their homeland, and the murders and lootings seemed to be ills of the past.

On the political level, however, sensitive relations were severely tried by the new constitution: because the new Republic's ministers, MPs and bureaucrats were each elected and recognised by only one of the two ethnic groups, they saw themselves as exclusively representing either Greeks or Turks, never both. As quarrels over taxation, development programmes and questions of infrastructure arose, the two sides came into conflict, each bent on keeping the larger slice of the cake for itself.

The government and the executive were preoccupied by endless quarrels over resources. Political representatives of both ethnic groups showed little if any interest in genuine cooperation. Indeed, many of them saw the collective state as only a temporary solution. Greek nationalists continued to demand *enosis*, while more and more Turks called for *taksim* (partition).

A return to violence

This uneasy peace lasted for three years. In spite of difficulties, the economy managed to recover, and in foreign affairs Cyprus became a committed member of the non-aligned states. But at the end of 1963, President Makarios called for a far-reaching revision of the constitution which would have deprived the Turkish Cypriots of many of their guaranteed rights. He insisted that the minority's right of veto, and the ethnic quota system in the police, army and administration be scrapped. The Turkish Cypriot side refused to support his proposals, and the Turkish government threatened to intervene if they were introduced unilaterally. The situation finally came to a head at Christmas 1963: fighting broke out in Nicosia, and soon spread to the rest of the island. Former partisans of the EOKA and the Turkish Cypriot terror unit TMT were reactivated.

The police and the army divided into their constituent ethnic groups and Turkish Cypriot ministers and people's representatives walked out of the parliament. Widespread civil violence ensued, started by the same nationalists responsible for the bloodshed of the 1950s. Ever since, the island's Greek and Turkish communities have been blaming each other for triggering hostilities. According to the Greek Cypriots, the Turkish Cypriots had attempted to achieve partition by starting a rebellion. In the opinion of the Turkish Cypriots, the Greek Cypriots had wanted to exterminate the Turkish minority and introduce *enosis*.

Over 500 people were killed during the summer of 1964. It was only when a United

then on the US saw him as insecure and unreliable, a kind of "Castro in priest's clothing", who had dealings with communists and was threatening to turn Cyprus into "the Cuba of the Mediterranean".

The conflict ended peaceful coexistence for the island's ethnic groups once and for all. The majority of Turkish Cypriots sought shelter in rural enclaves and urban ghettos. Their leaders, who supported the partition of the island, ensured that no further contact with their former neighbours took place.

The Greek Cypriots, with all the state power to themselves, began a trade embargo. Soldiers

Nations peace-keeping force arrived that the violence was brought to a halt. When the fighting was at its peak, the Turkish air force attacked Greek Cypriot positions and for a while it looked as if Turkey was threatening to invade. War between NATO partners Greece and Turkey looked increasingly likely. The US sought a diplomatic solution to the problem, and suggested that the island be divided between Athens and Ankara, with both zones belonging to NATO. President Makarios, however, rejected this suggestion out of hand. From

patrolled the borders separating the rival ethnic groups: Greek Cypriots were forbidden to enter Turkish Cypriot ghettos, while Turkish Cypriots suffered harassment if they entered Greek-controlled areas. Closed off and isolated in this way, the minority became dependent on relief packages, and their standard of living steadily worsened.

In the junta's shadow

The situation began to relax in 1968, when Makarios lifted the embargo. Turkish Cypriots were once again allowed to work and live wherever they wished. The Greek Cypriots' desire for *enosis* began to fade in the face of a

LEFT: Sir Hugh Foot, the last British governor.
ABOVE: march for independence.

burgeoning economy and the military junta in Athens, and only the most extreme nationalists still supported union with the Greek military dictatorship. Talks between the two ethnic groups began, under the auspices of the United Nations. The Turkish-Cypriots wanted a bizonal federation with a weakened central government, but the Greek Cypriots would not comply, fearing that it might help to pave the way towards partition. Negotiations took place nonetheless.

As the situation on Cyprus calmed down, tensions rose between the governments in Athens and Nicosia. The Greek military dicta-

torship felt that Makarios was trying to provoke friction by offering asylum to persecuted democrats and by not imposing press censorship that existed in Greece. Criticism of the Cypriot president also grew more vocal in the US. With the help of the 950-strong force of Greek soldiers and officers stationed on Cyprus and a nationalist terror group known as EOKA-B, the Greek junta decided to try to rid itself of Makarios. But its attempts to assassinate the archbishop failed.

Police units loyal to the government helped put many EOKA-B terrorists behind bars, and for a while it seemed as if Makarios had gained the upper hand.

Greek military attack

On 15 July 1974 the island's capital of Nicosia was rocked by gunfire. The presidential palace went up in flames. Terrorists and soldiers supporting the Greek junta embarked on attacks all over the island. The Republic and its defenders never stood a chance. The soldiers interned thousands of democrats and members of left-wing parties, and murdered their wounded rivals even in hospitals. News of Makarios's death was broadcast over the radio. Only the Turkish-Cypriots were left unscathed by the junta (so as to give Ankara no excuse to intervene). The longed-for *enosis* with the "motherland" had happened overnight, but it was a very different union from the one Greek Cypriots had imagined. The majority supported their elected government, and could only watch helplessly as the Greek military took control.

But one part of the Greeks' plan went hopelessly wrong: President Makarios had managed to escape from the burning presidential palace and find his way to the British Sovereign Base of Akrotiri where he was out of the junta's reach. Nikos Sampson, a right-wing radical who had been involved in the mass murder of Turkish Cypriots during the civil war of 1963–64, was proclaimed president in his place. The coup was announced as an internal affair of the Greek Cypriots. Athens was convinced that Turkey wouldn't intervene in Cyprus. How such a grave misjudgement could have been made has not yet been discovered. Relevant documentation is still lying inside a safe in Athens.

At daybreak on 20 July, five days after the coup, Turkish motor torpedo boats landed on the north coast. The Turkish air force dropped bombs on the island's capital. This time, unlike 1964, the United States did nothing to stop Turkey from carrying out its plans. This "peace operation", as the propaganda termed it, seemed to be quite justified under international law because the Cypriot constitution condoned intervention by the guarantor powers should it be necessary. The troops quickly succeeded in occupying an area to the north of Nicosia where many Turkish Cypriots lived; the Muslims rejoiced at being liberated from the Greek military dictatorship.

LEFT: Canadian and UN flags fly over Nicosia.
RIGHT: a British gunner digs in.

The "mini-junta" in Nicosia was just as surprised by the invasion as the larger one was as it looked on from Athens.

Two days later, the Greek military dictatorship fell as a result of the Cyprus fiasco. The chief of the mainland's junta, Ioannides, had tried to force his country to go to war with Turkey, but his own officers had refused orders. In Makarios's absence, the post of president in Nicosia was taken by Glavcos Clerides, the head of parliament, and Konstantin Karamanlis took over in Athens. Democracy had thus been restored – but the human tragedy on Cyprus had only just begun.

In defiance of the United Nations Security Council resolution, the Turkish army of invasion refused to withdraw, and on 14 August, despite intensive talks held in Geneva, the Turkish soldiers marched onwards.

Tens of thousands of Greek Cypriots ran for their lives, leaving all their possessions behind. Thousands were taken prisoner. Any who returned for any reason were shot. Turkish tanks rolled across the island, encountering almost no resistance. Two days later the Turks had achieved the objective of their operation: 37 percent of the island was occupied and partition was a reality. ❑

THE TRAGEDY OF WAR

Following the Turkish invasion, nearly 165,000 Greek Cypriots fled from the north to the south. For years afterwards they were forced to live in refugee settlements. Unemployment in the south, after the Turkish invasion, stood at 39 percent. As far as the Turkish Cypriots were concerned, a minimum of 55,000 of them fled from the south to the safe haven now provided by the occupied north.

Once the invasion had begun, the terrorists and junta soldiers inflicted bloody reprisals on the Moslem communities in the south, and the legal government of the island was in no position to stop them. Paramilitary units massacred the entire male Turkish Cypriot population of several villages, old and young alike. Likewise, since 1974, more than 1,600 Greek Cypriots, soldiers and civilians have disappeared. Many of them have appeared in International Red Cross lists of prisoners-of-war in internment camps in mainland Turkey. The war of 1974 radically changed Cyprus.

Since that time, an impenetrable line has extended across the island, and Greek and Turkish Cypriots have been living in strict separation from one another. Most of those still living in the "wrong" sector were resettled in 1975. Nearly every family on the island lost at least one of its members in the fighting. Around 6,000 people died in that bloody summer of 1974.

THE SEARCH FOR UNITY

For nearly a quarter of a century, UN-sponsored negotiations have repeatedly foundered on the incompatible demands of the Greek and Turkish Cypriots

In the immediate aftermath of the 1974 catastrophe, southern Cyprus was confronted with an enormous task. The refugees had to be provided with housing; farmers needed land, workers needed jobs and the self-employed needed the opportunity to start again. Unemployment in the Republic of Cyprus for the second half of 1974 was 59,000.

By the following year almost all of the 45,000 or so Turkish Cypriots living in the southern part of the island had been resettled in the Turkish-occupied zone. They, like their Greek compatriots in the north, left house and home behind. The better homes and the more valuable land were snapped up by the Greek Cypriot refugee families, sometimes after rental agreements had been entered into with their rightful owners. Moreover, all Turkish Cypriot-owned housing and land was officially registered and even today Turkish houses in southern Cyprus can be identified by the registration number painted on their outside walls.

Legally, the Turkish houses on the island are still the property of their former owners. Unsurprisingly, the refugees have shown little inclination to invest in renovation, and the properties are dilapidating fast.

Despite hardships, many refugees have managed to do quite well in southern Cyprus's newly affluent society; they have built their own houses, and they have progressed to good jobs. Some, in fact, are doing better now than they were in the north, and although if you ask anyone if they would like to return to their former home the instinctive answer is a resounding "yes", the reality is that such a prospect may not be quite so desirable. Quite a few of them would find their former homes in ruins, for many of the buildings left behind in the north have not been occupied since 1974.

Greek Cypriots cannot and will not be allowed to forget the dramatic events of 1974. *"Den Xechnoume"* – "We have not forgotten" – is flashed every evening on Greek Cypriot television screens. In Pafos it appears in shoulder-high lettering on the façade of a school building.

Reunification intent

The declared intention of the government of the Republic of Cyprus is the reunification of Cyprus. Greek Cypriot politicians have proposed some far-reaching compromises since the beginning, but there have been no breakthroughs in negotiations so far.

UN Security Council resolutions and resolutions by the General Assembly have called for the withdrawal of Turkish troops. "The Security Council requires that all states acknowledge the sovereignty and territorial integrity of Cyprus... (and) demands that foreign military intervention in Cyprus cease immediately," ran the text of the United Nations resolution of 20 July 1974, the very day the Turkish invasion began. The United Nations Security Council also condemned the self-proclaimed "Turkish Republic of Northern Cyprus" on 18 November 1983.

These, and many other resolutions, have made no difference.

Plan for peace

Some areas where agreement might be found have, however, been identified. The basic outline of a solution to the conflict was prepared as long ago as 1977. In that year the President of the Republic of Cyprus, Archbishop Makarios, met Rauf Denktash, leader of the Turkish Cypriots, in Vienna. The talks resulted in what is known as "the four guidelines", which were agreed upon by both politicians, and it is worth quoting them in their entirety:

No Solution

All talks, both direct and indirect, between the Greek Cypriot and Turkish Cypriot sides have so far failed, even though the UN General Secretaries have tried everything in their power to find a solution.

erative system and certain practical difficulties that may arise with respect to the Turkish Cypriot population should be taken into account.

"**4**. The competence and function of the central government will guarantee the unity of the country while taking the bizonal character of the federation into consideration."

A new federation

Although they were formulated a generation ago, the four "guidelines" listed above comprise the most important step so far

"**1**. We shall strive towards the foundation of an independent, non-aligned, bizonal - federation.
"**2**. The size of the territory administered by the respective communities shall be discussed in the light of economic viability and ownership of land.
"**3**. Fundamental issues such as freedom of movement, freedom to settle, property rights and other specific matters are open to discussion, whereby the fundamental basis of a bizonal fed-

towards reunification. The document lays the foundations of a future federation. Unlike the stipulations of the 1960 constitution, according to this document, the new federation would be composed of two federal states, a Greek Cypriot one to the south and a Turkish Cypriot one to the north.

The second paragraph, relating to the size of the respective federal states, implies a reduction in the size of the region at present occupied by Turkey; a result of the invasion has been that, in northern Cyprus, 18 percent of the population now occupies roughly 37 percent of the island's surface area. This imbalance is the basis of a Greek-Cypriot territorial claim.

LEFT: guarding the Green Line (*see page 81*).
ABOVE: as refugees from northern Cyprus flooded into the south, emergency housing mushroomed.

The third point touches on the question of the provision of basic liberties for all citizens of the Republic in every part of the Republic – a question that is still a bone of contention between the conflicting sides.

The final point makes it clear that the aim of these endeavours is not a loose union between two states but a single, joint federation, with a central governing authority representing the whole of the country.

The distribution of power between the central government and the island's various districts remained unclear. The Greek Cypriots expressed their desire for a powerful central

posed new borders have already been circulated among diplomats in Nicosia. The latest version provides for a reduction in Turkish Cypriot territory of 10 percent, which would give around 90,000 of the Greek Cypriot refugees the chance to go back their former homes.

The question of individual liberties is a lot harder to settle. Here, the Greek Cypriot side insisted until recently that freedom of movement, the right to settle and property rights should be guaranteed to all citizens in every part of the federation, pointing out that such freedoms are an accepted feature of any democratic state. It was the intention that all Greek

authority, while the Turkish Cypriots were in favour of strong district authorities.

The "four guidelines" contained two fundamental flaws: firstly, they did not include the question of finding international guarantors for the new federation; and secondly, the issues of individual liberties and of territorial rights in general were left unresolved.

Overcoming stumbling blocks

The easiest question to resolve is that of the size of the two federal states. Even the Turkish Cypriot leader, Rauf Denktash, was aware that the sector now occupied by the Turkish Cypriots should be reduced in size. Maps showing pro-

Cypriot refugees be given the right to return to their homes. The Turkish Cypriot side, however, rejects this right. It argues that if all the refugees were allowed to return, the Turkish Cypriots would become a minority in their own land.

The property issue is a controversial one, for most of the fields and houses presently farmed and inhabited by Turkish Cypriots are actually Greek Cypriot property. Compensation is probably the only way of achieving a solution.

Turkish immigrants

The "four guidelines" agreed on by Archbishop Makarios and Rauf Denktash make no mention of the settlers who have immigrated to the

northern sector from Turkey. Their transfer to Cyprus from Anatolia on the Turkish mainland has changed the island's demography. They have filled the underpopulated occupied sector, and increased the number of Muslim inhabitants on the island. Between 70,000 and 80,000 Turkish settlers now live in the occupied sector. What is to become of them would be another essential part of any peace negotiations.

Although they have now been there for more than two decades – and many have actually been born there – the Republic of Cyprus says that, since they are foreigners, they should leave the island immediately; members of the Turkish Cypriot leadership believe that most immigrants should remain and be granted Turkish Cypriot citizenship.

Also disputed is the presence of Turkish troops in the north and the question of international guarantors for such a federation. The Greek Cypriots reject Ankara's guarantor status out of hand. For the same reason they also demand the total withdrawal of all Turkish occupying forces. In contrast, the Turkish Cypriots – including the Opposition – insist on the minority receiving protection from Ankara and reject the withdrawal of the Turkish army; at most a reduction in the troop presence is offered. The Republic of Cyprus has begun discussing the possibility of giving the UN guarantor status over the new federation and its constitution.

Given the failure of negotiations so far, United Nations mediators have come up with a new strategy. So-called "confidence-building" measures have been introduced. As well as a reduction in military forces, youth exchange programmes and a more liberal approach to "cross-border traffic", a project involving economic co-operation between the Greek and Turkish communities have been proposed. It was hoped that an improvement in the Cypriot Turks' economic prospects would increase the willingness of the Turks to compromise. Wages in the Republic are, in fact, four times higher than in the north.

However, agreement has not so far proved possible on any such confidence-building measures. At the end of 1994 the North Cypriot Parliament officially declared that it had aban-

doned its aim of creating a federation with the Cypriot Greeks. Instead, closer ties would be sought with Turkey.

Gloomy outlook

Developments in the 1990s have intensified both the military and diplomatic pressures surrounding the search for a solution, at the same time as opening up new opportunities for a settlement. The end of the Cold War, removing the threat of a Soviet thrust into the eastern Mediterranean, also ended the always uncertain cooperation between those ostensible NATO allies, Greece and Turkey. They have since

come several times to the brink of war over disputed territorial claims in the Aegean Sea. Both sides are building up their military forces. Opposing warplanes routinely "buzz" each other in disputed areas. Cyprus could easily become an explosive ingredient in this already incendiary mix, especially as Greece and Cyprus have signed a defence agreement, which provides for joint military exercises and for Greek air and naval units to use bases at Pafos in western Cyprus.

Southern Cyprus's economic progress has enabled it to acquire modern weaponry, ranging from tanks and artillery to rocket launchers and surface-to-air missiles. Although not giving the

---

LEFT: barbed-wire blight from a divisive war.
RIGHT: Turkish Cypriot leader, Rauf Denktash.

Cyprus National Guard parity with the 35,000 Turkish troops in the north, these would allow it to put up a better fight should it come to armed conflict. In 1998, Cyprus was planning to deploy Russian-made S300 anti-aircraft missiles, Turkey was vowing to attack them, and Greece was warning that an attack would mean war with Greece. The killing of two Greek Cypriot protesters by Turkish military and paramilitary forces inside the UN buffer zone in 1996, as well as that of a third Greek Cypriot who apparently strayed into the zone, showed that guns have not been abandoned as an option.

the EU would not accept the preconditions.

Under UN auspices, the Cypriot President Glafcos Clerides met with Turkish Cypriot leader Rauf Denktash in Vienna. As usual, the talks went nowhere, with Denktash taking most of the international heat for intransigence. As far as membership of the EU was concerned, with Turkey rebuffed and the Turkish Cypriots not represented at the accession talks, the northern Cyprus authorities announced that they would pursue integration of their zone with Turkey.

For anyone looking for chinks of light in a gloomy situation, it can be said that the out-

While sabres were rattling noisily in the background, Cyprus's journey towards membership of the European Union was progressing, and new settlement initiatives from the EU, the United Nations and the United States were making their tortuous way through diplomatic channels. In 1997, Cyprus was included in the next wave of EU candidates, at the same time as Turkey was being shoved to the back of the queue. The Turkish Cypriots wanted to be at the accession talks, but as representatives of the Turkish Republic of Northern Cyprus, and only if Turkey was included in the list of EU members in the same wave. Despite wanting the Turkish Cypriots to join the Cypriot delegation,

look is probably no darker than before. The various initiatives at least had not been abandoned – on the contrary, their sponsors were determined to press ahead with them. The European Union was counting on Turkey's irritation with it to eventually subside, and on a way to be found to bring the Turkish Cypriots aboard the European train.

As the 1990s come to a close, the biggest question mark looming over the S300 missiles. If Cyprus deploys them, and Turkey attacks, all bets on the future would be off. ❑

LEFT: the north-south border crosses a street in the divided city of Nicosia.

Along the Green Line

A white jeep, flying the blue-and-white flag of the United Nations, rumbles its way across the broken tarmac of what used to be the city centre of Nicosia and is now a wasteland of overgrown buildings and wrecked cars sprouting flowers in their torn upholstery.

Ruined houses contain whole colonies of cats. Barriers of sandbags protect the dug-outs of the Greek Cypriot and Turkish soldiers. Here, only a few metres from the bustle of the city, the silence is frightening. No Cypriot is allowed to cross this closely-guarded no-man's-land. The burned-out houses lining Odos Ermou and melted neon signs remind us that this is the former heart of the city.

A thin, lifeless strip of land, the so-called "Green Line", only 60 ft (20 metres) wide in places, dissects the old part of Nicosia. It crosses the town's ancient fortifications, divides its districts, and then extends to the old airport, today the operational headquarters of the UN troops. The demilitarised buffer zone dividing the island is 112 miles (180 km) long, and extends from Kokkina in the northwest to Famagusta in the southeast. UNFICYP (United Nations Force in Cyprus) has been a familiar feature of life on Cyprus since as early as 1964. It was originally called in to end the civil war between Greek and Turkish Cypriots. After 1964, its most urgent task was to separate the Turkish Cypriots and their paramilitary units from the National Guard of the Republic of Cyprus. Since the Turkish army invaded northern Cyprus in 1974, the UN force has ensured that the Cyprus National Guard and the Turkish soldiers have kept to their side of the demarcation line.

About 1,200 soldiers are stationed in Cyprus, with Great Britain, Austria and Argentina providing the largest contingents. On account of the high costs invloved in such an operation, some countries such as Denmark and Canada have withdrawn their troops. Part of the 50 million dollars required to meet the costs of the troops is now being provided by the Republic of Cyprus.

A dirt track leads to an inspection post, from which the respective armies' ceasefire lines can be easily observed. Here, Turks and Greek Cypriots have dug primitive-looking shelters. The beach, distant and inaccessible for the UN troops, can be seen through binoculars. As seven Austrians sitting in a corrugated-iron shelter on a small rise verify, one of the worst things about their job is boredom. The blue-helmeted soldiers are on duty 24 hours a day for two weeks at a time, and invariably nothing happens. Elsewhere, though, the buffer zone is not as lifeless as it is in Nicosia. In many areas farmers are still allowed to cultivate their fields. And the Austrians have an entire village to supervise in their zone: in Pyla, a village between the two battle-lines guarded by military police, Greek and Turkish Cypriots still live in relative harmony.

The UN peacekeeping force has the situation mostly under control. The only danger of military escalation has been in Nicosia, where soldiers on both sides frequently start sparring. But it is seldom that

shots are exchanged. "Keep the peace and make the peace" is the troops' motto.

For genuine peace, Cyprus still has a long way to go and the chances of any union are as slim as ever. This is despite the fact that in the opinion of most Cypriots, reunification would pose no problems at all. Meetings held on neutral ground between women's groups and peace campaigners are making this increasingly clear. In the north and south of Nicosia there is little trace of the so-called "hereditary enmity" between the Greeks and the Turks.

It is clear that it is not culture, character, religion or language which divides the population. The greatest divisive force is politics. ❏

RIGHT: UN peacekeepers on patrol.

CONTEMPORARY CYPRUS

After the troubled times of the past, the Greek Cypriot south now enjoys comparative prosperity – at least compared with its Greek and Turkish neighbours

The most striking feature of modern Cyprus is the jagged line that cuts clear across the island, dividing it into two armed camps and making movement between the two sectors difficult if not impossible. But how much of that reality do you actually notice on the ground? Much of the time, surprisingly little, unless you go looking for it. Most visitors are too busy trying to find a little free space at the beach, puzzling over maps of mountain tracks, or filling up on *meze* and local wine at their local taverna, to worry overmuch about a situation that has been set in political concrete since 1974.

If that wasn't so, the Cypriot economy would all but collapse. So you'll find few complaints from ordinary Cypriots on either side of the line if you concentrate on having fun and leave someone else to worry about geopolitics.

An economic success story

Southern Cyprus has rebounded from the economic disaster of the Turkish invasion to such an extent that it is now three to four times richer, per capita, than Turkey and the north, and also wealthier than Greece and most of the rest of non-EU Europe.

This was no mean achievement, considering the legacy of the events of 1974. The Republic was burdened with 180,000 refugees and had suffered the loss of the island's best agricultural land as well as its main tourist centres, Keryneia and Famagusta. In addition, the international airport, occupied by the UN, was closed to civilian traffic.

Since those dark days, tourism and construction have boomed side by side, as new hotels, apartment blocks and leisure facilities have been built to meet the needs of a steadily growing number of visitors. The refugees from the north contributed to growth in both sectors, as they provided a ready supply of labour and a

massive and immediate demand for housing. Agriculture, shipping, trade and manufacturing have also underpinned the economic expansion. More recently, they have been joined by a fast developing financial and services sector, as Cyprus capitalises on its role as an offshore business centre and a bridge between Europe

and the Middle East and Gulf regions.

Even without civil strife and invasion, this would have been a notable feat. In the last decade of British colonial rule, the island was hugely underdeveloped. Most Cypriots scratched a thin living from agriculture or in the copper, iron and asbestos mines. Independence gave an immediate boost to the economy, as long overdue irrigation schemes made agriculture more productive and a consumer manufacturing base was established. Between 1960 and 1974, Cyprus achieved a higher standard of living than any of its neighbours, with the exception of Israel.

Recreating and surpassing that level of pros-

PRECEDING PAGES: a Turkish memorial.
LEFT: keeping up with developments.
RIGHT: Glafkos Clerides, elected president of the Republic of Cyprus in 1993 and again in 1998.

perity since 1974 has put Cyprus optimistically on course for European Union membership.

The social scene

The social benefits have also been immense: today, instead of unemployment there is a labour shortage, despite the fact that many Cypriots work at two jobs (it's not uncommon for people to have a "regular" job and when that is over to get down to business on the family farm. "Guest workers" – some, though certainly not all, of whom

> **HARD CASH**
>
> Most analysts ascribe the economic upswing to the sharp rise in tourism, an industry which now draws in more than 2 million visitors a year and is a vital source of hard currency.

imported pick-up to take him to and from his orchards or vineyards. While in the countryside, with its rough and ready dirt-tracks, these are as much practical requirements as status symbols, the same cannot be said for many of the four-wheel-drive RVs office workers use for shopping at their local supermarket.

The face of most towns and villages has changed for ever as shady old houses are demolished in favour of brash villas and apartment blocks, whose construction standards may not

are miserably exploited – have been brought in in large numbers to meet the shortfall, mostly from eastern Europe, the Indian subcontinent and the Philippines. Cyprus's powerful and well-organised trade unions regularly manage to push through generous wage rises for employees. The quality of social care, measured by the average life expectancy, the infant mortality rate, the number of doctors per thousand inhabitants, and the standard of education, show that southern Cyprus stands comparison with any wealthy industrialised Western nation.

Greek Cypriots now demand, and many can apparently afford, the good life. Rare is the farmer who does not have an expensive

be of the highest, but which are indelible signs of the modernity and affluence their owners crave. Cypriots themselves occasionally worry that their drive to be Western, rich and cosmopolitan is changing them in ways that they may live to regret. Stress is on the rise, even if it has some way to go before it reaches Western levels – but generally they are too tired from working at one of their several jobs to reach any conclusions.

Big spending

The income from tourism has made it possible to finance the enormously high expenditure on imports, such as foreign cars (these days a

Greek Cypriot family that does not own at least one car is a rarity). Not the least of these imports has been military equipment. Cyprus is after all, effectively in a state of emergency, with a large and well-equipped foreign military force on its territory. Some of the fruits of the expanding economy have been expended on strengthening its defence forces.

The Greek Cypriots have not relied solely on tourism, a notoriously fickle industry, and in this region in particular, prone to sudden debilitating shocks, such as the Gulf War. They also invested in the necessary modern infrastructure to provide a bedrock for further economic

source of labour. Most crucial, however, was the fact that Cyprus was now able to take advantage of the market represented by the increasingly rich Gulf states, where industrial products, including shoes, clothing, paper and synthetic goods, all found a ready market. In recent years exports have also been successfully targeted at the European Union.

A good image

The authorities in southern Cyprus have had a lot of success in promoting the island as an ideal location for doing business with the Middle East and the Persian Gulf. At the same time

development and to compensate in some measure for the amenities which had been lost in the invasion. It included new airports at Larnaka and Pafos, new harbour facilities at Limassol and Larnaka, a well-developed network of roads, including a motorway from Nicosia to Larnaka, Limassol and, when the project is complete, to Pafos, and modern telecommunications facilities. Perhaps the greatest achievement of the south Cyprus economy has been its successful industrialisation. To begin with, the refugees provided a cheap

the number of "offshore companies" registered in southern Cyprus is continuing to rise. Among them are banks, insurance companies, architectural firms, real estate companies and consultancy firms. The offshore sector, taking advantage of favourable tax and ownership regulations, has been a major factor in growth of the services sector, boosting employment in such white-collar jobs as financial services, commercial and tax law and consultancy.

Cyprus, due partly to its non-aligned status during the Cold War, and partly to AKEL, its Communist party,had strong links with the former USSR and Eastern Europe. Since the collapse of communism, these links have taken on

LEFT: Cyprus offers classic attractions to visitors .
ABOVE: Larnaka's airport, a hub for many tourists.

a more commercial nature. On the one hand, guest-workers from these countries are helping to meet Cyprus's labour shortage. More noticeable, however, is the prevalence of wealthy Russians. Some 100,000 Russian tourists visit every year, many of them on spending splurges for everything from waterfront villas to designer sunglasses; they often pay cash on the nail in US dollars. They have helped Cyprus's economy, and the tourist industry in particular, to survive a few lean years in the mid to late 1990s. Questions could be asked about the origins of at least some of the Russians' wealth, but few people are willing to ask them.

Taken altogether, the effect of these developments is that southern part of Cyprus is no longer and underdeveloped country. Success has its dark side, however: the construction boom, steadily increasing industrialisation and intensive farming methods are taking a heavy toll on the environment, and the level of foreign debt has grown to dangerous proportions.

In the late 1990s, there were increasing signs that the economic model that had proved so successful for 25 years was under strain. The tourist industry professed itself to be in a more or less permanent state of crisis, not so much because overall demand had dropped as because the supply of accommodation and

other facilities was continually increasing, and a limited number of tourists had to be shared out among too many businesses. This could be seen in everything from hotels operating at a small fraction of their capacity, to the ridiculously low prices charged for car hire at off-peak times. The message for tourists was to shop around for bargains that were there for the taking. Competition from lower-cost destinations, such as Turkey, was taking its toll at the lower end of the market, and there were too few (the Russians always excepted) big-spending, upmarket tourists to go around.

Manufacturing also took a hit as failure to invest in new products and processes damaged its ability to compete. The reputation of the country's big merchant fleet was at a low ebb, with Cypriot-flagged ships being seen as prime suspects for safety violations in European ports. Cyprus's own ports were also said to be in crisis due to over-powerful unions, restrictive practices and corruption. Cyprus Airways, the national carrier, suffered from high cost structures and inflexibility. Agriculture was threatened by several years of near-drought which had left the island's freshwater reservoirs all but empty. These and other indicators were a wake-up call to Cyprus, as it pursued membership of the European Union and opened itself to the world economy, that if it was to remain successful it had to adapt.

Political brands

Politics permeates Greek Cypriot life in many ways. Goods manufactured by the Co-operative movement (linked with the PEO trade union) are associated with the left wing of the party spectrum. Thus there is "leftist" brandy (produced by co-operatives) and "rightist" brandy (produced by private firms). Even what local *kafeneion* a villager goes to regularly is a certain indicator of his political affiliation. Sport also falls into left/right categories. No Conservative would cheer a victory by the club Omonia Lefkosia, because the club has political affiliations with the Communists. If Olympiakos wins rather than Omonia, however, then it's a victory for the right.

During the decades since independence in 1960, Greek Cypriot politics has been characterised by sharp antagonism between the Communists and Conservatives. On one side there is the progressive party of the Working people (AKEL), formed in 1941, and the successor of the Communist party KKK, which was forbidden under British rule. AKEL and the trade union federation affiliated to it, the PEO, have traditionally looked after farmers' and workers' concerns, thereby gaining substantial influence. The opposing side was initially represented not by an actual party, but by the Archbishop and his followers, the clergy and the business establishment.

Following independence, the Democratic Front was founded as a Conservative collective movement. Only since 1968, when this party broke up, has Cyprus had a modern party system.

However, since the Turkish Cypriots withdrew from all government bodies in 1964, their posts have remained vacant, and the 24 seats reserved for them in the 80-seat House of Representatives have been left empty. The Republic of Cyprus has a presidential system. The president can appoint and dismiss ministers, and decides policy matters in general. The voting procedure allows for the best-placed candidates after a first ballot to go on to face a second one to determine who becomes president. The House of Representatives, elected by proportional representation, has only a legislative, not executive function. ❏

By that time the Communists, with no Social Democratic opposition, were firmly entrenched.

The Republic of Cyprus's political system is derived from the London and Zurich accords, which formed the basis of the island's independence. Greek and Turkish Cypriots were given separate municipal administrations and separate representation in the government and the law courts. The president was a Greek Cypriot, while his vice-president was a Turkish Cypriot.

LEFT: visitors to Cyprus have been quick to discover that bargains are there for the taking.
ABOVE: turning a back on political messages.

PATTERNS OF ALLEGIANCE

Even today a politician's place of origin and his family's reputation can be far more decisive than his ideological position when it comes to elections. The close connection between individuals, families and politics is evident when you compare election results in one small area. In some villages the Communists have been overwhelmingly successful for decades, even though the inhabitants do not give the impression of being radical left-wingers. The next village will vote for the far right – but the voters themselves are far from being right-wing extremists. Some of this is changing as the island modernises and old patterns of allegiance fade.

ENVIRONMENTAL PROTECTION

There is always a price to be paid. The downside of the whirlwind economic growth in southern Cyprus has been the effect on the environment

Salt used to be extracted commercially from the Salt Lake at Larnaka, but now pollution from jetliners using the busy international airport nearby has made the salt unfit for human consumption. Pink flamingoes still feed in wintertime in the lake's shallow waters, swallowing a garnish of hydrocarbons

along with the pink crustaceans that give them their special colour.

The coastal regions have been the hardest hit by the effects of economic development. In some places frenzied building has destroyed the once scenic aspect for good, and the resulting mess threatens to drive away the very tourists whose demand encouraged the construction boom in the first place. The Agia Napa-Protaras-Pernera corridor south of Famagusta has been heavily developed, likewise the coast along Larnaka Bay and Limassol Bay. Pafos started later than its cousins but with the opening of the airport there it moved quickly to catch up. To the despair of environmentalists there seems little to stop the development juggernaut. Zoning rules and regulations exist, but where one form of construction – hotels for example – is discouraged, other forms – villas and apartment complexes – move in to take up the slack. Planning rules are routinely relaxed, even to the extent of allowing the building of a giant hotel complex on the edge of the Akamas Peninsula, an area that is under government consideration for national park status (it's a leisurely consideration, to be sure, and has been so for at least ten years).

The case of the Akamas

The drive to achieve national park status for the wild and scenic Akamas has become a *cause célèbre* for environmentalists. Greenpeace's Mediterranean director regularly jets in from the organisation's regional headquarters in Malta to rally the local troops and launch actions to prod the government. It is not just starry-eyed greens, however, who say that a national park is needed to preserve the area's flora and fauna, scenic charms and historic sites. A report from the World Bank makes the same case, and the European Union is watching how Cyprus handles the matter. In 1998, the Cypriot government had yet to legislate.

The north coast around Polis and Latsi, then eastwards to the demarcation line has so far escaped the fate of resort areas developed over the last 25 years. Local people there are, however, fighting tooth and nail against the restrictions that have been applied to them. They not unnaturally resent outsiders telling them what they can and can't do with their land and don't see why they alone should be denied the chance to raise their standard of living.

Lara Bay, north of Pafos, has become a symbol of how serious the plight has become for wildlife. This is the last resort for endangered green and leatherback turtles, a refuge where pregnant females are not too fearful to come ashore and lay their eggs and where their nests are protected. The turtles' other beaches are already fully occupied by sunbathers.

There are several ironies in the development versus preservation stakes. One is that hoteliers at Agia Napa don't want the Akamas Peninsula developed – not so much because they are unenthusiastic about more competition (which they are, in fact), but because they want somewhere for their guests to be able to go on daytrips where they can see something other than more hotels.

Another is that among the best protected areas of the coast are those that lie within the boundaries of Britain's two Sovereign Base Areas. Only small-scale development is permitted here – commercial development, that is. Military development has a higher priority and has been responsible for eyesores such as the forest of radio antennae on the Akrotiri Peninsula. The British forces also conduct occasional live-fire exercises in the Akamas Peninsula and there are warnings to visitors not to pick up items that might explode and kill them.

The tree campaign

In the search for a genuine environmental success story, you have to abandon the beaches and head inland, particularly to the Troodos mountains, where the forests that once blanketed the island are being painstakingly restored, tree by tree.

In the ancient world, Cyprus was known as the Green Island, a description undoubtedly awarded on account of its forests. The Apostle Paul reported that he had to pick his way through thick forests on his journey from Famagusta to Pafos, even on the plains. This wealth of trees, together with a favourable geographical location in the eastern Mediterranean, made Cyprus into an important exporter of wood and a centre for shipbuilding. Alexander the Great kept part of his fleet here.

When an inspection was made of the island's forests at the start of British colonial rule, officials claimed that the Ottoman Empire had virtually destroyed this great natural resource. The plain of Mesaoria was a treeless steppe. Nearly all the fruit trees had been axed: people preferred to forgo their yields rather than turn them over to the tax collectors. The only remaining forests were in the mountains.

The British paid close attention to the state of Cyprus's forests. The first Forestry Commission in the British Empire was set up in Cyprus and as early as 1879 the first forestry laws were passed. In stark contrast to all other aspects of colonial administrative practice it was the maintenance and regeneration of the forests rather than their economic exploitation which was the main consideration.

The British left behind 670 sq. miles (1,735 sq. km) of forests, 19 percent of the whole island. Their method of reporting forest fires with a network of "forest telephones", remains a model system even today. Since 1951 knowledge about the care and regeneration of

Mediterranean forests has been developed at the Cyprus Forestry College in Prodromos.

Since taking over from the British, the work of the Cypriot Forestry Commission has not always gone smoothly. During the wars of 1964 and 1974 large areas of forest went up in flames. The Turkish invasion of 1974 alone led to the destruction of 16 percent of the state-owned forests. These areas were reafforested in the period up to 1982.

Today, all over Cyprus, terraces which had been barren for decades are being replanted and, with the aim of promoting more environmentally friendly methods, the work is done without bulldozers. ❑

LEFT: more beautiful than concrete.
ABOVE: the Forestry College, set up by the British.

THE FACE OF CYPRUS

The island of Cyprus owes much in terms of its physical characteristics and climate to the azure waters of the Mediterranean which lap the coastline

Like Aphrodite emerging from the sea foam, Cyprus rose dripping out of the primeval Tethys Sea, which lay between what are now Eurasia and Africa during the later Palaeozoic Era and into the Mesozoic.

By the Cretaceous Period, some 90 million years ago, two chains of islets had formed from the tips of mountains and volcanoes forced up from the sea floor by the slow-moving collision of the African continental plate with the European plate – these were the basis of today's Troodos and Keryrneia mountains. Erosion and continuing raising of the land laid down the Mesaoria Plain and the coastal low-lands.These broadly defined geological formations are still the main features of Cyprus's topography.

The Mesaoria ("Between the Mountains") Plain occupies the middle of the island, along with a more rolling westward extension called the Morfou Plain. The plains merge along their southern fringes with the foothills of the Troodos massif, which dominates the west and rises in waves to the 6,340-ft (1,951-m) summit of Mount Olympus (Khionistra), the island's highest point. South and west of the Troodos lies rugged, hilly country fringed by a narrow coastal plain. The sharp-edged Keryneia range lines the northern coast from about Cape Kormakitis in the west to Cape Apostolos Andreas in the east, fading out at either end.

The peninsulas

Distinctive appendages to the main body are a quintet of major peninsulas, whose configuration led commentators in ancient times to compare Cyprus to a spread-out sheepskin. The Karpas peninsula in the northeast forms the tail, with the Cape Kormakitis and Cape Gkreko peninsulas the hind legs, and the Akamas and Akrotiri peninsulas the forelegs. Nowadays, a frying pan is a more popular image of the island's shape, and given the summer heat,

perhaps a more appropriate one, but it is a misshapen frying pan.

Troodos mountains

The Troodos mountains are far and away the most conspicuous geographical feature on the island. They are visible from all over the centre

and west. Their central core, roughly 18 miles (30 km) long, consists of igneous rock. Mount Olympus itself is composed of dunite. Over the course of millions of years the dunite was gradually transformed into serpentine, leading to the mining of asbestos in the upper Troodos (a process that has left massive scarring of the mountainside around Amiantos and has now been stopped). The landscape is undulating and spacious, with light and dark browns and shades of grey.

To the east is the Pitsylia district: a rugged, hilly and sparsely populated region dotted with villages, that gradually fades away towards Nicosia and the Mesaoria. To the northwest lies

PRECEDING PAGES: the wild shores of Pafos; Cyprus is renowned for its abundance of fruit and flowers.
LEFT AND RIGHT: Troodos trees and landscape.

Tilliria, with a wild and scenic landscape that manages to make Pitsylia seem tame and densely populated by comparison.

North of the mountains are the gentler landscapes of the Marathasa and Solea valleys, rich agricultural country thick with orchards, and a lack of dense natural forest cover that opens up spectacular views, as far as the sea in one direction and up towards the mountains in the other. Just off the southern fringe of the Troodos is the Commandaria wine region, while off to the west and the long, slow

> **BEST FOOT FORWARD**
>
> There is almost nothing in Tilliria apart from sopme of Cyprus's most testing settings for hill and forest hiking.

descent towards Pafos, are more vineyards and wine villages.

The Keryneia massif

The other mountainous region of the island, the Kyrenia massif (also known as the Pentadaktylos, "five-fingered", range after one of its mountains, which has five separate peaks; and as the Besparmak mountains in Turkish), stands in stark contrast to the Troodos. Characterised by rough rock walls and steep precipices, it is largely formed of hard, compact masses of whitish-grey limestone. To the north and south the range divides into numerous small valleys and ravines. On the northern slopes, the hard

limestone is covered by much softer clay, resulting in a very varied coastline. The mountains crowd the northern coast, rising up steeply a short way inland from the sea and looming over the coastal settlements like a sharp-toothed saw. Deep river valleys, swollen in spring with mountain torrents, lead from the Keryneia range to the coast. The isolated villages on the slopes are linked by narrow roads, some of which climb right up to the mountain ridges. Beyond, forest tracks lead across nearly the entire length of the massif, providing magnificent views of the steep limestone walls, fabulous rock formations and forests. Clear paths pick their way through bright, dry pine forests, which rarely become dense and dark. Up here you can move easily between views of the north coast on one side, and down into the plains on the other.

The Mesaoria plain

The Mesaoria plain between the Keryneia and Troodos mountains extends from Morfou in the west to Famagusta in the east. It used to be forest-covered but the trees have long since been chopped down, leaving behind a steppe that would admirably suit the description "windswept", except that there is rarely very much wind. In places, erosion of the alluvial soil has exposed the underlying sandstone and other rock. Rivers have carved up the landscape and water and sand have shaped it. The Mesaoria has been dubbed the breadbasket of Cyprus, but large parts of it frequently lie fallow (this may have more to do with depopulation since 1974 than with lack of fertility).

The coastline

In the Troodos region and up in the Keryneia range, the land tends to drop down quite steeply before it reaches sea level. In spite of this incline, most of Cyprus is distinctive for its relatively flat coastline. And it is here that, apart from Nicosia, the main towns are located. Larnaka, Limassol, Pafos, Morfou (a short way inland), Keryneia and Famagusta are neatly spaced out around the coast.

The areas around the towns of Morfou and Famagusta contain broad expanses of flat coastline. To the southwest of the island, too, near Pafos, and also in Akrotiri Bay and around

Larnaka, the coastline is broad, with smooth flat beaches.

Although steep sea-cliffs are a rarity, some can be found at the points where the Troodos massif runs steeply towards the coast on its north and its south sides: between Pomos and Kokkina in the north, and to the west of Cape Aspro in the south. In the extreme northwest of the island, northeast of the Akamas forest, there are further stretches of rocky coastline, but the wide-open expanses of sand unprotected by cliffs are equally attractive. Visually stunning and varied stretches of coastline occur wherever the chalk of the hill country meets the sea. The hilly landscape near Kourion, for example, drops sharply to the narrow strip of intensively farmed land beside the sea; what trees there are here have been bent inland by the prevailing onshore wind.

The coastline of the Keryneia range is even more varied, low and steep with slabs of limestone jutting out above the clay below. It is worth visiting this coastal zone, which extends from Cape Kormakitis in the northwest to Cape Plakoti in the northeast, to study the rock formations and characteristic coastal flora. Among the best beaches are those along the broad sweep of Famagusta Bay and reaching along the coastline of the Karpasia Peninsula, where they are extensive and almost entirely deserted.

Akamas and Karpasia

The Akamas and the Karpasia peninsulas, separated by the entire width of the island (as well as by the transient man-made scar of the demarcation line), though quite different in character, are equally notable places. The Akamas is short, squat and rugged; the Karpasia is long, thin and more rolling. Each may eventually become a national park, although the authorities on either side of the great divide seem to be in no hurry to establish them.

Rivers, springs and lakes

The map of Cyprus shows a large number of quite small rivers flowing straight into the sea from the hills and mountains. However, most hold water only in the winter and spring, and dry up with the onset of summer. Yet during sudden summer thunderstorms, a dried-up riverbed can turn into a torrent in little more than half an hour. Much of the island's distinctive appearance comes from the deep valleys created by these rivers, with their broad gravel beds. The longest river in Cyprus is the Pedieios, which rises near Machairas monastery in the hills southwest of Nicosia, and flows into the sea near Famagusta. Together with the River Gialias, with which it flows parallel, it irrigates the Mesaoria plain. The Gialias has been dammed in two places to form reservoirs.

Two springs in the Keryneia range are both called Kefalovryso. One is near Kythrea and

the other near Lapithos. Several more springs, shaded by plain trees, can be found in the Troodos mountains below an altitude of roughly 5,250 ft (1,600 m). Some of them, such as the spring near Kalopanagiotis, are rich in minerals and for centuries have been used for therapeutic purposes. The only major lakes in Cyprus are the saltwater lakes near Larnaka and Limassol, which were originally lagoons. Over the millennia they became separated from the sea. They are rich in bird life, particularly during the December and April migrations between Europe and Africa. They have been joined by a constellation of artificial lakes, to preserve as much fresh water as possible. ❑

LEFT: coastline on the road to Vouni.
RIGHT: Avgas Gorge on the Akamas Peninsula.

ISLAND OF FLOWERS – A BOTANIST'S DREAM

Cyprus is one of the most rewarding places in Europe to see wild flowers, thanks to the island's position in the Mediterranean Sea.

Spring arrives early in Cyprus, making it heaven for botanists and hell for gardeners. March to April present a magnificent cornucopia of flowers and fragrances: hillsides resemble giant rock gardens and brilliant patches of untended waste ground outdo northern Europe's carefully tended herbaceous borders with ease. The flowers are at their best in the inland parts of the Akamas peninsula, the high Troodos mountains, and the limestone hills of Keryneia in northern Cyprus.

The richness and diversity of the flora are due in part to the proximity of three continents (Europe, Asia and Africa), partly to the favourable climate, and partly to the variety of habitats. Winter rains followed by a warm, frost-free spring, produce a season's flowers compressed into just a few weeks before the summer's heat become too much. By May or June the flowers are over, the seeds for next year's show are ripening, and greens are fading to brown to match the tourists on the beach.

Except in the cooler, higher Troodos mountains, most plants go into semi-dormancy to survive the arid summer. The first rains of autumn, which could be in early September but may not be until late November, tempt a few autumn bulbs into flower but also initiate the germination of seeds – plants that will grow and build up strength during the winter in pre-paration for the following spring.

▽ **CYTINUS HYPOCISTIS**
Often overlooked, this remarkable plant is a parasite living on the roots of the *Cistus* (below). It emerges only to produce its own white or yellow flowers.

◁ **CISTUS CRETICUS**
Flowers of the *Cistus* family occur in pink, purple and white. This resilient plant rarely shows signs of suffering from the presence of the *Cytinus*.

△ **CYCLAMEN**
Several types of cyclamen are found in Cyprus. The commonest is *Cyclamen Persicum*, the ancestor of the cultivated cyclamen.

△ **NARCISSUS TAZETTA**
Fragrant *Narcissus* adds November colour to rocky hillsides and marshes.

◁ **CISTUS SALVIIFOLIUS**
Cistus species smother the hillsides in May. They thrive after fires and can swiftly re-colonise burned areas. In turn, they give way to regenerating trees.

△ **SPIRANTHES SPIRALIS**
Most orchids flower in the spring, but the unusual spiralling flowers of "autumn ladies' tresses" appear, as is suggested by its common name, in the autumn.

▽ **SCILLA CILICICA**
This blue squill is found in limestone crevices in Cyprus and Asia Minor, flowering in the early part of the year.

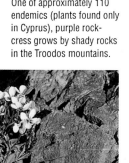

▽ **ARABIS PURPUREA**
One of approximately 110 endemics (plants found only in Cyprus), purple rock-cress grows by shady rocks in the Troodos mountains.

△ **RANUNCULUS ASIATICUS**
A spectacular and elegant buttercup with poppy-sized flowers occurs in white, pink and red as well as shades of bright yellow.

CALLING ALL ORCHID FANS

Orchis simia, the monkey orchid (above), and the naked man orchid, *Orchis italica* (below left) are among the over 50 species of orchids found in Cyprus.

Orchids thrive in undisturbed sites, particularly on the Akamas Peninsula where the displays in March can be spectacular; however, different species require different soil types, so those that are abundant on limestone will be absent from nearby serpentine, and vice versa. Often they grow near the protection of a spiny bush that discourages grazing goats.

Some are easy to identify while others, such as the brown-lipped bee- and spider-orchids, are subject to much taxonomic debate and you will need a comprehensive, up-to-date identification guide to tackle these. (Common names derive from real or fancied resemblances in the individual flowers.)

Needless to say, orchids should not be picked, but should be left to spread their seed and for others to enjoy in their natural habitat. When photographing them be careful not to trample on other plants nearby.

THE CYPRIOTS

"In neither speech nor genius, has the Cypriot any resemblance to either Turk or Greek." The people of Cyprus are something else altogether

In 1879, a publication called *British Cyprus*, which was printed in London, contained the following words by W. Hepworth Dixon: "What are the Cypriots? The Cypriots are neither Turks nor Greeks, neither are they an amalgam of these two races. From Larnaca to Keryneia, from Paphos to Famagusta, you will seek in vain for any sample of these types. In neither face nor figure, in neither speech nor genius, has the Cypriot any resemblance to either Turk or Greek. Nowhere have I seen a Turkish figure, nowhere a Grecian profile. It is safe, I think, to say, that not a single Turk exists in Cyprus. not a single Turk lives on Cyprus."

Cypriots are never described simply as Cypriots. The word is always prefaced by the qualification Greek or Turkish, in recognition of the two very different ethnic groups which inhabit Cyprus: the Greek-speaking Greek Orthodox community and the Turkish-speaking Sunni Muslims. The question of whether they exist as a single people is up to the islanders themselves to decide, and cannot be answered by sociological study.

With half of the population looking to Athens and Europe and the other half towards Ankara and Turkey, the gulf between the communities continues to widen rather than close. The slogan "Proud to be a Turk" is picked out in white stones high on the slopes of the Keryneia mountains, and is visible for miles around. Turkish and Turkish Republic of Northern Cyprus flags, flutter all over the northern part of the island, just as Greek and Republic of Cyprus flags adorn almost every church and town hall in the southern part.

Peaceful coexistence

To begin with, following colonisation by the Ottomans, there were few incidents of social conflict between the Muslim settlers and the indigenous Orthodox Christian population. In fact, the two groups joined forces several times to fight their oppressors in Constantinople (Istanbul). Marriages between the Muslim and Christian communities were unusual, on religious grounds, but in everyday life it was quite difficult to tell the two ethnic groups apart. It was only the growth of nationalism during the

19th century that produced the social and political conflicts that were later to erupt so violently.

In 1960, when the British Crown Colony of Cyprus was finally given its independence, the new Republic's constitution defined the Greek and Turkish Cypriots as two separate ethnic groups. At that time the members of both groups still lived in ethnically mixed villages and cities. Purely "Greek" or "Turkish" areas were few. In most cases, neighbours lived together in peace and celebrated their festivals together. Many villages operated communal cooperatives. Agricultural products were marketed on a mutual basis.

PRECEDING PAGES: tying the knot in a courtship dance.
LEFT: the Orthodox face of Cyprus.
RIGHT: most women still play a traditional role.

Today, these two communities have not laid eyes on each other for a quarter of a century. Their only knowledge of one another's activities is generally gained via television. Nevertheless, the north and south, Greek Cypriots and Turkish Cypriots, have more in common than they would care to admit. In their daily life, their food and drink, their gestures and temperament, Greek Cypriots and Turkish Cypriots are Cypriots. In spite of the propaganda put out by both communities, 400-year-old traditions often prove more influential than a few decades of politics.

One of the saddest aspects of today's division is the widespread inability on both sides, on the part of politicians and ordinary people alike, to imagine the other side's pain. Greek Cypriots too lightly dismiss the trauma that Turkish Cypriots went through in the 1960s in their isolated enclaves, subjected to harassment, armed attack and murder by terrorists and Greek Cypriot regular forces, and cannot appreciate that Turkish Cypriots might genuinely have welcomed the protection of the Turkish army. Turkish Cypriots, in their turn, have no real appreciation of the anguish felt by Greek Cypriots that their homes, their churches and their farms have been invaded, nor for the fate of their 1,600 missing from the 1974 conflict (a

figure that equates to 640,000 Americans if relative population sizes are compared).

Relaxed pace

Anyone who is familiar with Athens and Istanbul will be amazed at the relaxed pace of life in Nicosia. Despite congested traffic jams, car horns are used far less frequently here than in the capital cities of the respective motherlands, for Cypriots tend to be calmer in their reactions to life's daily irritations than either the Greeks or the Turks. Similarly they follow political developments at home and abroad with less passion, even though they have more than enough

reason to get aggravated. Greek Cypriot society, in particular, is more markedly cosmopolitan than it may first appear. Almost everyone has been abroad at some time or other, not least to visit friends and relatives. Until the 1950s Cyprus was still a poor country and thousands emigrated to improve their prospects.

Today, there are large colonies of Greek Cypriots in New York and Australia, and there is a 100,000-strong community in London.

Those who remained at home have retained a strong link with the diaspora. One important factor contributing to the country's cosmopolitan feel was the lack of a university. This situation changed in 1992 when the University of

Cyprus opened. Until then most students had to go abroad and most went to Athens, but many also studied in Britain or the US. This has contributed to a keen awareness of what is going on outside the island. A side-effect for visitors to Cyprus is that they very rarely have problems communicating. Most people have a good command of English.

Still a male society

That said, society is still very traditional in its outlook and Cypriot women are conservative.

EUROPEAN VIEWPOINT

Greek Cypriots consider themselves Europeans as a matter of course, even though their island is geographically part of Asia. They look to Athens, Paris or London for inspiration and orientation.

virtuous, the history of Cyprus would be less eventful and much happier."

The cafés are still the domain of the menfolk, and they are the centres of political discussion. In the villages the café is the forum for political decision-making too. As a rule, Cypriot women are unwelcome in such cafés. There are still only a few women members of parliament (out of 50). Although the attitude persists that a woman's main role is to look after the household and the children, more and more

For centuries fanciful male travellers have liked to ponder on whether they retain any of the characteristics of the goddess Aphrodite. Most decided not. In the opinion of one Charles Lewis Meryon, writing in 1846, "They were not in general beautiful, nor was their dress graceful... Seen from behind they resembled nothing so much as a horse in a mantua-maker's showroom, with a dress appended to it." A more recent visitor, the humorist George Mikes, said: "I cannot suppress my feelings that had the Cypriot girls been just a shade less

women are working after marriage, and in the villages women have always shared the farming work with their menfolk.

The Turkish Cypriots' attitude to life is more Near Eastern than that of their Greek Cypriot counterparts. The influx of tens of thousands of Turkish settlers may have had the desired effect of creating a stronger relationship with Turkey, but it has also caused a mounting wave of protest against "Anatolisation" among indigenous Turkish Cypriots. Immigrants from mainland Turkey are certainly more deeply rooted in Islam, and their adherence to such observances as Ramadan is much more strictly enforced than among Turkish Cypriots. ❏

LEFT: a break on the hilltop, western Cyprus.
ABOVE: a male-dominated society persists in Cyprus.

THE RURAL EXODUS

The farmer's life in the mountain areas of Cyprus has never been romantic; rather, it is a constant struggle with nature

Drive into the pretty Troodos mountains conservation village of Lasanias and you might think that all the inhabitants have run away and hidden indoors at your approach. The streets are deserted, seemingly permanently. When someone finally does put in an appearance it is an old lady dressed entirely in

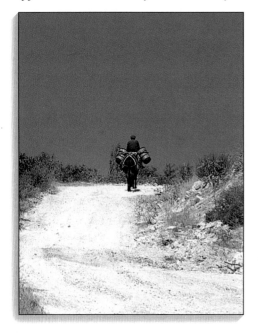

black, and she soon vanishes back inside her house. Lasanias may be an extreme example, but is indicative of a problem that has struck almost all of Cyprus's villages, especially the remoter ones. Most of their people have left, and those who remain are old. An average age of 60 is common in the mountain villages. Like the head of Janus, rural Cyprus has two faces: here decline, there (usually near the coast) the victim of rampant building activity, as holiday homes and apartments spring up like mushrooms.

The steep character of the countryside and the barren stony ground make the farmer's life unadulterated hard-work. An antiquated system of land rights, retaining elements from the

Ottoman era, provides an additional difficulty: a farmer's tiny parcels of land often lie far apart from each other, for example, and over 100 different farmers sometimes have legal claims to the yield of one single olive tree. What's more, droughts and plagues of locusts can strike at any time.

Of course, the 20th century has brought some improvements for Cypriot farmers: new agricultural techniques have been introduced and the feudal system of tributes, under whose yoke generations of farmers had laboured, was abolished in the 1920s. The British were responsible for abolishing the exploitative system of money-lending, and the introduction of a close network of rural cooperatives.

Even today, agricultural life in the mountain areas of Cyprus, where irrigation is impossible, could support a limited number of people. However, people's demands have changed. In former years farmers were content with bread, olives, and wine, and dressed themselves in a single *vraka* (baggy trousers). Any surplus money which they managed to save was invested in the future of their children, in particular the compulsory dowry (*prika*) for their daughters. Today, although people can find a husband for their daughters without a dowry, expectations concerning their own living standards have risen sharply: the material wealth of employees in the cities is demanded in the country too – television brings news of the latest products and fashions to even the remotest home.

In the 1950s, when Cyprus was still under British rule, large building projects demanded workers outside the agricultural sector. Since the 1960s industrial and trading companies in the large Cypriot cities have also needed workers, as have the massive hotel developments. The result was a massive migration from the remote mountain areas to the towns and their suburbs.

Villages within a radius of 12 miles (20 km) from Nicosia, Limassol and Famagusta experienced rapid growth. People worked in the cities but lived in the village, where land prices were still affordable. They tended their own vine-yard or olive grove at the weekend, and con-tracted a fellow villager to cultivate the land.

In the Pafos district, things were more prob-lematic. Until the end of the 1970s there was neither industry nor tourism to any significant extent. In contrast to Limassol or Nicosia, Pafos was just a large village without any supra-regional significance. Income supplements were only available to a limited number of sea-sonal workers in the plantations of the southern coastal areas or in the mines on the edge of the Troodos mountains (these are now exhausted and have been closed). The only possible option for many, especially the young and well-educat-ed, was migration to another region. Between 1960 and 1973 this district was the only one in Cyprus to experience a reduction in the number of its inhabitants – not even the high birth rate amongst the resident population could make up for the loss through migration.

The crisis of 1974 and the division of the island brought the Pafos district further popula-tion losses. During the course of 1975 all the Turkish Cypriot inhabitants had to leave their homes to be resettled in the Turkish occupied north of the island. In the space of one year the district lost some 15,000 inhabitants, a quarter of its total population. Only a few of the Greek Cypriot refugees took the opportunity of set-tling in the abandoned Turkish villages or areas. The prospects of making a reasonable liveli-hood from farming were simply too poor to persuade people to start a new life here.

In the past few years, however, with the rapid growth of tourism, the economic conditions in the district have changed fundamentally. The coastal area of Pafos has experienced its first boom since the heyday of the ancient cult of Aphrodite, and now its tourist industry is also suffering from a shortage of workers. There is hardly a single *Pafitis* (as the inhabitants of the district are known) who has to leave his home village to find work. Yet whilst these newly-created jobs are of enormous significance for the region, the old farmers in the *kafeneion* of Lyso or Fiti are left pondering an uneasy ques-tion: will the young people, who are today working in the hotels as receptionists, bar staff, cooks and chambermaids, be able to maintain

their relationship with the rural world of their parents, or will they become irrevocably alien-ated from their roots?

This relationship can only be maintained by continuing the business of farming, even if it is only as a sideline. The old stooped farmer knows the situation better than anyone else: Cyprus's rural communities thrive on village unity. What's more, to many foreign visitors, the whole appeal of Cyprus is its traditional life style and values.

Seen from this point of view, all those pro-jects which are aimed at bringing about funda-mental improvements in agricultural life and

the rural infrastructure (such as schools and water supplies) are of enormous importance. Until now the beneficiaries of the new large Pafos Irrigation Project have been mainly the landowners on the coastal plain. But other locations in Cyprus are also benefiting from schemes, in particular the Pitsilia Integrated Rural Development Project on the southern edge of the Troodos mountains.

The achievements of such projects should not be measured in terms of the relationship between the costs incurred and the resulting improvements in productivity. Rescuing rural Cyprus from the circle of resignation, apathy and decline is what matters. ❑

LEFT: the way out.
RIGHT: priest and farmer.

CELEBRATIONS

In keeping with their love of worldly pleasures, the Greek Cypriots adore
celebrations and festivals, each occasion usually being accompanied by a feast

Witnessing a wedding in Cyprus is a real experience for the traveller, even though only a few of the original customs and rituals are still adhered to (for example, the length of the celebration has been re- duced from a week to only half a day, and the stipulation that weddings may take place only on Sunday has been relaxed).

Most couples marry in the summer months; leap years are avoided because they are considered unlucky. The festivities begin with the dressing of the bride and groom in wedding finery, usually to a musical accompaniment. Then it's off to church, the time of the ceremony depending on the number of other weddings taking place that day. The guests attending the one-hour-long ceremony – during which the couple is crowned with pearls – are usually too numerous to fit inside the church.

Afterwards, the festivities begin with the "making of the bed", the symbolic setting up and decoration of a mattress: married women carrying the future couple's bedclothes (an important part of the dowry) dance around the mattress and make the bed. Guests then decorate the finished bed with coins and banknotes.

By around 8pm, most of the guests have arrived. Each guest is offered a drink and a plate piled high with the wedding supper – traditionally a range of set dishes: fried slices of potato, cucumber, tomatoes, *kleftiko* (lamb roasted in a sealed oven or sealed earthenware pot) and *pastitsio*. Women carrying large bowls distribute *resi* (crushed wheat porridge, a speciality that no self-respecting wedding omits), and *kourabiedes* (baked almond pastries).

At this point the dancing starts, and lasts until about midnight: there's the *tsifteteli*, a simplified form of the belly dance, which men and women do separately in pairs, or the *rembetiko*, a dance dating from the war of Asia Minor, in which a single individual performs to

PRECEDING PAGES: festival in Agios Neofytos. **LEFT:** the *choros tou androjinou* – wedding donations gratefully received. **RIGHT:** a Turkish festival in Bellapais.

the syncopated clapping of a circle of friends. Once the evening is quite far advanced, it's time for the *choros tou androjinou*, danced only by the bridal couple. This is when the guests shower money on the bride and groom. The couple literally disappear under long chains of banknotes, all pinned together. The song has a

number of optional choruses – depending on how long the bombardment lasts. Finally, towards midnight, the guests disperse.

Christenings

Festivities celebrating engagements and christenings are similar, but on a more modest scale and without any dancing.

Greek Orthodox christenings differ in many important respects from the common Northern European version. The main difference is that the child is naked and completely immersed in water. He or she is then oiled and dressed in fine clothing. The godfather (only one) provides each guest with a baptismal gift, usually a small doll or animal decorated with sweets, and sometimes even a photograph of the baby. The ceremony is followed by a grand party for at least 100 guests.

Name-day celebrations are also very popular with the people of Cyprus. They are held on particular days each year by numerous monasteries, and are similar to country fairs (without the merry-go-rounds). A large area in front of the monastery fills up with stalls and booths selling everything from household goods and clothing to souvenirs, cassettes, toys, nuts and honey. Sweets are particularly popular, especially *loukoumia* (a kind of Turkish delight),

fee entitles one to sample the various types of wine on display and to attend all the theatrical and musical activities. An estimated 100,000 visitors manage to consume an impressive 30,000 litres of wine.

Excuses for a festival in Cyprus are not hard to find. Limassol – and recently Pafos, too – holds its own carnival celebrations in March every year, complete with parades, parties, music and masked balls, and in the summer the firm of Keo hosts a beer festival, similar to the one organised by Carlsberg in Nicosia. There are several cultural festivals in the summer, including the ancient Greek Drama Festival.

chewing gum, *daktyla* (almond cakes with syrup), *lokmades* (small round cream puff pastries fried in oil) and the ever-popular *soutsoukos* (strings of almonds dipped in grape juice and then dried).

Visitors interested in more than just shopping might try their hand at one of the numerous games, where prizes include live canaries.

City festivals

The biggest city festival is the Limassol wine festival, held for 12 days every September. The tradition, started by the wine producers, began in 1961 and was only briefly interrupted for a four-year period by the Cyprus crisis. The entry

In May, every town has its own flower festival, with a procession through the streets and competitions among the children for the best flower arrangements. Before partition, two of the most spectacular festivals were the Orange Festival in Morphou and the Carnation Festival in Varosha; both have fallen victim to the political situation.

There are also the numerous small harvest festivals and fairs (*panegyri*) in all the larger villages of the island, as well as the Dionysos Festival in Stroumpi and the Cherry Festival in Pedoulas. On these occasions, old and young celebrate in the village square, with music, dancing, feasting and drama.

Pagan superstitions

As the Cypriots are a deeply religious people, a great number of church festivals are celebrated, but their significance is rather different from what one might expect, for they feature a fascinating blend of pagan superstition and Christian rites.

Families attribute little importance to Christmas, for example, but New Year's Day is celebrated with at least one *vasilopitta*, a cake made of baked semolina. A coin is hidden inside the cake, and whoever is fortunate enough to find it is assured of good luck in the coming year. Another custom is to throw olive leaves on to

is a water festival of pagan origin in honour of Aphrodite, but it has developed into a Christian festival to mark the Flood. The whole thing culminates in an enormous fair, with music and dancing and readings by local poets.

In May, the towns along the coast celebrate Christ's baptism by lowering crucifixes into the water. And in Larnaka on 18 April, citizens hold a procession headed by the icon of St Lazarus, patron saint of the city. The Assumption of the Virgin on 15 August and the Day of the Holy Cross on 14 September are also important church holidays, when fairs are held at many of the monasteries.

hot ashes, and watch the way they curl; from this, it is maintained, one can predict whether wishes will be fulfilled. *Lokmades* (doughnuts) are an integral part of the Epiphany celebrations on Cyprus; it is customary to throw the first doughnut out of the frying-pan and on to the roof of your house, in order to pacify any lurking evil spirits.

Pentecost is not generally marked. An exception is the popular religious festival unique to Cyprus known as Kataklysmos, which coincides with Pentecost and is held in Larnaka. It

LEFT: a lute player.
ABOVE: motherly embrace for a new bride.

NORTHERN CELEBRATIONS

In the North the festivals correspond to the main Turkish ones and the holiday calendar is again a mix of religious occasions and official commemorations. The two largest religious festivals are the Id-ul-Fitr at the end of the fasting month of Ramadan, and the Id-ul Adha a little later in the year. These are usually celebrated with family get-togethers and the giving of sweets and presents to children. Unlike the south, they don't go in for big bashes but there are occasional folkloric performances at Famagusta and Keryneia castles and unpredictably timed harvest festivals on the Mesaoria plain in thanksgiving for the orange, strawberry and watermelon crops.

Easter time

Without doubt, the most important church festival is Easter. Preparations begin a full 50 days in advance with the onset of fasting, and a strictly vegetarian diet. During Holy Week this diet becomes even stricter – just pulses and vegetables. On Orthodox Good Friday (which falls after the Catholic one) the Epitafios procession, led by a coffin containing a figure of Christ, is held in the villages, and every icon is draped in black cloth; then on Easter Saturday preparations get under way for baking *flaounes*, pastries filled with a mixture of egg, cheese and raisins.

In the evening villagers gather in church for the service celebrating the Resurrection. Everyone holds a candle, and children are given sparklers. At midnight the priest announces Christ's Resurrection with the words "*Christos anesti*" (Christ is risen), to which the answer resounds: "*Alithinos anesti!*" (He is truly risen!). Then the candles are lit, and the square in front of the church blazes with light. After the service, Easter soup is served, and many people stay out even later. On Easter Sunday, familes sport new clothes and go to the countryside for a picnic of grilled *souvla* (skewered lamb) and hard-boiled eggs that have been painted red.

Greek national holidays are also observed in the southern part of Cyprus. Greek Independence Day, for example, is celebrated on 25 March, and "Ohi" Day (celebrating Greece's defiant "no" to the Italians in 1940) on 28 October. Cyprus has its own Independence Day too, of course, on 1 October.

Making music

A few words about music in Cyprus. As mentioned above, the melodies most often heard at festivals are *tsifteteli* and *rembetiko* songs: they are happy, light, rhythmical and generally about romance and everyday affairs, without much depth. But there are other types of music too, ranging from disco and Greek pop to classical music and traditional folk songs. The latter come in various categories: emotional love songs, working songs, children's rhymes, humorous songs, wedding songs, dirges and laments as well as ballads with mythological, Christian, social or political content.

Musical instruments are equally varied. As well as the common instruments of pop music – the bouzouki, drums, accordion, violin and synthesiser – there are a number of very ancient instruments, some dating back to Byzantine times. Some of these are confined to the Turkish culture, such as the *'ùd* (a short-necked lute), the *zornà* (a kind of oboe), the *davul* (a two-headed cylindrical drum) or the *kàsàt* (small finger cymbals), and others are found only in Greek music: the *laoudo* (long-necked lute), the mandolin, the *aulos* (reed pipe) and the *tambuchin* (large frame drum), as well as the kettledrum, the trumpet and cymbals used in parades. These traditional instruments are gradually dying out, however, due to the increasing appetite for modern pop music. The Turkish Cypriot music of today is similar to the music of mainland Turkey, with the main instrument being the *sas* (a kind of balalaika).

Attempts have been made by modern musicians to rescue at least some of the island's old melodies. The Trio Giorgalletto, a male-voice group belonging to a musical family that has been famous on the island for decades, frequently goes on international tours. The group also performs on big festive occasions and for radio and television. ❏

LEFT: a member of the musical Giorgalletto family.
RIGHT: celebrations in the streets of Limassol.

FOOD AND DRINK

*Scarcely a conversation takes place without coffee, beer or brandy
being proffered, and invariably a small snack too*

Food and drink in Cyprus are an integral part of any and every social occasion. The Cypriots love food. No surprise, then, that the country's cuisine is so broad. The island's geographical position and its history have resulted in an interesting mix of Greek, Turkish, Arabic and English culinary influences.

It is at the weekend, above all, that fathers take their families out to eat, and groups of up to 15 people are not uncommon. These kinds of gatherings are informal, and the table is literally strained to breaking-point under the sheer number of different dishes. Plates are piled high, and everyone tries a little bit of everything (leaving a clean plate is considered unusual).

A little of what you fancy

This style of dining stems from the Cypriot preference for *meze* (meaning "mixture"), usually a little of everything that's available that day in that taverna or restaurant and, on occasion, augmented by ingredients brought by the customer – for example, snails they have selected at the local market. There's no better way of getting a general idea of the cuisine than the *meze*, because it offers the widest range of Cypriot food in one sitting. A *meze* always includes a few Cypriot specialities, in particular *halloumi* cheese (produced by thyme-fed goats). The dishes are well seasoned, but not over-spicy. No one need fear stomach upsets, and oil and fat are used moderately.

Although Cyprus is an island, the price of seafood here is high: this part of the Mediterranean is not rich in fish, and many species have to be imported deep-frozen. Typical Cypriot seafood dishes include small, deep-fried fish and rings of cuttlefish.

The traditional Cypriot dishes that can be found are often modified, doubtless as a result of English influence which is still so much in evidence all over the island. Unfortunately it's

no simple matter to find genuine, unadulterated local food, especially in the more touristy areas. Restaurants in the main resorts tend to offer steaks, cutlets and other international dishes, all of which arrive with the compulsory helping of oversized chips. The really simple and delicious local food (pumpkin slices fried in butter, wheatmeal pilau, broad bean stew, and the like) remains unobtainable for the majority of visitors, because such dishes are not generally considered to be a "full meal".

Nor, when sitting down to dine, should one expect the food to be all that Greek: the salads rarely contain sliced onion, and the *talattouri* (similar to the Greek *tsatsiki*) contains only a dash of garlic. Unlike in Greece, however, the food does arrive hot.

One particular favourite with Cypriots is game. Ducks, game birds and rabbits, and also, unfortunately, the *ambelopoulia* – a species of small songbird – are the usual targets of the island's enthusiastic hunters.

PRECEDING PAGES: traditional *meze*.
LEFT: making no bones.
RIGHT: *souvlakia*, always a favourite.

The food in northern Cyprus is closely related to that served in mainland Turkey, with meat and vegetables much in evidence.

A drop to drink

Unlike the Greeks (and the tourists, too), the Cypriots are not great fans of ouzo. Retsina is drunk rarely. Beer, however, is extremely popular (there are two locally-produced brands, Keo and Carlsberg), as is brandy. The latter is excellent, and there are various types. Brandy Sour, a long drink con-

as that of Pliny the Elder, attests to the quality of the grapes, and especially their size. Mark Antony gave Cyprus to Cleopatra, as a token of his love for her, with the words: "Your sweetness, my darling, is like the Nama wine of Cyprus." In the mid-14th century the German pilgrim Ludolf von Suchen wrote: "In all the world there are no greater or better drinkers than in Cyprus." And legend has it that Sultan Selim II ordered the invasion of Cyprus after tasting one of the island's wines.

Another important event in the history of Cypriot wine was the invasion of Cyprus by Richard the Lionheart, and his sale of the island to the Knights Templar; the latter were concentrated around Limassol, notably in Kolossi, where they had their "Grand Commandery" (later taken over by the Knights Hospitaller), which gave the island's famous Commandaria wine its name. Richard is reputed to have later said: "I must go back to Cyprus, if only to taste its wine once again." It was around that time that the Nama wine was rechristened Commandaria.

Even today, this wine, probably the most famous of Cypriot wines, is produced using the same age-old methods, including fermentation in open jars. The grapes are grown in a restricted area of the southern Troodos mountains and the wine's special merit lies in the way it is blended and "aged". It is sweet and heavy, tastes rather like Madeira, and should really be classed as a fortified wine. There are several different types available.

sisting of brandy, lime juice, angostura bitters and soda, is a wonderful pick-me-up after a hard day on the beach.

Cyprus sherry (Emva Cream being the most popular) is well known outside Cyprus. Less familiar to outsiders are the various liqueurs made from the island's fruits. Especially delicious is *Filfar*, made from oranges and reminiscent of Grand Marnier. And to quench the thirst of those not keen on alcohol, the island also stocks the full range of internationally known soft drinks – the empty cans that litter the roadside give a good idea of the range.

But the wines of Cyprus are worthy of particular note. Much written evidence, as early

Today, wine-making is still one of the country's most important sources of income. The sunny, mild climate and the fertile soil make it a natural industry. The main wine areas can be found in the Limassol and Pafos regions, and on the slopes of the Troodos mountains. The large wine factories of the four main producers, Sodap, Keo, Loel and Etko, are all based in Limassol and Pafos. Along with the government, they have encouraged the import of several European grape varieties, in particular several from France. The main importer of Cyprus wine is still Great Britain. ❑

LEFT: Cyprus wines, little known abroad, can be very palatable. **RIGHT:** Cypriot sherry, a major export.

CRAFTS

Many cottage industries, unable to compete with imported goods, are disappearing from Cyprus, but there are people trying to keep traditions alive

The twin village of Lefkara (population: 1,300) nestles in a picturesque setting at the foot of the Troodos mountains. This attractive collection of buildings, with unusual red roofs, is said to have been a popular summer resort with ladies of the Venetian period. Kato Lefkara, the lower part of the village, is tiny, with narrow, winding streets. It has a shop that provides basic necessities, two *kafeneions*, where the male population of the village meet, and a small church.

Pano Lefkara, the upper part, is larger. Here, restaurants and shops have sprung up around the market-place where the tourist buses pull up and the side streets are flanked by souvenir shops, selling silver and gold jewellery and tablecloths. These, magnificently embroidered, hang outside nearly every shop. In good weather, the women of the village sit outside their houses and work at their broderie anglaise, embroidering motifs on cotton and linen. The store owners are only too happy to invite any passing strangers to take a look around.

Da Vinci's choice

Lefkara is the centre of lace-making in Cyprus. The industry has gained a worldwide reputation for its intricacy and beauty. Leonardo da Vinci is said to have purchased some *lefkaritiki* lace-making for the altar of Milan Cathedral (a sample hangs in Lefkara in his memory). At the turn of the century, men from Lefkara were travelling halfway round the world selling embroidery, some of them to North America, while their wives stayed sewing at home. Records show that in 1910, some £1,720 worth of Lefkara lace was exported, a handsome sum at the time.

The base material for the lace is Irish linen. Creating, say, a tablecloth can frequently mean several weeks' hard work, and so prices can be

high – though not prohibitively so. The end product is unique: no piece of Lefkara embroidery is the same as any other.

Four main companies, each employing some 150 workers, look after the manufacture and marketing of lace in Lefkara. The village also contains several fine stone houses – one of

which, the House of Patasalos, contains a Museum of Folk Art – devoted to the history of lace and silverwork of the area.

Thanks to its buoyant lace-making industry, Lefkara has prospered, and there is no danger that the village will decline, but other cottage industries are not faring so well and so official Handicraft Centres have been set up with the aim of keeping the island's handicrafts alive. Their workshops still use traditional methods. The employees, many of whom are refugees from the Turkish-occupied sector, keep old techniques alive which would otherwise have been forgotten. Handicrafts made on a private basis are also sold here.

PRECEDING PAGES: modernisation has brought sweeping changes to traditional crafts.
LEFT: pottery in Kornos.
RIGHT: a young practitioner of an ancient art.

Anyone buying goods at any of the Cyprus Handicraft Service (CHS) shops in Limassol, Larnaca, Pafos and Nicosia can be sure that their purchase has been handmade.

Embroidery and lace is made in other villages apart from Lefkara. Colourful cotton embroidery is a speciality of several remote villages, such cloth being the traditional cover for dowry chests. In the wine village of Omodos, elderly ladies embroider quilts and tablecloths.

Crafts under threat

Indeed, without the Cyprus Handicraft Service, production of the handsomely carved wooden

from the inedible bottle gourd are no longer needed by a world used to canned drinks and glass bottles. Gourd flasks can sometimes be seen hanging outside restaurants, often in the guise of lamps.

Wickerwork and basketry is still being made. Colourful wickerwork baskets and platters are a very common sight. Decorative wicker plates, with perforated rims, are often used as bowls. The craftsmen tend to be elderly refugees, who want to earn extra money to supplement their pensions.

Weaving mills were once widespread on the island, but the ancient looms in the remote

bride's chests (*sandouki*), made of pine, cedar or walnut, would have died out. In the old days these chests used to contain the daughters' dowries and jewellery. These days the Cypriots use ordinary wardrobes, but the old chests – the fronts of which are usually decorated with flower and tree motifs – are still used for ornamental purposes. The town of Lapithos on the north coast of the island, the former centre of chest-making, has been under Turkish occupation since 1974.

Another craft that has almost disappeared is the manufacture of gourd flasks, an industry which used to be found wherever bottle gourds grew. Artistically decorated gourd flasks made

mountain villages are rarely used these days. In the Handicraft Service workshops, on the other hand, they are in use daily. Silkworms are bred here, too, and their threads are spun into fine cloth for dresses and skirts.

All that glisters

Gold and silver jewellery is still produced today, albeit on a much smaller scale than in years gone by. Most of Cyprus's goldsmiths and silversmiths, whose premises used to share a street in Nicosia, disappeared long ago.

Copper artefacts are usually antiques, with a correspondingly high price-tag. Small-scale metalworking, however, is still done in the traditional way; here, the piece to be duplicated is placed in a metal frame, which is then filled with a special type of sand on two sides. When the mould is opened the original is carefully removed, and liquid metal is then poured into the sand-mould.

Ceramics for storage

Pottery, made of the local red clay, is still widespread. Here it's possible to differentiate between larger, simply-constructed pieces and smaller, finer work. The largest specimens,

WATER COOLERS

Even in the broiling heat of summer, water stays pleasantly cool in large unglazed clay pitchers. They often stand on metal tripods and can also be used as flower pots.

still made, and look much like they did in the last millennium.

Small pottery ware is a speciality of the Pafos region. Clay figurines, glazed vases, candlesticks, bowls and complete coffee services are all available. Some are colourfully decorated with flower patterns, others are more simple, with geometrical designs. The latter, with their line patterns, are strikingly reminiscent of their ancient counterparts. Some of the decorative forms date back to the Early Neolithic Period.

round storage jars often measuring up to 3 ft (1 m) in diameter, are commonly found lying in gardens and outside houses. Called *pitharia*, these jars were formerly used for storing oil, olives, water or wine. The potters who made them were held in high regard, and used to travel from village to village creating them on the spot – without even using a wheel.

Alas, *pitharia* are now rarely produced; their enormous size and incredible weight make them unsuitable for modern-day living. Large, simply constructed clay pitchers, however, are

LEFT: coppersmith at work.
ABOVE: Lefkara, renowned for its lace-making.

The pots are formed using simple wheels, and are then hand-painted. Beware, however, pottery depicting Greek gods, especially with inscriptions in English – these are usually cheap, mass-produced imports.

Craftsmen are struggling to compete with the cheap, factory-produced equivalents saturating the market: the chairmakers, for instance, who used to make the old wooden chairs with wickerwork seats and arms, are a vanishing breed; their chairs may be hard-wearing, but plastic ones are cheaper.

Everywhere the competition from industry is gaining ground. With refrigerators readily available, who needs *pitharia*? ❏

PLACES

*A detailed guide to the entire island, with principal sites
clearly cross-referenced by number to the maps*

Cyprus is characterised by the striking differences between
ancient traditions and new, fast-moving, Western-influenced
developments. On the one hand, archetypal Mediterranean
landscapes with mountain villages and isolated forest areas; on the
other, brand-new farms employing modern methods of agriculture,
and cosmopolitan cities with seemingly endless suburbs. Sometimes
tradition and modernity coexist: not far from the hyper-modern
blocks of flats in the city of Nicosia, for example, are the tranquil
labyrinths of the old city, full of mysterious alleys.

Some of the island's most famous sites have been victims of earthquakes and art thieves, and their extant remains are thus modest. Yet
there are still many spectacular sights, in particular the Byzantine
churches and monasteries in the Troodos mountains, with their
wealth of frescoes and icons, the splendid Roman mosaics in Kato
Pafos and, in the North, the ruins of the Hellenistic-Roman city of
Salamis, and the Gothic abbey of Bellapais, captured so memorably
in Lawrence Durrell's *Bitter Lemons*.

The places section of this guide begins with Limassol, a popular
tourist destination and convenient springboard for visiting Kolossi
and Kourion, proceeds to Larnaka (ancient Kition) and moves on to
the burgeoning resort of Agia Napa at Cape Gkreko. It then crosses
to the southwest of the island, where Pafos offers the best of archaeological Cyprus, and thence to the island's wilder fringes, such as
Polis, and into the Troodos mountains. Lastly, from the divided capital of Nicosia, it hops into northern Cyprus.

Those who want to travel to the North should take into account the
political difficulties. The Cypriot population is unable to cross the
demarcation line between the two territories, and tourists can only do
so subject to considerable restrictions. Normally, tourists are given
permission to make only a day trip from Nicosia to the Turkish-
occupied part of the island. It is therefore assumed that your journey
is of this type, and alternative tours, embracing the main sites, have
been devised. Entering northern Cyprus via Turkey is against the
regulations of the Government of the Republic of Cyprus and travellers who do so are forbidden from crossing into the south.   ❑

PRECEDING PAGES: Pano Lefkara, in the Troodos mountains; Petra tou Romiou,
mythical birthplace of Aphrodite; on the road in southwest Cyprus; Kourion's
Early Christian basilica.
LEFT: fishing boats in the harbour at Pafos.

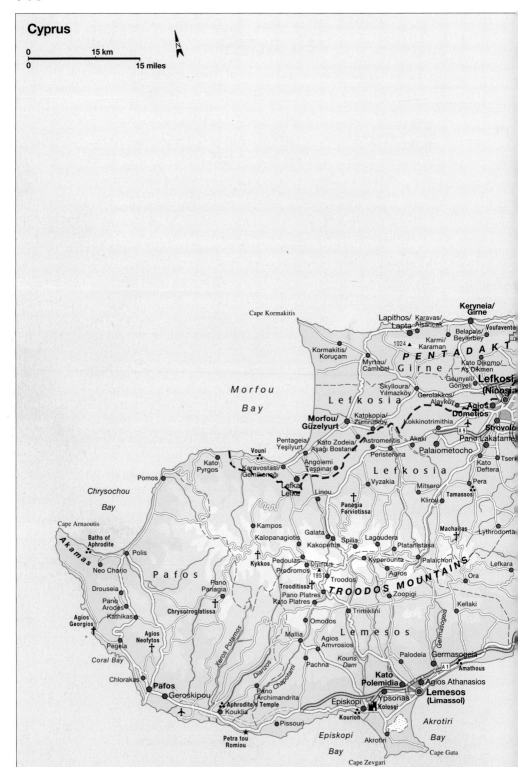

Cyprus

0 — 15 km
0 — 15 miles

N

Cape Kormakitis

Morfou
Bay

Keryneia/
Girne
Lapithos/ Karavas/
Lapta Alsancak
Belapais/ Voufavento
Karmi/ Beylerbey
Karaman
1024 ▲
PENTADAKT
Kormakitis/ Myrtou/ Kato Dikomo/
Koruçam Cambel Aş Dikmen
Girne Geünyeli/ Lefkosi
Skylloura/ Gönyeli (Nicosia)
Yilmazköy Gerolakkos/
Lefkosia Alayköy
Morfou/ Katokopia/ Agios
Güzelyurt Zümrütköy Kokkinotrimithia Dometios
Strovolo
Pentageia/ Kato Zodeia/ Astromeritis Akaki Pano Lakatame
Vouni Yeşilyurt Aşağı Bostanı A 9
Kato Peristerona Palaiometocho Tseri
Karavostasi/ Taşpinar Kato
Gemikonağı Angolemi Deftera
Kato Vyzakia Lefkosia Pera
Pomos Pyrgos Lefka/ Linou
Lefke Mitsero Klirou Tamassos
Chrysochou Panagia
Bay Forviotissa Machairas
Lythrodonta
Cape Arnaoutis Kampos Galata
Baths of Kalopanagiotis Spilia Lagoudera Platanistasa
Aphrodite Kakopetria Palaichori Lefkara
Akamas Polis Kykkos Pedoulas Kyperounta Ora
Neo Chorio Prodromos Olympus Agros
Pafos 1951 Troodos TROODOS MOUNTAINS
Drouseia Trooditissa Zoopigi Kellaki
Pano Pano Platres
Pano Panagia Kato Platres
Arodes Chrysorrogiatissa Trimiklini Germasogeia
Agios Kathikas Omodos Lemesos
Georgios Agios Mallia Palodeia Germasogeia
Agios Neofytos Amvrosios Amathous
Pegeia Pachna Kouris A 1
Coral Bay Dam Kato Agios Athanasios
Chlorakas Polemidia Lemesos
Pafos Pano Chapotami Episkopi Ypsonas (Limassol)
Geroskipou Archimandrita Kolossi
Aphrodite's Temple Kourion Akrotiri
Kouklia Pissouri *Episkopi* *Bay*
Petra tou *Bay* Akrotiri
Romiou Cape Zevgari Cape Gata

Xeros Potamos
Dianzos
Germasogeia

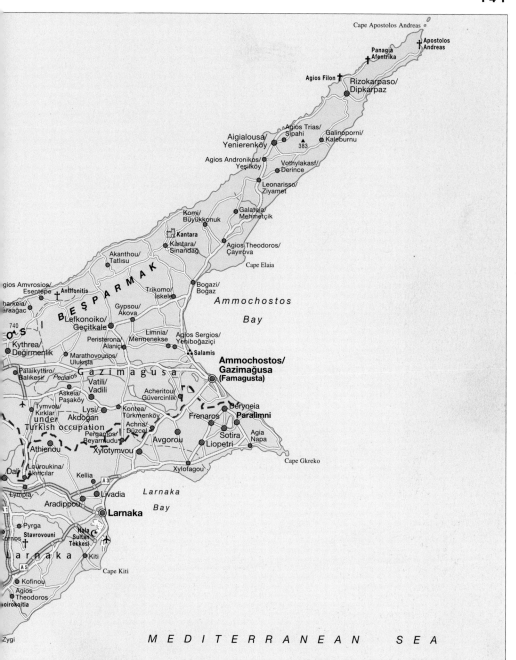

Cape Apostolos Andreas

Apostolos
Andreas

Panagia
Afentrika

Agios Filon

Rizokarpaso/
Dipkarpaz

Agios Trias/
Sipahi

Galinoporni/
Kaleburnu

Aigialousa/
Yenierenköy

383

Agios Andronikos/
Yeşilköy

Vothylakasf/
Derince

Leonarisso/
Ziyamet

Komi/
Büyükkonuk

Galateia/
Mehmetçik

Kantara

Kantara/
Sinandağ

Agios Theodoros/
Çayırova

Akanthou/
Tatlısu

Cape Elaia

gios Amvrosios/
Esentepe

Antifonitis

Trikomo/
İskele

Bogazi/
Boğaz

B E Ş P A R M A K

Ammochostos

harkeia/
araağaç

Lefkoniko/
Geçitkale

Gypsou/
Akova

Bay

O S I

740

Kythrea/
Değirmenlik

Peristerona/
Alaniçi

Limnia/
Mermenekse

Agios Sergios/
Yeniboğaziçi

Marathovounos/
Ulukışla

Salamis

**Ammochostos/
Gazimağusa
(Famagusta)**

Palaikythro/
Balıkesir

Pediaios

G a z i m a g u s a

Vatili/
Vadili

Askeia/
Paşaköy

Acheritou/
Güvercinlik

Tymvou/
Kırklar

Lysi/
Akdoğan

Kontea/
Türkmenköy

Deryneia

Frenaros

Paralimni

under

Achna/
Düzcel

Pergamos/
Beyarmudu

Avgorou

Sotira

Agia
Napa

Turkish occupation

Athienou

Xylotymvou

Liopetri

Cape Gkreko

Dali

Louroukina/
Akıncılar

Kellia

Xylofagou

A 3

Lympia

Livadia

Larnaka

Aradippou

Bay

Larnaka

A 1

Pyrga

Stavrovouni

Hala
Sultan
Tekkesi

rnos

Kiti

L a r n a k a

A 5

Cape Kiti

Kofinou

Agios
Theodoros

oirokoitia

Zygi

M E D I T E R R A N E A N   S E A

LIMASSOL AND THE SOUTHWEST

Limassol may not quite live up to its billing as the "Paris of Cyprus" but it does have a certain appeal. One in three visitors to the island heads for the Bay of Amathous, Limassol's "riviera"

Map on page 144–5

L ying on Cyprus's south coast, **Limassol ❶** is big, brash and bustling. With 150,000 inhabitants, it has grown at breakneck speed since 1974, just about tripling its population thanks to an influx of Greek Cypriot refugees from the north and a subsequent boom in industry, services and tourism. With Cyprus's main port, Famagusta (Ammochostos) in Turkish-occupied territory, Limassol took over as the Greek Cypriots' shipping hub.

Not all the effects of this enforced growth have been pleasant. Little thought, care or imagination has been devoted to the process of expansion. Limassol (Lemesos to Greek Cypriots) has swallowed up hapless villages along its rim and its outer suburbs are edging up into the foothills of the Troodos mountains, while at the same time big resort hotels have sprouted all along the bay to the east. In compensation, Limassol has a scenic setting, is cosmopolitan in the way port cities tend to be, and has nightlife, shopping, dining and drinking venues in abundance.

LEFT: alms-seeker outside a Limassol mosque.
BELOW: musician in medieval garb performing at Limassol Castle.

Soldiers' haunt

The British soldiers, who are stationed at the military base on the Akrotiri peninsula to the west of Limassol, and who spend their free time in the nearby city, are as characteristic of Limassol as the locals who have made their living from trading since time immemorial. Nowadays the export of fruit and vegetables is the most significant branch of the local economy.

In the area around Limassol there are extensive citrus fruit plantations of lemon, orange and grapefruit trees. Moreover, Keo, in the west of the city between Odos Fragklinou Rousvelt and the coast, has established itself as Cyprus's largest manufacturer of alcoholic drinks. The firm's complex comprises a brewery, winery, and a distillery for schnapps; it is possible to go on a tour of the facility during normal working hours. Wine-growing has a long tradition in the region; the most important vineyards stretch along the southern slopes of the Troodos mountains, interspersed with nut bushes and plantations of cherry, apple, pear and peach trees.

Every year, in September, Limassol is the scene of a wine festival, and the celebrations even outdo the local spring carnival. The Arts Festival in July completes the varied cultural calendar, which is increasingly orientated towards the tourist trade.

The approach road from Larnaka is lined solidly with hotels, broken only by restaurants and nightclubs. Limassol has not only taken over Famagusta's role as

Visitors to Limassol castle.

the main port on the island but also its position as the leading tourist centre.

New business centres and industrial estates have sprung up, actively helped by the government of Cyprus with tax concessions and ongoing improvements in the infrastructure. Amongst the new ventures are numerous banks – not the usual massive skyscrapers, but buildings which blend discreetly with the surrounding cityscape. Considerable numbers of Russians also live in Limassol and many of them brought money to the town.

Ancient history

Archaeologists are not able to give a definitive account of the origins of Limassol, not least because of the modern superstructures which have been built over the ancient remains. Various tombs from the Early and Middle Bronze Ages, whose burial gifts – mainly ceramics – can be dated to the end of the 3rd century BC or to the 2nd century BC, are proof that there were settlements in the city around this time (the discoveries are displayed in the local museum).

In the suburb of Agia Fyla, which lies to the northwest of Limassol, a cemetery was discovered from the Late Bronze Age (around 1300 BC). It has been proved that the ancient coastal settlement of Nemesos, or Lemesos, which gave its name to the modern city, was situated here. At that time, however, the settlement was in the shadow of the more important nearby coastal cities of Amathus (today Amathous, to the east of Limassol) and Kourion (further west on the other side of the Akrotiri peninsula), and so played only a very minor role.

After a number of severe earthquakes in the Byzantine era, the rebuilding of the area under Emperor Theodosius II (AD 408–50) was concentrated on the area of present-day Limassol, to the detriment of the previously more significant

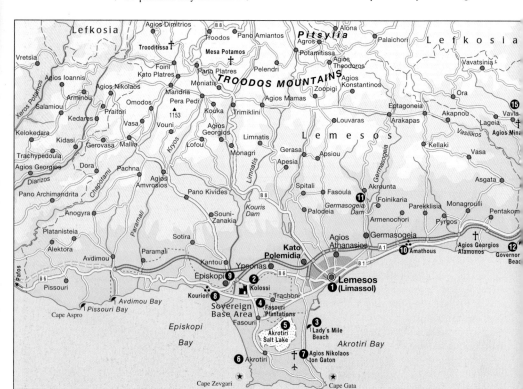

settlement at Amathous. The port of Theodosias, named after its builder, was founded anew in the wide bay. In the following period Theodosias was also the see of the bishops, the most significant of whom was Leontius (AD 590–668).

During the Third Crusade King Richard the Lionheart, on his way to the Holy Land, chose Limassol as a landing place for his army and a base for conquering Cyprus. The marriage of Richard and Berengaria of Navarre took place in the citadel of Limassol, and the Spanish noblewoman was thereby crowned Queen of England. Before the bridegroom continued his journey to the Holy Land he sold the island of Cyprus to the crusading Order of the Knights Templar, who subsequently sold it to Guy de Lusignan.

In the following period the city was fortified, and continued to serve the crusaders as an important base from which they could fend off attacks from the Saracens. It also provided accommodation for the Hohenstaufen emperor Frederick II, both on his way to the Holy Land in 1228 and on his return in the following year. The Lusignans and the Knights Templar contributed to the economic upturn in the city, as did the Order of the Knights of St John of Jerusalem (the "Hospitallers") later. In 1303 the last Grand Master of the Templars, Jacques de Molay, took his leave from the city, having been ordered back to France by Pope Clement V, where he was burned at the stake six years later.

Having suffered many severe earthquakes, Limassol was set on fire by the Genoese in 1371 and plundered by Egyptian raiders in the first half of the 15th century. What was left was then destroyed by the Ottoman Turks in 1539. As early as 1480 the oriental traveller Felix Faber was complaining about the deplorable state of the city. The only building of any consequence left was a single church, and that was virtually ruined (even here the bells had been stolen).

Map on page 144–5

Blacksmith at work in the backstreets of Limassol.

BELOW: tombs of Limassol Castle's past occupants.

Southwestern Cyprus

The continuing decline of the city was described by a succession of European visitors who followed in his tracks.

There were already tensions between the established Greek population and the Turkish-Ottoman newcomers. One traveller who saw Limassol soon after the devastating earthquake of 1584 reported that the entrances to the modest dwellings of the Greeks were so low that you had to bend down to enter them. Their purpose was to prevent Turkish knights from using them as stables for their horses. As late as 1815 an English traveller described Limassol as a run-down settlement of 150 mud houses, in which the proportion of Greeks to Turks was two to one.

The city's only importance at that time was based on the shipping of wine. In 1881 Limassol had over 6,000 inhabitants. When the export of wine was increased considerably towards the end of the 19th century, and the rebuilding of the harbour had been finished, the city quickly recovered its former prosperity. The capacity of the old harbour was soon no longer sufficient, and a new complex was built to the southwest of the city, complete with fire-fighting equipment and ship-repair yards.

Around the town

The coastal road, with its four lanes and grassy central reservation, starts from the old harbour and runs to the north. The first section is Odos Spyrou Araouzou (the Tourist Information Office can be found at number 27). From then on the street is officially known as Odos Oktovriou 28, after the Greek national holiday. Hotels and restaurants serving fresh fish are sprinkled between shops and residential buildings, along with bars and English-style pubs.

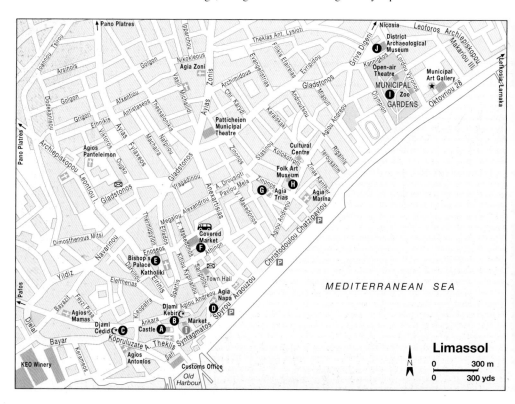

Limassol

Just a little way from the road to the north of the old harbour (but hidden from the road itself) is **Limassol Castle** , in the middle of a small fenced-off area. This now serves as a museum. On the way there from the coast, you pass a small roundabout, near which is a **Reptile Museum**, run by an immigrant from Pakistan, and an excellent fish taverna, reputed to be the oldest in the city. Outside, two live pelicans attract the attention of potential customers.

The Castle

At the beginning of the 14th century the Crusader citadel (tel: 05-330419; open daily; entrance fee) was built on the ruins of the Byzantine castle. Part of the eastern wall of the castle was still standing and was integrated into the western wall of the citadel. The marriage of Richard the Lionheart and Berengaria took place in the chapel of the Byzantine castle, followed by the coronation of Berengaria as Queen of England by the Bishop of Evreux.

King Janus (1389–1432) handed Limassol Castle to the Knights of St John of Jerusalem, who had made their headquarters in the castle of Kolossi. They also carried out further renovations to the castle of Limassol. After 1570 the Turks moved into the castle and totally rearranged the internal layout (the Great Hall had already fallen in after one of the supporting pillars had collapsed in 1525). Up to 1940 the castle served as a prison for the British administration, and for a while as an army headquarters. Extensive restoration in 1950 included reinforcement of the vaults.

With the division of the island, the Medieval Museum in Nicosia lay right on the border between the Greek and Turkish halves of the city. As a result the exhibits were moved, with the financial support of the Amathus Ltd shipping

Map on page 146

TIP

Those of squeamish disposition should avoid visiting the snake terrarium at the Reptile Museum shortly before the close (7pm), when the animals are fed with small rodents.

BELOW: sturdy walls of Limassol Castle.

company, to Limassol Castle, and since then they have been housed there in the new **Cyprus Medieval Museum.**

The entrance to the castle leads into a small ante-room. From here you can enter the lower-lying, almost quadrangular Gothic Great Hall to the right. On the left-hand side, spread over two floors, there is a group of smaller rooms, which can be reached via a central corridor. These rooms house objects from the Byzantine and medieval periods.

The most spectacular exhibits are the three silver plates discovered among the famous "Lambousa Treasure" in 1902. Unfortunately a further six from the same collection were smuggled abroad and can now be found in the Metropolitan Museum in New York. The plates, which date back to AD 620, show scenes from the youth of King David. They were discovered in the ancient town of Lapithos, which now lies on the north coast of Cyprus, in the part of the island now under Turkish occupation.

From both the Great Hall, and from the smaller rooms on the left, there are steps leading up to the roof of the castle. From here there is a good view over the port and, above all, over the old city. The two minarets, which tower over the city, provide a lasting reminder that a significant Turkish population once lived in Limassol.

Heading north

BELOW: fresh fruit and vegetables and lots more on sale at the Covered Market.

The Episcopal church and its neighbouring **Bishop's Palace** can be reached via Odos Eirinis, which begins at the citadel, crosses Odos Ankara and then continues further north. Two turnings further to the east lead to the **Covered Market**, where fruit, vegetables, meat, and poultry are on sale.

If you follow Odos Agiou Andreou to the north away from the coastline you can make a short detour to the right, to the **Holy Trinity** church (**Agia Trias/Hagia Triados**) ⑤, which can be easily seen from the road. Going back to the turn-off and continuing along Odos Agiou Andreou, leads to a corner house (number 253) standing alone on the left-hand side at the junction of Odos Othonos and Odos Amalias. Since 1985 this has housed the **Folk Art Museum** ⑪ (Mon–Fri; entrance fee), where agricultural implements and traditional furnishings, ceramics and textiles are on display.

Map on page 146

A little further along, on the same side of the street, is the **Cultural Centre**, with rooms for art exhibitions and a library. If you turn into Odos Kannigkos at the top end of Odos Agiou Andreou, you reach the northern edge of the **Municipal Gardens** ①, which contain an open-air theatre and a raggedy little zoo, and are the setting for the Limassol Wine Festival in September. A little further along the coast road, at 103 Odos Oktovriou 28, is the Municipal Art Gallery (open Mon–Fri; entrance fee).

The garden area to the north houses the **District Archaeological Museum** ① (tel: 05-330157; open daily; entrance fee), which was set up in the 1970s. The majority of the exhibits here are from the discoveries at Kourion and Amathous, along with a number from other sites in the region around Limassol. The exhibitions are organised both thematically and chronologically: the first display case documents the history of Cypriot ceramics. Other interesting artefacts include terracotta figures. The larger sculptures nearby reveal both Greek and Egyptian influences, the latter being most obvious in the monumental and ornately decorated capital from Amathous, which bears the unmistakable cow-head of the Egyptian goddess Hathor. ❑

The remains of the Castle gate.

BELOW: reminder of a once-substantial Turkish population.

THE TURKISH DISTRICT

After visiting the castle you can walk between the two mosques, the **Djami Kebir** ❸ ("the large mosque") in the east and the **Djami Cedid** ❻ (also known as the Köprülü Haci Ibrahim Aga Mosque) in the west, and appreciate the typical Turkish architecture of the area, which was once the Turkish commercial district. Particularly notable are the pronounced oriels on the first floors which lean over the street. On some of the houses you can still see Turkish inscriptions, and the further west you go, the more often you come across Turkish street names: Odos Agiou Andreou joins Odos Ankara, which at its western end fans out into a mass of small Emirs and Pasas. Here the Djami Cedid (Köprülü Haci Ibrahim Aga Mosque) towers above the river bed of the Garyllis – invariably bone dry.

In the immediate neighbourhood of the Djami Kebir there is a **Turkish bath**, and, just a little further east, the **Agia Napa** church ❹, consecrated with St Veronica's veil (offered to Christ on his way to the Crucifixion), rises up between the promenade and Odos Agiou Andreou. The present church, built in 1903, houses a series of icons preserved from its early-18th century predecessor. Further on, Agios Andronikos church hides in a cul-de-sac, accessible only from the waterfront.

KOLOSSI AND KOURION

*Take the scenic route to the knights' castle of Kolossi
and to Kourion, perched on a bluff over the sea – the most
spectacular archaeological site in the South*

Limassol itself wasn't always the centre of power: during certain periods this role was enjoyed by the fortress of **Kolossi ❷** (open daily; entrance fee), which dominated the Episkopi Plain in the western hinterland of the city. King Hugo I, a member of the Lusignan nobility, handed the fortress over to the Knights Hospitaller during the 13th century.

This area was economically important for a long time as a result of its sugar cane plantations. *Zucchari de Cipro* appeared on European trading documents as long ago as the beginning of the 14th century. Nowadays it is the vast citrus fruit plantations, known as *Fasouri*, which shape the appearance of the landscape and form the economic backbone of the region.

About 9 miles (15 km) west of Limassol the castle of Kolossi of the Order of St John, rises up above the fertile landscape of the plain of Episkopi. Its walls contain not only a fortified tower with living quarters but also a sugar-processing factory for the cane sugar which was grown in the area at the time.

The countryside surrounding Limassol was given to the Order of St John by Hugo I (1205–18); in return he received their support in battles against the Muslims. When the Christians lost Syria to the Arabs following their defeat at Acre in 1291, the Order of St John chose Cyprus as their headquarters. They stayed here until 1310, at which point they founded their own state on the island of Rhodes, where they remained until driven out by the Turks in 1522 and forced to flee to Malta.

LEFT: Kourion's spectacular theatre.
BELOW: the castle of Kolossi.

In Cyprus they had to compete with the Knights Templar for possession of the castle of Kolossi. It was only after the Templars were proscribed by the Pope in 1308 that the Knights of St John were able to take proper possession of the castle. In fact they received not only the castle itself but also 60 neighbouring villages, their property and their serfs.

Along with oil, wheat and cotton, the main products were wine and sugarcane. The **Hall of the Sugar Factory** – near the aqueduct used for transporting the water necessary for sugar production – has survived into modern times. A mill stone with a diameter of 11 ft (3.2 m), used to press out the juice from the cane, also still exists.

The Knight von Gumppenberg mentioned the place in his *Pilgrim's Travels*: "We rode to a house, that of the Knights of St John, and sugar grows there and the house is called Koloss."

But Kolossi was not alone in being a sugar-producing area. There was stiff competition from nearby Episkopi, in the form of the Venetian noble family, the Cornaro. As various historical documents prove, there were continual disputes between the two families over the rights to use the water in the region. In

The royal coat of arms on the tower of Kolossi castle.

BELOW: the Hall of the Sugar Factory.

the end, Catarina Cornaro, widow of the last king of Cyprus before the island was taken over by the Venetians in 1489, dispossessed the Knights of St John and took possession of the castle and its factory. Moreover her nephew, the Cardinal Marco Cornaro, was then appointed Commander of the Order of St John. An inscription from 1591, which Murad, Pasha of Cyprus at the time, had carved in the south wall, is evidence that the Ottomans, who had conquered the island some 20 years before, carried on this lucrative industry.

Near the sugar factory is the **fortified tower** with its three floors. It rises from a quadrangular ground plan whose sides measure 52 ft (16 m). Its present structure was built in 1454 on the remains of a previous building dating from the time of the crusades. The semi-circular foundations of the original building and a well on the east side of the fortified tower have survived.

A group of coats of arms has been chiselled into the east wall within a cross-shaped frame. In the middle, directly under a crown, is the royal coat of arms divided into four parts and comprising the emblems of the Kingdom of Jerusalem, the Lusignans, the Kingdom of Cyprus and Armenia. This royal coat of arms is flanked by that of the Grand Masters of the Order, Jean de Lastic (left) and Jacques de Milli (right). In the lower arm of the cross is the emblem of Louis de Magnac, one-time Grand Commander of Cyprus who is believed to have commissioned the building of the new fortified tower.

At that time, this *donjon* could only be entered via a drawbridge leading to the first floor. After going through a further entrance gate, at one time protected with a machicolation, visitors proceed to a kitchen, with an open fire, and a day-room with paintings of scenes from the crusades. These paintings can be dated from the coat of arms of Louis de Magnac. A spiral staircase leads up to

the second floor and two living rooms, one of which has a fireplace (the same coat of arms can be seen on the chimney). The staircase leads up to the roof. Going down instead of up, visitors proceed to three vaulted chambers in the basement, two of which have wells.

Lady's Mile and Fasouri

On the way from Limassol to Kolossi, on the southwestern edge of the city, is **Lady's Mile Beach ❸**. It lies inside the territory of the British Sovereign Base and is mostly used by British service personnel and their families (actually it's mostly deserted). A long stretch of fine golden sand, it has a less than scenic view across to the Limassol harbour installations. Lady's Mile apparently got its name because it was the place the colonel's wife walked her horse, or had it walked for her, back in the rose-tinted days of empire. Inland from here are the **Fasouri Plantations ❹**, whose air is heady with the tang of citrus fruits.

The roads in the area are lined with cypress trees that serve as wind breaks protecting the orchards. Sadly the prettiest such road, where overhanging cypresses once formed a tunnel of trees, must have broken one wind too many, and most of the trees were deemed a hazard to traffic and chopped down.

Flamingos and cats

Kolossi lies at the northern end of the Akrotiri peninsula. Crossing the peninsula in the direction of the coast to the south, you come to the basin of the large **Akrotiri Salt Lake ❺**, which is usually dried out. Whole colonies of flamingos can be seen here when the lake bed fills up in winter, and migrating birds also use the area as a stop-over en route to and from Africa. As with the salt lake

Simple gardens visible below Kolossi castle.

BELOW: luscious citrus fruits are abundant in the region.

near Larnaka, however, no salt is extracted here any longer. In the immediate neighbourhood is a British military air base – photography is strictly forbidden – and the small village of **Akrotiri** ❻, which gave its name to the peninsula.

On the edge of the village is a modern monastery which has replaced the abandoned monastery of **Agios Nikolaos ton Gaton** ❼ (St Nicholas of the Cats), to the eastern edge of the military airport. The eastern tip of the Akrotiri peninsula, Cape Gata, also takes its name from the felines which the monks in the old monastery employed to defend them against snakes. Today, the nuns who have replaced the monks in residence at Agios Nikolaos maintain the tradition of being kind to cats. Masses of lazy felines lounge in the garden and in the shade of the cloister, and not one of them looks as if it would know what to do with a snake if it suddenly came fang to whisker with one.

Kourion

To go from Limassol to visit the impressive ruins of **Kourion** ❽, (open daily; entrance fee) which stand in solitary splendour on a massive rock ledge 230 ft (70 m) above the sea, take one of the public buses which leave from Limassol Castle throughout the day. What you see on arrival, however, dates only from the Hellenistic, Roman and Early Christian times: the relics of the pre-Hellenistic capital of the local kingdom of Kourion have still to be discovered.

Most of what we know about this period comes from the writings of Herodotus. According to him, the victory of the Persian invaders during the Persian wars in 497 BC, following their suppression of the Ionian rebellion, was made possible only by the cowardly retreat of Stasanor, the King of Kourion. As a result, Pasicrates, the last king of Kourion, supported Alexander the

BELOW: enjoying the acoustics and the views at Kourion.

Great as naval leader in the fight against the Persians during the siege and storming of Tyre from a position off the Lebanese coast.

During the period of the Roman Empire, the city flourished both economically and as a centre for the worship of Apollo, a cult which soon gave way to Christianity. The basilica, built in the 5th century, eloquently testifies to the early importance of Christianity, but when Arab invastions in the 7th century prompted the relocating of the bishop's residence to neighbouring Episkopi, Kourion lost its status and fell into decline.

Map on page 144–5

Sites to see

Today the ruins of Kourion (*Curium* in Latin) extend across three areas. Coming from Limassol, you reach the most imposing of the sites first. A gravel path leads off the asphalt road to the left and gives an impressive view over the sea. Following the road up the mountain in the direction of Pafos, you reach the **stadium** on the right-hand side after half a mile or so. Unfortunately all that remains is an elongated, oval-shaped wall. Near the stadium is a small basilica. Far more impressive are the ruins of the **Sanctuary of Apollo**, which are slightly off the asphalt road. A signpost indicates the way.

You have to pay an entrance fee to visit each of the sites, with the exception of the stadium ruins. This means that, although you will already have passed the first of the villa ground plans (with its mosaic-decorated floor) on the left-hand side at the junction of the aforementioned gravel road, you have to drive or walk to the little ticket house before gaining access.

Once inside the fenced-off area, if you stay on the inner-side of the fencing, parallel to the approach road, you come to the **House with Wells**, though the

A young theatregoer.

BELOW: Christian influence is evident in many of the mosaics at Kourion.

Looking east from the Temple of Apollo.

water has now run dry, and then to the **House of the Gladiators**, named after its mosaics of armed warriors in action (the names of the villas are inlaid in mosaic). Finally, near the asphalt road, you come to a villa with a mosaic scene (4th-century) depicting the legend of Achilles: in order to prevent Achilles from entering the Trojan War, his mother, Thetis, dressed him in women's clothes and hid him among the daughters of King Lykomedes. However, Odysseus blew his cover by displaying a range of weapons alongside a selection of jewellery and watching Achilles's reaction.

Another mosaic in the same villa, showing how Zeus, disguised as an eagle, kidnapped the young Ganymede, has been badly damaged.

In the area next to these villas is an sector where excavations, begun in 1975, are in progress. So far, a longitudinal **stoa** from Roman times has been uncovered, with accompanying rows of columns. The stoa measures 213 ft (65 m) long and 15 ft (4.5 m) wide and was built over part of an extensive Hellenistic house of unknown purpose. Parts of a **Roman forum** (meeting place) have also been dug out. This area can be easily recognised from the columns, whose shafts are not grooved vertically but fluted with winding threads.

Directly northwest of this area, archaeologists came across a massive **cistern**, which once fed a nymphaeum measuring 148 ft (45 m) long and 49 ft (15 m) wide.

Adjacent to this area, and in a superb location overlooking the sea, are the remains of a monumental **Early Christian basilica**, thought to have been commissioned by Bishop Zeno, who represented the diocese of Kourion at the Council of Ephesus. The main part of the church had three aisles and the nave included a choir stall, set in front of the apse on a slightly raised level, and at one

time separated by a choir screen. On both sides of the aisles you can still see long halls, the so-called *catechumena*.

The entrance hall (*narthex*) in the west, which lies sideways, stretches across the total width of all five aisles. Going further west you come to the deacon's rooms, and the bishop's private rooms. Going north brings you to an **atrium court**, which is surrounded by columns, with a watertank in the middle and further rooms on three sides. The baptistry used to be on the eastern side. Inscriptions and the remnants of the mosaic floor can still be seen.

At the southern end of the gravel path you come across the **theatre**, first built in the Hellenistic Period, but whose present size is the result of extensions made in Roman times (2nd century). Despite its size, it remains a rather modest building with just 3,500 seats (the theatre at Salamis can hold an astonishing 17,000 visitors). It was probably not restored by the Christians after the severe earthquake in AD 365 and so fell into decline.

Another complex of buildings worth visiting on account of the mosaics is the **annexe of Eustolios**, next to the theatre. The mosaics are thought to date from the 5th century. Fragmentary inscriptions refer to Eustolios (the builder), and Apollo (the former patron). It was probably originally a Hellenistic private villa, which was converted into a public baths at the end of the 4th century. Christian influences can be seen in the floor mosaics: floral, geometric (such as cross-shaped ornaments) and animal motifs rather than portraits of people; and one of the inscriptions in the floor mosaic makes it clear that the building did not need defensive features because it was already "surrounded by the most honourable symbols of Christ".

The long oval of the **stadium**, of which only the foundations are extant, lies

Map on page 144–5

The most important motif (in the frigidarium) is the bust of a woman holding a measuring rod which, according to the inscription, represents Ktisis, the personification of the creation.

BELOW: Sanctuary of Apollo.

Map
on page
144-5

*The area around the
Temple of Apollo is
believed to be the
oldest settlement in
Kourion, founded by
Dorians from Argos
in the Peloponnese.*

RIGHT: Kourion,
bathed in dawn
light.
BELOW: admiring
the Sanctuary of
Apollo Hylates.

between the areas described above and the Sanctuary of Apollo, and covers some 750 ft (229 m), of which the actual arena itself measures 610 ft (186 m). The rest of the area was occupied by the seven rows of seats, which could accommodate a total of 6,000 visitors.

The **aqueduct pipeline**, which comes from the mountains and provided the city of Kourion with water, goes past the Sanctuary of Apollo and along the southern wall of the stadium. To the west, a little way back, is the ground wall of an Early Christian basilica, dating from the end of the 5th century or the beginning of the 6th. According to archaeological discoveries, it was built to replace a pagan temple.

The hill is surmounted by the **Sanctuary of Apollo Hylates** (open daily; entrance fee), the protector of the woodland. The imported Greek god was merged with a long-established Cypriot god of vegetation. Two gates, the Pafos and Kourion Gates, lead into the sacred area of this syncretistic deity, who was worshipped only in Cyprus.

The passage to the latter is flanked by a bathing area and a square building with a courtyard in the middle (the *palaestra*). The south side of the trapezium-shaped courtyard, into which both gates lead, borders on five right-angled rooms, supported by columns and complete with stone seats.

From here a passage strikes north at a right-angle, past buildings which have a stoa in front. The passage is lined by two walled-in **worshipping areas** (so-called *temenoi*) and leads directly to the Temple of Apollo itself.

The smaller *temenos* on the eastern side has a small round altar in the middle. Excavations indicate that it was built as early as the 7th century BC. The middle of the larger *temenos* to the west is occupied by a fascinating circular monument, 59 ft (18 m) in diameter, said to be unique in the Mediterranean, dedicated to the "protector of the trees". The whole complex was probably built in the 1st and 2nd centuries AD.

Episkopi

The name of nearby **Episkopi** ❾ signifies that this village became the seat of residence of the bishop when the residence at Kourion was abandoned in the wake of the Arab invasions.

The village contains the **Kourion Museum** (open Mon–Wed and Fri 7.30am–2.30pm, Thur 3–6pm, except Jul and Aug; entrance fee), which displays selected finds from Kourion and its surrounding area, where evidence has been found of Early Stone-Age settlements, such as Erimi and Sotira, and the Bronze-Age settlement of Phaneromeni. One of its most fascinating, and moving, exhibits is a skeleton group of a young man and woman and a baby – surely a family group – lying huddled together in a vain effort at protection. They perished in the earthquake that levelled Kourion in 365.

Some 12 miles (20 km) west of the Sanctuary of Apollo, off the old coast road to Pafos, is **Pissouri Bay**, which has the best sand beach between Kourion and Geroskipou. As always in Cyprus, that means it gets busy and it is lined with tavernas (some of them very good, if rather expensive) and hotels. ❏

FROM LIMASSOL TO LARNAKA

The journey from Limassol to Larnaka offers a wide variety of attractions including the remains of Early Christian basilicas and prehistoric houses, lace-making, ceramics and monastic peace

C onsidering the important role which **Amathous** ⑩ played in the ancient world, both as a port and the seat of residence of the local kingdom, it is somewhat surprising that archaeologists didn't begin excavating the site (open daily; entrance fee) until as recently as 1980. What has been uncovered so far, on the coast about 5 miles (8 km) east of Limassol, has been very promising: it includes an Early Christian basilica, located directly on the bumpy coastal road, and the ruins of a sanctuary to Aphrodite on the **Acropolis Hill**, rising behind the road.

Other parts of the lower city, which probably stretched from the foothills of the Acropolis Hill to the south as far as the coast, have still to be excavated. Parallel to a river bed in the west, are the remains of a wall which ran from the southwesterly edge of the Acropolis to the sea. On the other side of the wall, not far from the Amathus Beach Hotel, local archaeologists came across a burial ground from the Archaic period. Remains of the old harbour site have been located under the sea.

According to legends recorded by Tacitus, the city was founded by Amathus, the son of Aerias, although Amathousa, mother of King Cinyras from Pafos, is also credited with giving her name to the city. For a time, it was an important trading base for the Phoenicians and during the Ionian rebellion it sided with the Persians. It remained an important port until the time of Richard the Lionheart, who destroyed it. The reason why the ruins give so little impression of the splendour of its ancient past is that, as so often in history, their stone served as building material for the projects of later eras – this time for the Suez Canal.

Fresh water and black sand

About 3 miles (5 km) inland from Amathous is **Germasogeia Dam** ⑪ and Germasogeia Lake, one of Cyprus's biggest freshwater reservoirs. The level of water behind the dam gives a good indication as to the state of Cyprus's reserves of drinking water.

A few miles beyond the ruins of Amathous, a side street leads from the main road to Larnaka and Nicosia to the convent of **Agios Georgios Alamanos**. The monastery was founded at the end of the 12th century, but its buildings, built into the side of the mountain, were erected more recently. Outside the monastery wall a stall offers visitors a selection of icons hand-painted by the nuns.

The next bay up the coast from Agios Georgios Alamanos, **Governor's Beach** ⑫ is noted for its black sands. A side-effect of its colour is that the sand soaks up even more of the sun's heat than regular sand – so watch out for toasted feet here. Keep going east on

LEFT: Stavronouni monastery.
BELOW: Lefkara is famous for its lace and silver shops.

the coast road and you'll arrive at **Zygi**, a fishing harbour with a line of pretty good seafood restaurants along the shore.

Prehistoric houses

The motorway from Limassol to Larnaka crosses an area believed to have been inhabited as early as the Early Stone Age; the round houses, which are characteristic of this period, have been found in both the village of **Kalavasos ⑬** and in the more famous **Choirokoitia ⑭**, both of which lie just to the north of the motorway. The motorway also crosses the two Late Bronze-Age cemeteries of **Agious and Agios Dimitros**, near Kalavasos. In Agios Dimitros two royal tombs have been discovered – including one belonging to a queen which contained gold-decorated grave goods.

The round houses of Choirokoitia, which measure up to 33 ft (10 m) in diameter, are packed tightly together and stretch over a steep slope halfway between Limassol and Larnaka (open daily; entrance fee). They were discovered in 1936, but excavations were halted in 1939 and not restarted until 1975. They are continuing today. This settlement, probably the oldest on Cypriot soil, dates from the 7th or 6th millennium BC.

Its location was probably selected for its defensive advantages; the Maroni river flows around the hill in a large loop, thereby providing extra protection. The proximity of the river also ensured that there was an adequate supply of water, and its detritus provided building materials for the lower layers of the rotundas. Only the carefully constructed foundations of the rotundas, measuring up to 3 ft (1 m) high, have survived. At one time lancet arches made from air-dried tiles stood on top of them.

BELOW: remains at Amathous.

Equally conspicuous is a wall-like construction dissecting the settlement. The theory that this is the foundation of a paved path, designed to make the steep climb easier for the people and their animals, has not been confirmed. It seems more likely that the wall marks the boundary of the settlement before it expanded. Its people lived from hunting, but also kept sheep, goats and pigs as domesticated livestock, and carried out a modest amount of farming. The discovery of objects crafted from obsidian rock is, in the view of some historians, proof of trading links with Asia Minor – the rock is not otherwise found on the island. The dead were buried either in lined graves under the floors of the houses, or outside the houses. The grave goods which accompanied them reveal the religious beliefs of the inhabitants. In the last phase of the settlement in the 4th millenium BC, when the first metal objects (made of copper) made an appearance in graves, the people also produced ceramics with typical "comb" patterns. Most of the discoveries are in the Cyprus Museum in Nicosia.

Map on page 144–5

Lace is on sale in many places in the area.

Villages and monasteries

If instead of returning from Choirokoitia to the motorway you continue north along the approach road, you eventually climb up to the village of **Vavla** ⓯ (after about half an hour). You will find that it is not the village but **Agios Minas** (St Menas) – the convent in the village – which is signposted. This was founded in the 15th century, but owes its present appearance to its rebuilding in 1740. The nuns sell icons, honey that is famous all over the island and grapes, grown in green houses outside the convent walls.

Beyond Vavla the road meanders gently downhill, passing picturesquely sited Kato Drys, believed to be the birthplace of the Cypriot national hero Neofytos

BELOW: bathing below the ruins.

(born in 1134), before joining a road that leads to the twin villages of Lefkara, which are situated at around 1,970 ft (600 m) above sea-level in the foothills of the Troodos mountains.

Kato Lefkara  is the smaller and lower-lying of the two villages. Most tourists, however, come to visit **Pano Lefkara** , usually to see and buy the elaborate cotton *broderie anglaise* lace which is produced here.

In summer, the narrow streets between the quaint-looking stone houses with red-tiled roofs are open-air workshops, for the women of the village prefer to practise their craft out of doors. The local men sell the filigree craftwork produced by their wives, named *Lefkaritika* after the place of their production, all over the island and beyond.

The local tradition of lace-making is said to have been started by Frankish and Venetian noblewomen who spent their summers in cool Lefkara, and whiled away their time lace-making. Leonardo da Vinci is supposed to have admired their craft and bought an altar cloth for the cathedral in Milan when he visited the village in 1481 (although there is no evidence that Leonardo was ever here). In the **House of Patsalos**, a small local museum (open Mon–Sat; entrance fee) has now been set up for lace and the region's equally famous silver work.

The **Tou Timiou Stavrou** (Holy Cross) church contains an exquisite silver cross, dating from the 13th century, which is the focal point of the annual Festival of the Holy Cross held each year on 13–14 September.

It is worth visiting **Kato Lefkara** to see the 12th-century mid-Byzantine frescoes in the **Archangel Michael** church. In 1865 a cache of sacred objects, including a bishop's mitre, was found in a hiding place under the floor; they date from 1222, when the bishop of Limassol was banished here.

BELOW: welcome to Stavrovouni.

The monastery of Stavrovouni

A steep, winding asphalt road leads to the oldest monastery in Cyprus – the **Stavrovouni monastery** (the Mountain of the Cross) – which lies at 2,192 ft (668 m) above sea-level.

Map on page 144–5

Women are prohibited from entering the monastery, as indicated by the sign at the start of the ascent, where the aged monk, Father Kallinikos paints and sells superb icons in a little hut. Photographic equipment has to be surrendered at the entrance to the monastery, and taking pictures is also forbidden on the stretch of the approach road which borders military territory.

By the last S-bend before reaching the monastery there is a small **chapel**. Beyond the monastery gate, a set of steep steps leads past the gardens to the monastic cells and the main church. Below and to the left of the fortified complex, is the **Constantine and Helena chapel**. This was constructed in the 17th and 18th centuries, virtually on the foundations of the main church which lies one level higher. You have to ask the monks for the key to this chapel.

The Empress Helena, mother of Constantine the Great, is regarded as the founder of the monastery. According to legend, she was stranded here in AD 327 on her way back from Jerusalem, and erected a cross made from cypress wood on the monastery hill. The cross was supposed to contain a nail from the cross of Jesus, and was therefore preserved as a relic. It is is said to have hung freely over the earth, without any form of suspension, until it was stolen by invading Mamelukes. Today a splinter of this cross is preserved in a silver cross in the church.

The view on a clear day from the monastery hill to the Troodos mountains and over the extensive Mesaoria plain to the Mediterranean is magnificent.

TIP

It is worth organising your trip from Larnaka to the Stavrovouni monastery so that you can also visit the Chapelle Royale just outside Pyrga.

BELOW: icon painter Kallinikos plies his trade.

Chapelle Royale

The Chapelle Royale or Royal Chapel (open daily; entrance fee) lies just outside the village of **Pyrga** . This small place of prayer, which is dedicated to Agia Ekaterina (St Catherine) and was extensively restored in 1977, acquired its name when it was established that it was founded by the Latin king Janus (1398–1423) in 1421. The founder and his spouse, Charlotte of Bourbon, can be recognised on one of the wall-paintings (they are kneeling down on either side of the crucified Christ and wearing crowns). In addition, the coat of arms of the House of Lusignan appears on the ribs of the vaulting. Other scenes, of Mary and the baby Jesus, the raising of Lazarus, the Last Supper, the washing of Christ's feet, and Christ's Ascension, are all easily recognised. Each scene is supported by inscriptions in old French, spoken in Cyprus at the time. Of the three doors which originally led into the little vaulted building, which had no apse, two were later walled in.

On the lintel above the southern entrance is a representation of a wheel, the emblem of St Catherine. About 4 miles (6 km) southeast of Pyrga you can see the ruins of a Cistercian monastery.

Classical styles are still popular when it comes to pottery.

Kornos and Kiti

It is also worth making a detour to **Kornos** ㉔, just west of Pyrga and not far from the motorway. Kornos is a centre for ceramic production, in particular the large-size jars known as *pitharia* used for storing water.

In the village of **Kiti** ㉑, descendant of the ancient settlement of Kition, you can find the **Panagia Angeloktistos** church (literally "built by the angels"). From an Early Christian basilica, which once stood here, only the apse now

BELOW: picturesque village of Pyrga.

remains, on to which a domed cruciform church was added in the 11th century – itself later rebuilt. Amazingly, the 6th-century mosaic decorations in the earlier apse have survived. They show the standing figure of Mary, with the baby Jesus on her arm, flanked by the two archangels, Michael and Gabriel. Although this motif dates from the time when the theological controversy about the worshipping of idols (the "iconoclastic controversy") had been settled, the style of the portrayal of the figures along the arch of the apse (first discovered in 1952) suggest that it came from an earlier period. Indeed so imposing is the style of the mosaic that it has been compared with those of the 6th-century Byzantine Emperor Justinian, Empress Theodora and their courtiers at the Church of San Vitale in Ravenn, Italy.

Later pictorial representations, such as frescoes from the mid-18th century, can be found in the church of **Agios Georgios of Arpera**, 1 mile (2 km) northeast of Kiti, not far from a dam on the River Tremithos. The church's founder, the Greek dragoman Christophakis, has immortalised both himself and his family here, in a picture over the northern portal.

Place of pilgrimage

Hala Sultan Tekkesi ㉒ (open daily; entrance fee) lies within sight of the International Airport at Larnaka, on the southern shore of Larnaka Salt Lake. (*Tékké* is the Turkish description for a Muslim monastery). The local holy woman is Umm Haram, reputed to have been an aunt of the Prophet Mohammed, on his father's side.

Accompanying her husband on the Arab invasion of Cyprus in AD 674, she had such a bad fall from her mule that she broke her neck and died. Her tomb

BELOW: looking across the lake to Hala Sultan Tekkesi.

Map on page 144–5

made the mosque (constructed over her burial place at a later date) an important place of pilgrimage for Muslims. Umm Haram is known reverently by the Turkish population as *hala sultan* ("great mother").

Another prominent tomb lies in a neighbouring room. Buried under an alabaster cenotaph with golden inscriptions is Chadija, the grandmother of King Hussein of Jordan. Chadija died in Cyprus in 1930. The picturesque mosque, situated in a palm grove and complete with fountains, owes its current appearance to the Turkish Governor of 1816.

In **Larnaka Salt Lake** ㉓, which borders the mosque to the east, you can see whole colonies of flamingos and migrating birds in winter. Fortunately the birds remain unaffected by the salt-mining once practised here – a state industry – as extraction was confined to the period from the middle of summer to the onset of the autumn rains. Then the fierce summer heat causes the water to evaporate and the level to fall so low that a salt-crust is left, which could be mined. The export of salt was already a flourishing business in the time of the Franks in the Middle Ages; nowadays it is no longer carried on, as pollution from the nearby airport has tarnished the salt.

On the left, after a few hundred yards along the extension of the approach road from the airport to the *tékké*, is an enclosed area where archaeological excavations have been underway since 1972. A team of Swedish workers is uncovering the remains of a Middle and Late Bronze Age settlement, thought to have rivalled Kition in importance. Among the most interesting discoveries so far is a bathing area, otherwise unknown in Cyprus in this period, and Cypro-Minoan inscriptions.

In 1978 a treasure trove containing 23 objects of solid gold came to light. Some of these pieces – into which agate, carnelion and rock crystals had been intricately worked – show distinct Egyptian influences. Informative documentation of the archaeological findings is provided in the museum at Larnaka Fort. According to this, the area was settled around 1600 BC and developed steadily until its abrupt destruction in the early 12th century BC, when it was swallowed up by the same severe earthquake which destroyed Egkomi and Kition. ❑

RIGHT: time to sit and reflect.

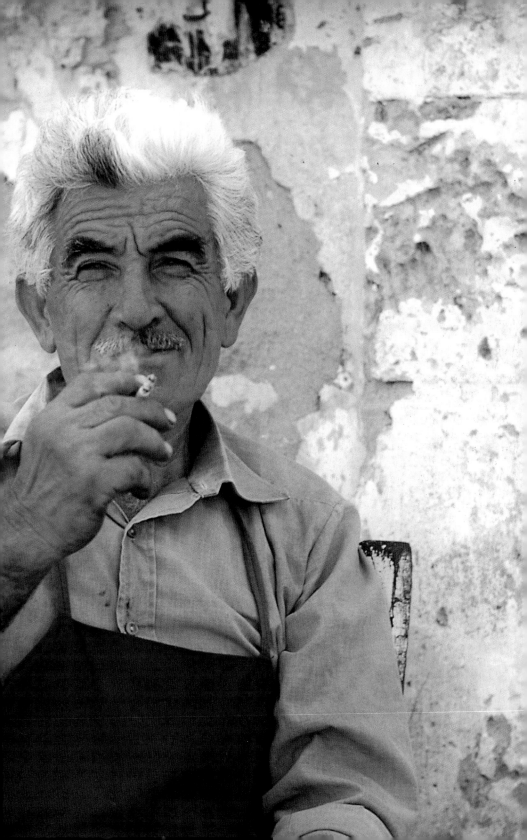

LARNAKA AND THE SOUTHEAST

Larnaka has managed to retain much of its historic character, despite the fact that it is the gateway for tourists to southeastern Cyprus – the most popular part of the island for holidaymakers

Maps:
Area 174
City 176

After Nicosia and Limassol, Cyprus's third-largest city is **Larnaka** . The important port of Kition (*Citium* in Latin, and *Kittim* in the Old Testament) is known to have occupied the same site, though extensive urban development has prevented archaeologists from uncovering more than a small part of Kition's remains. The ancient tombs which were found here seem to be the source of the city's modern name: Larnaka comes from *larnax*, a Greek word for sarcophagus. During the period of Frankish rule, when the salt mines in the large salt lake to the west of the port were its main source of industry, the town was known as "Salines" or "Salina".

Oil exporter

Today oil is the city's main export product. Being the second-largest port on the island, Larnaka is an important berth for tankers, and there are also regular ferry crossings to the Lebanon. Larnaka is also popular with yacht owners on account of its relatively cheap charges for winter mooring.

Under the Ottomans, although Nicosia was the capital, most of the consulates and embassies were based in Larnaka, along with representatives of foreign trading companies. With 13,000 inhabitants, Larnaka was even larger than the capital for a short time. Reminders of that period are the 33 arches on the road to Limassol. They originally formed part of an aqueduct built between 1746 and 1750 by the Ottoman governor. This 6-mile (10-km) pipeline, fed by several springs not far from the River Tremithos, supplied water to Larnaka until 1939.

Larnaka city

The events of 1974 brought profound changes to the city. Following the closure of Nicosia International Airport, the one at Larnaka was developed to take its place. Thousands of Greek Cypriots arrived, fleeing from the occupied north of the island. Despite the migration of the city's Turkish people in the opposite direction, the net effect was to treble the city's population of previously, 60,000. The Turkish community had settled mainly in the coastal areas in the southern parts of the city, as the street names testify. The fort marked the northern boundary of this area. Opposite the fort, you can still see the **Djami Kebir** , the "large mosque", which had previously been a Latin Holy Cross church.

The city's main thoroughfare is the wide coastal road (known at its beginning as Leoforos Athinon, and further up as Odos Ankara), which stretches

PRECEDING PAGES:
inside Agia Napa
monastery.
LEFT: Agios Lazaros
church (interior)
and (**BELOW**) the
entrance.

southwards from the port and the marina to the fortress. In its northern part it is an attractive seafront promenade, bordered by palm trees, ornamental street-lamps, and chic cafés with outdoor terraces. Parallel to the coastal road is an inviting (but usually crowded) sandy beach.

The southern end of the beach and the promenade is marked by a small **Turkish fort ❸** (open Mon–Fri; entrance fee). According to inscriptions above the entrance, this fort was constructed in 1605. Earlier this century, during the period of British rule, prisoners were interned here. In one of the buildings there is a small **Medieval Museum**, whose exhibits include documentation on the Swedish excavations from Hala Sultan Tekkesi. The inner courtyard of the fortress sometimes serves as an excellent open-air theatre.

If you make your way to the north of the fort, away from the coastal road and towards the centre of the city, you will arrive at **Agios Lazaros** church ❸ after a few hundred yards. The extension of this street past the church to the west leads on to **Agia Faneromeni** church ❹, built in 1907. It has two ancient stone graves but these are likely to interest only real fanatics of antiquity.

In the former church, the Lazarus whom Christ resurrected from the dead is supposed to be buried in an accessible crypt to the right of the main altar. After the miracle, the resurrected Lazarus is said to have travelled to Cyprus where he was ordained as bishop by St Barnabas, an office which he is claimed to have held for 30 years.

Icons of the saint are carried through the streets in an annual procession on the Sunday before Easter. The sacred building over the tomb, a multi-domed mid-Byzantine church, was founded by Emperor Leo VI (AD 886–912), following the discovery, in AD 890, of a stone sarcophagus bearing the name "Lazarus". The

A marble bust of Kimon, the Athenian commander who tried to regain Cyprus for the Greeks in 450–449 BC and who died on the island during his campaign, stands on the Larnaka waterfront.

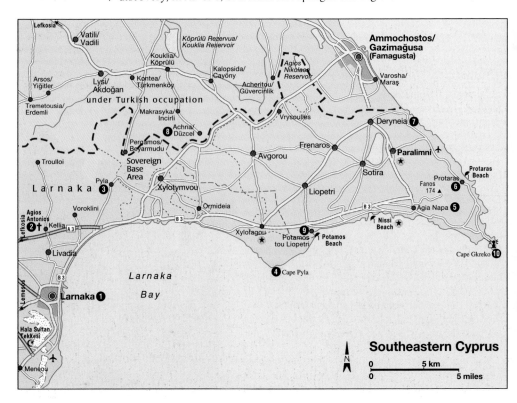

Southeastern Cyprus

relics of the saint were immediately transported to the Byzantine capital, Constantinople. From there, in 1204, they were taken by plundering crusaders to Marseille in France, a town which also claims Lazarus as a former bishop.

After the Ottoman conquest of Cyprus, the Christians succeeded, in 1589, in buying the church back. It underwent extensive restoration in the 17th century, and was extended by the addition of a bell-tower. Among the most notable features of the church are its baroque wood-carved iconostasis, and the Corinthian capitals at the base of the vaulted roof.

Behind the church is a small cemetery in which privileged 19th-century European diplomats and businessmen are buried. One of the most notorious foreign representatives, holding the offices of both American and Russian consul at the same time, was Luigi Palma di Cesnola. This accredited diplomat, who had been working in Cyprus since 1865, took treasures from a number of ancient graves in Larnaka and the surrounding area with the full permission of the Ottoman authorities. He exported his valuable discoveries abroad, mainly to the United States. The Cesnola collection now forms a large part of the stock of the New York Metropolitan Museum of Art.

A trio of museums

Continuing inland along Odos Agiou Lazarou and Odos Stadiou brings you to Larnaka's **Municipal Park ❺**, a not exactly huge triangle of trees, grass and flowers that nevertheless makes a good place of escape from the summer sun. Embedded in the park is the **Museum of Natural History** (open Tues–Sun; entrance fee), which counts among its exhibits a number of interesting dioramas, including one of pink flamingos at Larnaka Salt Lake in winter.

Map on page 176

Larnaka seafront promenade is a popular place for a stroll.

BELOW: the tomb of Agios Lazaros.

Pierides Museum, a rare 19th-century home which houses an interesting and varied collection.

BELOW: large congregations gather in Agios Lazaros church.

A local amateur archaeologist and art collector, Demetrios Pierides (1811–95) created a remarkable private museum in Larnaka, the **Pierides Museum** ❻ (tel: 04 652495; open Mon–Sat; entrance fee), which is also open to the public. The collection of exhibits, extending from the Early Stone Age to medieval times, is housed in the family's private house at 4 Odos Zinonos Kitieos, one of the few remaining examples of resplendent 19th-century villas.

The **Larnaka Archaeological Museum** ❼ (open Mon–Fri; entrance fee) in Plateia Kalogrenon is hard pressed to compete with the rich and representative collection in the Pierides Museum. Nevertheless it is still worth a visit. Among the ceramics and smaller items in the display cases on the right of the entrance room, and the free-standing statues to the left, are a number of exquisite exhibits.

To the right of the museum is the Catholic **convent of St Joseph** ❽, built in 1848, with an impressive wrought-iron fountain.

Kition

In the open-air area behind the museum remains from the ancient city of Kition have been excavated. Archaeologists believe they have discovered the acropolis of the city, although only a few relics have survived. Unfortunately the British occupying forces levelled the hill of ruins – known to the locals as Bamboula – in 1879 in order to obtain filling material with which they could reclaim a marshland area.

Excavations at other sites in the northern part of Larnaka have led to the discovery of a number of remains from the ancient city of **Kition** ❶ – for example, at the junction of Odos Agiou Epiphaniou and Odos Kimonos. The main archaeological area, however, lies further north, and includes, along

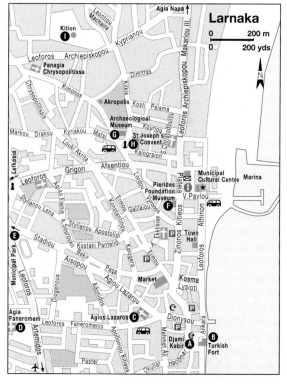

with the foundations of an important temple, a bronze-processing factory. Cyprus was an important supplier of copper during the 2nd century BC, particularly for the Hittite Empire in Asia Minor, in whose cuneiform script the island appears as *Alaschia*, but the bronze-processing factory in the north of Kition is more recent than that.

The excavation area is very confusing for visitors as a result of the various building phases from different historical periods which lie next to and over each other. For example, the original shrine from the Bronze Age was replaced by a temple for the goddess Astarte when the Phoenicians settled here in the 10th century BC and developed the city as an important export harbour. The new temple quickly acquired importance well beyond the region. After being rebuilt a number of times it finally burned down in 312 BC.

The Phoenicians extended their power over the island, from Kition outwards, and in the 5th century BC were able to conquer a number of other local city-kingdoms such as Idalion, Tamassos, Golgoi, Amathous and, between 450 and 411 BC, Salamis. Their success was due not least to the support of their allies the Persians. Zeno the younger (circa 336–264 BC), the founder of Stoicism, was also born in Kition (*see page 45*).

Archaeologists distinguish between three main periods in the history of Kition. The first phase, characterised by two temples with altars, separated by an artificially watered **Holy Grove**, probably began in the early 13th century BC and ended with the city's destruction around 1200 BC. The city was then re-built by the Mycenaeans. On the site formerly occupied by the shrine a large **temple complex** was built, measuring 110 ft (34 m) by 72 ft (22 m), thereby making it one of the largest of the Late Bronze Age temples in Cyprus. Between

Map on page 176

Just in case you forget that you're in the Mediterranean.

BELOW: older Larnaka residents have witnessed many changes to their home town.

Map on page 176

the temple and the nearby city wall there were extensive copper and bronze-processing plants which were directly accessible from the temple. In other shrines, which have been excavated a little to the east of the main temple, ivory carvings and bull-skulls have been discovered. The seafaring population, who lived from the export of copper, also presented a stone anchor as an offering.

Although the city was rebuilt after severe damage, following the earthquake around 1075 BC it was virtually depopulated. The third and last phase of the city's history was heavily influenced by the Phoenician invaders, whose large **Astarte temple** has already been mentioned. They took advantage of the favourable location of the city and turned it into a naval base. The extent to which the Assyrians had previously influenced the history of Kition can only be guessed: a basalt stele of the Assyrian king Sargon II (721–705 BC) was discovered here, on which he boasts about his power over the island. This now lies in a museum in Berlin.

Byzantine frescoes

The **Agios Antonios** church ❷, which lies on a hill to the north of Larnaka, is worth a visit on account of its mid-Byzantine frescoes. The oldest of the wall paintings date back as far as the early 11th century, making them some of the earliest Byzantine frescoes in Cyprus.

If you travel along the bay of Larnaka from the main city to the east, the village of **Pyla** ❸ can be reached by leaving the coastal road at the vertex of the bay and turning to the north. Pyla has achieved a degree of fame since the Turkish invasion in 1974: here, right on the Greek-Turkish demarcation line, is the only place on the whole island where the Greek and Turkish Cypriot populations still live side by side, albeit under the supervision of the UN peace-keeping force. The village square has both a Greek *kafenion* and a Turkish coffee shop. In the upper floor of a restaurant a blue-helmeted member of the UN peace-keeping force keeps guard, whilst on a rock spur directly above the village the Turkish military have set up a colossal silhouette of a Turkish soldier ready for battle with fixed bayonet.

You come to the cape of the same name, **Cape Pyla** ❹ on the far side of Larnaka Bay. ❑

RIGHT: Larnaka's old port, still thronging with boats.

AGIA NAPA

Since the 1970s, the formerly tranquil fishing village of Agia Napa has been turned into a typical Mediterranean hotel city. The largest tourist region of the whole island arose virtually from nothing

Map on page 174

The Cypriots call the very flat expanse of land south and southwest of Famagusta, the Kokkinochoria, "the red villages". Nowadays, the name tends to conjure thoughts of sunburnt tourists who populate its beaches, but initially it came from the fertile *terra rossa*, the soil tinged red by the presence of large amounts of iron and other metallic oxides.

At the beginning of the 1970s there was little here apart from potato crops. Visitors might have explored the coast to the west and north of Cape Gkreko with its string of idyllic sandy bays, and those interested in religious art and local crafts would have found the 16th-century monastery at **Agia Napa** ❺, the pretty village churches of **Liopetri, Sotira** and **Frenaros**, the 16th-century church of **Agios Angonas** (near Ormideia on the road to Avgorou) and the basket-making community of Liopetri.

The southeast corner of the island was at that time little more than an unexciting hinterland for the tourist centre of the then undivided Cyprus, the hotel suburb of **Varosha** in the south of the port of Famagusta.

A twofold invasion

None of the other formerly rural areas was turned so completely upside-down by the events following the Turkish invasion of 1974. The strengthening links with the urban centre of Famagusta were suddenly impeded by an impregnable demarcation line. The suburb of Varosha is today a ghost town, serving only as a pawn of the Turkish Cypriots in their negotiations with the Greek Cypriots. Its buildings are falling to pieces after decades of neglect.

By far the most important result of the invasion and division of the island, however, was the influx of refugees from the area around Famagusta. It led to a sudden quadrupling of the resident population. Large refugee settlements were created near the formerly rural villages and in the open countryside, for example in **Vrysoulles**. Within sight of their former home of Acheritou, now on the Turkish side of the border, nearly 2,000 refugees were given new detached family houses. Many of the refugees were soon able to find employment. To compensate for the demise of Famagusta and Varosha, hotels began to spring up like mushrooms in the latter part of the 1970s, in particular in Agia Napa, Paralimni and **Protaras** ❻.

Migrant workers

A third of Cyprus's tourist capacity is concentrated here. The booming construction and tourist industries have long since absorbed all the local workers and consequently the town must draw on a daily influx of commuters from the economically depressed Turkish

LEFT: Nissi beach, near Agia Napa. **BELOW:** the tourist industry has taken over this part of the island.

Agia Napa offers plenty of fun for children.

occupied part of the island. Nobody knows exactly how large the number of commuters is, but what is clear is that a situation which both sides originally recognised as an emergency has led to the strictly guarded border becoming much more porous – at least in one direction – than officials like to maintain.

Away from the beach

Agia Napa's chief – indeed almost its only – historical attraction is its 16th-century **monastery**, sandwiched between pizza parlours and boutiques, and attendant **Folk Museum** containing examples of prehistoric threshing boards. Backing up its firm commitment to the sea, Agia Napa has developed attractions to go along with it. Cyprus's highly regarded Pierides Foundation, usually more concerned with cultural matters, has established a **Marine Life Museum** (open Mon–Sat; entrance fee) on the premises of Agia Napa Town Hall, while at **Nissi Beach**, west of the town, you can see the performing dolphins and sea lions of **Agia Napa Marine Park** (open Wed–Mon; entrance fee).

Demarcation

There is hardly anywhere better than the surrounds of Agia Napa to appreciate the division of Cyprus. From a specially built high platform at a café on the northern outskirts of **Deryneia ❼**, you can look with binoculars across the demarcation line, past Greek Cypriot, UN, and Turkish positions, to the ruined hotel towers of **Varosha**, the abandoned suburb of Famagusta. The 33 hotels that line the long narrow beach are unmaintained and derelict but the return of Varosha has great symbolic importance to the Greeks. It would be of practical benefit too, if the 40,000 former Greek residents could be resettled there. For the

BELOW: you'll find no shortage of souvenir shops.

time being, however, it remains a negotiating pawn and figures high on the agenda of any intercommunal discussions.

Anyone making the journey along the demarcation line on the former connecting road between Larnaka and Famagusta, now little used, should also take a look (from a distance) at the deserted village of **Achna ⑧**, immediately behind the Turkish positions.

Near Achna the Turkish "Green Line" borders directly on the territory of the British base of Dhekalia, one of the two British military bases on the island. Here is a miniature Britain, complete with a military hospital, housing estates built of brick, a golf course, a gliding field, clubs and pubs.

Of course not many people go to Agia Napa to immerse themselves in Cyprus's tragic recent history. West of the resort, at **Makronisos Beach**, surrounded by toasting bodies, there is a complex of Hellenistic and Roman rock tombs (open permanently; free), whose excavation was paid for by local hoteliers. Just 2½ miles (4 km) further west on the Larnaka road is **Potamos tou Liopetri ⑨** fishing harbour, a typically colourful Mediterranean scene, with a fine family-run seafood restaurant beside the boats.

Going east from Agia Napa, but still within cycling or even walking range, is scenic **Cape Gkreko ⑩**, a great place for snorkelling and scuba-diving, but whose tip is unfortunately occupied by military and civilian (Radio Monaco International!) satellite communications gear.

The cape can be reached on foot in just under two hours from Agia Napa, but sections of the path cross quite rough ground. There is no proper footpath along the east coast to Protaras and Pernera but some of the testing trails around the cape are popular with dirt-bike riders. ❑

Map on page 174

TIP

The Agia Napa area offers beach holidays with every possible amenity, but if you're looking for isolated bays, traditional villages and authentic cuisine, you should probably head somewhere else.

BELOW: home of Cyprus potatoes.

WINDMILLS AND LIMESTICKS

The red soil of this area made Kokkinochoria one of the richest agricultural regions on the whole island. Water used to be abundant here. Creaking wind pumps, a feature typical of the region, drew water from under the ground and it was even stored in a lake during the winter. But intensive agriculture has caused the water table to sink and for many years now the area has needed the added benefits of artificial irrigation. Most of the windmills have long since been replaced by motor pumps drawing water from deep bore holes. And today water is received mainly via a pipeline from a new dam upstream from Limassol. The farmers of Avgorou and Xylofagou have specialised in growing potatoes and now harvest up to three crops a year. Growing demand has made the Cyprus potato one of the island's most important exports.

A less palatable culinary export from this area is pickled birds, mainly to the Middle East. Like tourists, migratory birds like to stop and relax here but for some, especially the small fig-eating Blackcaps, this becomes their final resting place. Legislation has been passed outlawing the use of limesticks and fine mist nets to trap the exhausted birds, but as long as there's a ready market for the delicacies the cash rewards are a tempting incentive.

PAFOS AND THE WEST

*For anyone wanting to trace the Hellenistic and Roman worlds of
Cyprus, Pafos will provide some of the highlights of their tour.
This is also an area of considerable scenic beauty*

Map on page 188

Lefkosia/
Nicosia

Pafos

The Pafos district, in the west of Cyprus, can look back on a truly glorious past: in the ancient world **Pafos** ❶ (Paphos) became a place of pilgrimage for the whole of the Hellenistic world, being a centre for the fertility rituals of Aphrodite. "The Paphian" was one of the names given to the goddess Aphrodite, who according to mythology rose out of the foaming waves off the coast. Here, more than in any other area of Cyprus, you are continually encountering spectacular evidence of the past, and no doubt the earth is hiding further treasures for archaeologists to discover.

Craggy coast

The beauty of this area lies particularly in the dramatic changes between its craggy coastline, steeply terraced vineyards, and the thick pine forests on the slopes of the Troodos mountains. As the moist west winds from the sea get trapped on the edges of these mountains, this part of Cyprus gets more rainfall than the eastern or central areas. Bizarre cloud patterns decorate skies even in summer. The sea wind brings a very warm and even climate to the coastal region, so bananas and other tropical fruits thrive.

The Troodos mountains also form a natural barrier with the rest of the island. As early as the 19th century the Troodos region had a reputation for lawlessness; livestock rustling was common, sometimes leading to bloody family feuds.

The region remained virtually untouched by the modernisation and industrialisation which happened around Nicosia and Limassol in the past few decades. Instead it remained, a somewhat backward, poor hinterland, from which the population began to migrate. Pafos became the most sparsely populated district in Cyprus: in 1982 it contained just nine percent of southern Cyprus's population.

However, all that changed with the building of an airport in 1984 and the rapid development of tourism. Nowadays Pafos ranks a close third behind Agia Napa/Protaras and Limassol in terms of the number of hotel beds, and is developing faster.

A journey through the Pafos area provides insights into the variety of settlements in Cyprus, and into modern-day rural life. Nowhere else on the island is as interesting in this regard: rich agricultural villages, dilapidated mountain settlements, communities destroyed by earthquakes, Turkish Cypriot villages sliding into ruin, refugee settlements and smart holiday villages are all here.

Pafos is one of the smallest of the Cypriot district capitals, with just 36,000 inhabitants. The urban communities in the surrounding countryside amount to a further 18,000 people.

PRECEDING PAGES:
bringing in the
grapes.
LEFT: Tombs of the
Kings, Nea Pafos.
BELOW: vineyards
near Pafos.

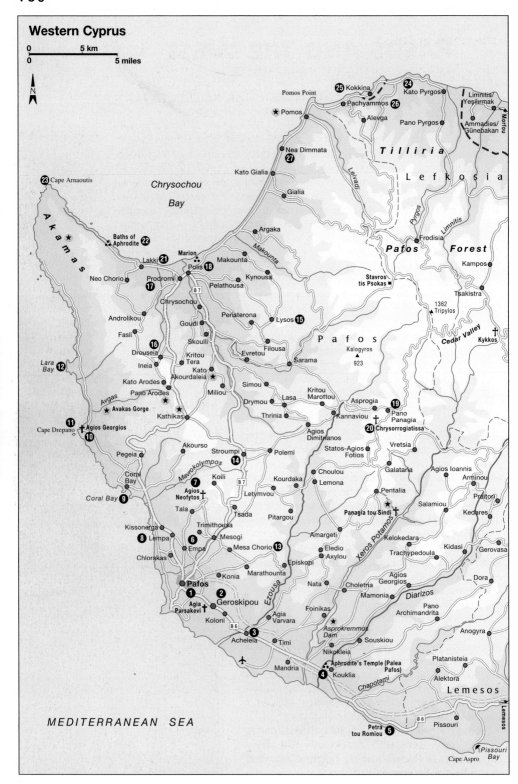

Western Cyprus

0 ——— 5 km
0 ——— 5 miles

N

Cape Arnaoutis ㉓

Chrysochou

Bay

Pomos Point

㉕ Kokkina

Pomos

Pachyammos ㉖

Kato Pyrgos ㉔

Alevga

Pano Pyrgos

Limnitis/
Yeşilırmak

Ammadies/
Günebakan

Morfou

Nea Dimmata
㉗

T i l l i r i a

Kato Gialia

Gialia

Levkadi

L e f k o s i a

Frodisia

Argaka

Makounta

P a f o s   *F o r e s t*

A k a m a s

Baths of
Aphrodite ㉒

Lakki ㉑

Marion

Neo Chorio

Prodromi
㉗

Polis ⑱

Makounta

Kynousa

Pelathousa

Pyrgos

Limnitis

Kampos

Tsakistra

Stavros
tis Psokas ■

Chrysochou

Androlikou

Goudi

Peristerona

Lysos ⑮

P a f o s

1362
Tripylos

Cedar Valley

Kykkos †

Fasli

Drouseia

⑯

Skoulli

Kritou
Tera

Evretou

Filousa

Sarama

Kalogyros
▲
923

*Lara
Bay* ⑫

Ineia

Kato
Akourdaleia ★

Miliou

Simou

Drymou

Lasa

Kritou
Marottou

Asprogia

Pano
Panagia ⑲

Kato Arodes

Pano Arodes ★

Thrinia

Kannaviou

⑳ Chrysorrogiatissa †

Avgas

★ Avakas Gorge

Kathikas

Agios
Dimitrianos

Vretsia

Cape Drepano ⑪

✝ Agios Georgios
⑩

Akourso

Stroumpi

Polemi

Statos-Agios
Fotios

Galataria

Agios Ioannis

Arminou

Pegeia

⑭

Choulou

Lemona

Praitori

Kedares

Mavrokolympos

Koili

Kourdaka

Pentalia

Salamiou

Kidasi

Gerovasa

*Coral
Bay*

⑦

Agios
Neofytos ✝

Letymvou

Panagia tou Sindi ★

Coral Bay ⑨

Tala

Tsada

Pitargou

Amargeti

Kelokedara

Trachypedoula

Dora

Kissonerga

Trimithousa

⑥

Mesogi

Eledio
Axylou

Agios
Georgios

⑧ Lempa

Empa ★

Mesa Chorio ⑬

Episkopi

Nata

Choletria

Mamonia

Diarizos

Pano
Archimandrita

Anogyra

Chlorakas

Konia

Marathounta

Foinikas

Agia
Parsakevi ✝

① **Pafos**

② Geroskipou

Koloni

Ezousa

Agia
Varvara

Asprokremmos
Dam

Souskiou

Platanisteia

Alektora

B 6

③

Timi

Nikokleia

Aphrodite's Temple (Palea
Pafos)

Chapotami

④ Kouklia

L e m e s o s

✈

Mandria

Xeros Potamos

MEDITERRANEAN SEA

B 6

Pissouri

Petra
tou Romiou ⑤

Lemesos

*Pissouri
Bay*

Cape Aspro

The town of Pafos

Modern Pafos is divided into two distinct parts: the lower town, **Kato Pafos**, with its little harbour, and the upper town, **Ktima**, once the original town centre, which lies to the north on a 557-ft (170-m) high rocky edge.

The remains of the ancient city of **Nea Pafos** (New Pafos) are in modern Kato Pafos. Nea Pafos was founded around 320 BC. King Nikokles, the last ruler of the city-kingdom of Pafos, moved the capital here from Palea Pafos (Old Pafos), which is now an archaeological zone around the village of Kouklia, 10 miles (16 km) southeast of present-day Pafos. Shortly after the city's foundation, Cyprus fell into the hands of the Hellenistic Egyptian Ptolemies, and in the 2nd century BC Pafos became the capital of the Ptolemaic governor. After 58 BC, when the period of Roman rule over Cyprus began, Nea Pafos remained the capital as seat of the island's Roman proconsul.

One important event which is said to have taken place here, and which was to be of lasting significance for the Christian world, concerns the missionary work of the Apostles Paul and Barnabas: on their visit to Pafos in AD 47 they converted the proconsul Sergius Paulus to Christianity. If this is correct, then Cyprus was the first Christian-ruled area. The archaeological treasures of Nea Pafos also date from Roman times. They include the splendid mosaics in the Houses of Dionysos, Theseus, Aion and Orpheus (*see below*).

Kato Pafos

The focal point of life in Kato Pafos is the little **harbour**  with its string of fish restaurants. The catches of the fishing cutters in the harbour basin are among the largest on the island. Across the harbour lies the **fort** ❸ (open daily; entrance fee), built in 1592 by the Turks. The new tourist zone of Kato Pafos, complete with hotels, restaurants and discos, stretches along Poseidonos away from the harbour, as well as north along the road to Pegeia (Peyia).

The barren, rocky coast makes swimming less than ideal. All the same, the relatively late development of tourism has led to much better planning. Unlike in Limassol, here building is subject to strict control. Despite this, the coastline north and south of Pafos is rapidly filling up with tourist-related developments. There might be a couple of hotels less than would have been the case in "pre-enlightenment" days, but since the space thus saved is being occupied by villas and apartment complexes, the effect in terms of the amount of concrete poured is marginal. Pafos may have some way to go before it reaches the level of over-development of Agia Napa and Limassol, but it's well on the road and getting there fast. Kato Pafos in particular has a burgeoning, neon-lit nightlife zone, with discos, bars, fast-food eateries, karaoke, and lots of noise and bustle. The entertainment here is fast-paced and tending towards wild on summer evenings, but rowdiness has yet to make an appearance.

The town's Department of Antiquities is permanently holding its breath, for excavators on the building sites are constantly making valuable discoveries which have to be brought to safety.

Map on page 190

A new friend.

BELOW: one of the many tourist-related developments in Pafos.

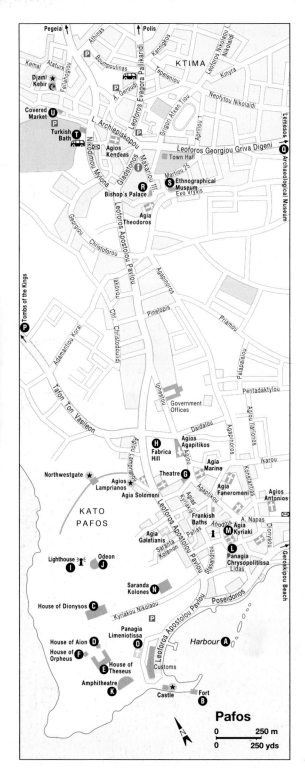

Pafos

0   250 m
0   250 yds

Archaeological Pafos

The ancient city of Nea Pafos covers some 235 acres (95 hectares). The main archaeological area lies to the west of Odos Apostolou Pavlou, which connects Ktima with modern-day Kato Pafos.

Nea Pafos was founded at the end of the 4th century BC by King Nikokles. Shortly after its foundation, Cyprus fell into the hands of the Egyptian Ptolemies. Around the time of the 2nd century BC, Pafos became the new capital of the island. In 58 BC, Cyprus fell to the Romans, and thenceforth was ruled by a Roman governor; Pafos nevertheless remained the capital of the island. The public buildings and the luxurious houses which have come to light during the excavations have revealed the important role played by Pafos during the time of the *pax Romana*.

Nea Pafos was affected by a number of earthquakes in the 1st century BC and then again during the 1st and 4th centuries AD. In the 4th century, following a series of devastating earthquakes, the city was razed to the ground, and its inhabitants fled. The city of Salamis was then made the new capital of Cyprus under the name of Constantia.

After the Arab invasions of the island in the 7th century, the decline of Nea Pafos continued at a steady pace, interrupted only by short periods of prosperity during the time of the French Lusignans and the Venetians, when a number of Gothic buildings were constructed. During the Ottoman Period (1572–1878) the inhabitants began to migrate to the hinterland – now occupied by the modern town of Pafos (Ktima) – with the result that the coastal region became almost completely deserted.

Such is Nea Pafos's importance that UNESCO has added the entire ancient city to its list of World Cultural Heritage Sites.

The houses of Nea Pafos (tel: 06-240217; open daily; entrance fee), with their wonderful floor mosaics, are of particular interest. The most famous are the House of Dionysos, the House of Aion, the House of Theseus and the

House of Orpheus. These names were given to the houses by archaeologists, and refer to the figures represented in their respective mosaics.

Map on page 190

The House of Dionysos ⓒ

This house came to light in 1962, when a chance discovery of the floor mosaic led to further excavations. It consists of an *atrium* (courtyard), from which corridors lead off in four directions. The other buildings of the house were arranged around this inner courtyard. The most impressive features are their mosaics of mythological scenes and geometric shapes.

Just to the left of today's entrance is a mosaic from the surrounding area, which shows Scylla, a mythological monster that is part woman, part fish and part dog. It is the oldest mosaic to have been found in Cyprus, and is peculiar in that it is made entirely of black and white pebbles. On the western side of the *atrium* are four scenes from Greek mythology. The first one on the left shows the death of Pyramus and Thisbe. The next scene show Icarus learning the art of wine-making from Dionysos. To the left of Icarus you can see the nymph Akme, and on the right-hand side is a group of figures drinking wine. The neighbouring scene shows Poseidon and Amymone and in the fourth scene Apollo is pursuing the nymph Daphne.

The large reception or dining hall (*triclinium*) to the west of the *atrium* shows the reception of the triumphal procession of Dionysos on his return from his Indian adventure. The rest of the room is decorated with scenes from the grape harvest. Other mosaics depict more mythical figures, such as Narcissus, Hippolytus, Phaedra, Ganymede with the eagle, and allegories of the four seasons. The building dates from the end of the late 2nd or early 3rd century.

ABOVE AND BELOW: mosaics inside the House of Dionysos.

The House of Aion D

Excavations began on the House of Aion in 1983 and have so far uncovered only a small number of rooms. The largest of them, probably the reception hall, is decorated with a large mosaic depicting five mythological themes. The first picture at the top on the left shows the beautiful queen of Sparta, Leda, with the scheming Zeus in the form of a swan. In the next picture, at the top on the right, you can see the young Dionysos sitting on Hermes's lap, before being handed over to Tropheus, while the nymphs are preparing Dionysos's first bath. The middle – and largest – picture shows a famous beauty competition, known as the Judgement of the Nereid. The winner of this competition is Queen Cassiopeia, who is being crowned by a winged female figure. The centre of the ensemble is dominated by the figure of Aion, the symbol of eternal life and judge over all people. The picture at the bottom on the left shows the triumphal procession of Dionysos, although only the chariot has survived the ravages of time. The last picture shows the aftermath of a musical competition between the satyr Marsyas and Apollo, god of music – Marsyas is being led away to his death after losing.

However extensive the development in the rest of Pafos, the headland between the harbour and the lighthouse is unlikely to be touched; the area is thought to contain as many archaeological treasures as it has already revealed.

The House of Theseus E

This building lies close to the House of Aion. It was built in the 2nd century and has undergone numerous alterations over the course of the centuries. Its mosaics date from the 3rd and 5th century. Its size and, above all, its architectural plan have led experts to conclude that it must have once served as the house of a Roman governor. The house consists of a large inner courtyard, from which the rooms radiate.

The most impressive mosaic decorates one of the vaulted rooms on the south

BELOW: the first bath of Achilles, House of Theseus.

side. The mosaic, which dates from the 3rd century, was restored in the 4th century and has a beautiful geometric motif. The medallion at its centre portrays the battle between Theseus and the Minotaur in the Labyrinth of Crete. Next to this are varied depictions of the island of Crete.

On the floor of the large room on the southern side of the villa is another interesting picture. This shows the new-born Achilles having his first bath. Next to his parents, Thetis and Peleus, are his two trophies and the three Fates. The mosaic dates from the 5th century.

Map on page 190

The House of Orpheus ❻

This house is situated to the west of the House of Theseus. Systematic excavations begun in 1982 have so far uncovered a building with many rooms, which are laid out around an *atrium*, itself encircled by colonnades (*peristylon*), with baths in the northeastern corner. The original building dates from the end of the 2nd century or the beginning of the 3rd century – when Nea Pafos was at its zenith. Like most of the buildings in the area, the house was decorated with rich floor mosaics and splendid frescoes.

The most important mosaic decorates a room on the northeastern side. This shows Orpheus with his lyre, surrounded by figures, and playing his heavenly music. The inscription under Orpheus is probably the name of the owner or the founder of the house. Two further mosaics, on the floor of a room to the south of here, are also worth finding. The first shows with impressive simplicity the battle between Hercules and the mythical lion Nemea. The other shows an Amazon standing against a blue background, carrying a horse's bridle in her left hand and a double axe in her right.

BELOW:
taking a break.

The lower rows of seats in the Roman Odeon have been restored.

The public buildings

The **Theatre** (open permanently; free), which lies in the northeastern corner of the old city, above the hill known as **Fabrica** ⓗ, is one of the most important buildings in this region. It is possible to visit the upper rows of the *koilon*, which are carved into the rocks. The lower part of the *koilon*, the orchestra and the stage, were all built out of stone. An inscription on one of the stone seats indicates that the theatre dates from the Early Hellenistic Period.

On the western side of Fabrica Hill you can visit a complex of underground rooms (open permanently; free) which have been carved into the rocks. The size of some of these rooms is staggering and their original purpose remains a puzzle even today.

Further west still, on the other side of the main road, is the so-called **Guard's Camp** (open permanently; free). This consists of two underground rooms, cut out of the rocks, one of which is rectangular and the other circular. It is thought that they had nothing to do with the camp, but belonged to a subterranean altar from the Hellenistic Period.

On the other side of the main street, on a hill, is the **Northern Gate** of Nea Pafos, whilst a further hill in the west can be identified as the **Northwestern Gate**. These gates probably formed part of the city wall which King Nikokles built at the end of the 4th century BC. The wall began and ended at the harbour, and it is still possible to make out its full length. Close to the sea the wall was built from massive stones, augmented in certain places by rock hewn out of the sea bed. In certain places the wall included multi-sided towers.

BELOW: an eager lemon-seller, Pafos.

Near the Northwestern Gate you can see both the wall and the towers. Traces of the gate's door have survived until today, together with the ramp, which led to the sea. There are also a number of emergency exits (sally ports), which connected Nea Pafos with the plain outside.

The hill in the west, where the **Lighthouse** ⓘ now stands, seems to have been the Acropolis of Nea Pafos. To the south of the lighthouse are the remains of buildings, whilst the Roman **Odeon** ⓙ (open permanently; free), dating from the 2nd century, lies on the slopes of the hill. The lower row of *koilon* around the semi-circular orchestra have been restored. Only the foundations have survived from the stage house (*skene*). The audience came into the odeion via two side entrances and a corridor to the rear of the *koilon*.

To the south of the odeion you can visit the **Asklepeion** (open permanently; free), which was the healing centre and altar of Asklepios, the god of medicine. A corridor connects this building to the odeion. Its architectural plan consists of a centrally-located arched hall, surrounded by two rectangular rooms. The building dates from the 2nd century.

The surviving foundations of a row of Corinthian columns reveal that the *agora*, dating from the 2nd century, was located to the east of the odeion. It consisted of a courtyard with rows of columns. From this courtyard you could ascend, via three steps, to the stoa and the shops, which lay behind. A number of columns, capitals and other remains have survived.

A little way to the south of the Odeon-Asklepeion complex is evidence of a small **Hellenistic altar**. All that remains now are its foundations, carved into the rock, and the steps which led up to it.

Beyond the city boundaries to the east is the altar of **Apollo Hylates** (open permanently; free), from the end of the 4th century BC. It consists of two rooms, both carved into the rocks. Two engraved inscriptions, one over the entrance and the other on the inside, reveal that the altar was dedicated to the god Apollo. From various inscriptions that have been uncovered we know that Aphrodite, Zeus, Artemis and Leto were also worshipped in Pafos.

Also worthy of mention are the remains of the Roman **Amphitheatre ⓚ**: this consists of a hill with an oval-shaped bowl in the middle, which lies to the northwest of the fort.

Byzantine and medieval

Without doubt the most impressive building of the Early Christian period is the **basilica**, known as **Chrysopolitissa ⓛ** (formerly Panagia Akroditissa), in the eastern part of Pafos, adjacent to the modern church of **Agia Kyriaki ⓜ**. The basilica, an imposing building which was constructed at the end of the 4th century has since undergone extensive reconstruction. It is one of the largest early Christian basilicas to be found in Cyprus to date. Originally it had seven aisles, but this was reduced to five during reconstruction in the 6th century. The nave was fitted with a double floor, a characteristic which is found only in Cyprus. Four granite columns still support the eastern part of the roof.

In the western part of the church is the **narthex** and the *atrium* with a fountain in the middle surrounded by rows of columns. A corridor leads in a south-

Map on page 190

BELOW: Chrysopolitissa basilica dates from the Early Christian period.

westerly direction to a building which is thought to have served as residence for the bishop of Pafos. The most important decorations in the basilica are the floor mosaics, which date from various periods. They comprise mainly plant and geometrical motifs, but near the shrine three pictures have survived from the 4th century depicting inscriptions and stories from the Old Testament.

Many of the floors were provided with new geometrical patterns during the 6th century: the floor of the nave must have been particularly impressive as it was embellished with multi-coloured stone slabs (*opus sectile*). A column on the site is known as **St Paul's Pillar**, and is said to be the one to which St Paul was tied and scourged.

The basilica survived until the middle of the 7th century, when it was destroyed during the Arab invasions. A small church was then built on the same spot. This was also destroyed in 1500, in order to make space for the current Agia Kyriaki church.

During the Frankish and Venetian periods (1192–1571) Pafos was the seat of residence of the Latin bishops and, as a result, a number of important new buildings were constructed. One of them lies directly northeast of the Agia Kyriaki. Here are the remains of the **Franciscan church**. From the foundations it is possible to recognise a building with three aisles, which was probably constructed at the end of the 13th century or at the beginning of the 14th. The architectural feature of two arches above a double column is especially interesting.

BELOW: St Paul's Pillar, scene of the saint's beating.

On the main road to Kato Pafos are the meagre ruins of the **cathedral of the Latins**, built in the 13th century. All that remains now is its southwestern corner. On the way to the mosaics – on the right-hand side on a hill – are the remains

Map
on page
190

of a medieval castle, known as **Saranda Kolones**  (open permanently; free), which means "the 40 columns". It was named after the old granite columns incorporated into the castle which previously lay scattered over the area. The central section of the castle is surrounded by a mighty wall and moat. The castle has four massive corner towers. In the central courtyard the roof was supported by arches; some of the *pessoí* (the supporting piers) were later converted into toilets.

A large kiln can still be seen. This is said to have served as a heater (*praefurnium*) for water. There are also a number of stalls here. The outer wall was protected by eight towers of different shapes; in the centre of the wall were seven steps which ended in an emergency exit leading to the moat.

We can only speculate about the original construction of the castle, and it is difficult to put a precise date on it. However, we do know for certain that is was devastated by an earthquake in 1222. Later, in the 13th century, during the period of the Lusignans, it was replaced by a smaller **fort** (open daily; entrance fee) near the harbour. What can be seen there today is the remains of a much larger building that was constructed around the core of a Frankish fortress. The Venetians had the fortress extended, but abandoned it when they realised that it was going to prove impossible to defend it against the Ottomans in 1570. An inscription directly above the main entrance shows that the fortress was finally restored by the Turks.

Behind the restaurants at the harbour are the remains of an early Christian basilica, **Panagia Limeniotissa** , which was built around the 4th or 5th century. The building was divided into three aisles by two rows of columns; the narthex and the *atrium* were to be found in the western section. A number of

Time for a snooze.

BELOW:
the massive arches
of Saranda Kolones.

floor mosaics can still be seen; in a room in the northeast of the building is a wonderful example of an *opus sectile*. The Arabic inscriptions from the second half of the 7th century indicate that the Arabs made use of this room during their invasions of Cyprus.

The Necropolis

According to ancient tradition, cemeteries (*necropoleis*) were always situated outside the walls of a city. In Nea Pafos the enormous necropolis extends from the town in all directions. The graves of the northwestern necropolis are known as the **Tombs of the Kings** ⓟ (tel: 06-240295; open daily; entrance fee) because of their imposing character rather than the regality of their inmates. In fact, they were used by the nobles of the Ptolemaic dynasty as family graves. The tombs, which are carved into the rocks, were built over a period of 600 years, between the 3rd century BC and the 3rd century AD. They are small, cubic graves without any form of decoration. There are over 100 tombs in all and the largest of them display an impressive architectural plan, having been cut into the rocks with the greatest of precision.

The two most important **peristyle tombs** can be reached by going up a flight of stairs leading into an open central courtyard, the *atrium*. The tombs are arranged around the courtyard and the columns are examples of the Doric style. Traces of a number of frescoes reveal that the rocks were intricately painted at one time. A neighbouring tomb reveals a different architectural form, consisting of a compact cube in the centre, which is surrounded by wide corridors. Unfortunately, only a small section of the decoration and its coloured stucco has survived.

BELOW: Tombs of the Kings.

The necropolis served as a place of refuge during the persecution of the island's first Christians. Tomb number 5 was later converted into a kiln and was used for firing medieval ceramics. Tomb number 6, on the other hand, was used as a chapel, and it is from this that the region takes its name – *Palioeklissia*, which means "the old church".

Pafos Archaeological Museum

Away from the hustle and bustle of the tourist trade, the **Pafos Archaeological Museum** ⊙ is the first thing you encounter as you arrive in the upper town of Ktima from the Limassol.

The first hall of the **museum** (tel: 06-240215; open daily, Sat and Sun to 1pm only; entrance fee) contains finds from the neolithic and Chalcolithic periods (8000–2500 BC), the Bronze Age (2500–1050 BC), and metal objects and pieces of golden jewellery from a number of other periods. In the centre of the hall is a mummy of a girl, discovered in the village of Lempa, which dates from the 3rd century BC.

There is also an important collection of ceramics from the Chalcolithic period in the museum. They have a red pattern on a white background and are among the earliest and most beautiful ceramics which have been found on Cyprus. In addition, a collection of surgical tools from Roman times is worth seeing. They came from a tomb now lying under the Annabelle Beach Hotel.

In the second hall finds from the Geometric (1050–750 BC), Archaic (750–475 BC) and Classical periods (475–325 BC) are displayed. Besides the Cypriot vessels with their beautiful paintings and sculptured decorations, you can see the black-on-red receptacles which were imported from Attica. The most significant

Map on page 190

In Pafos, not all the art is ancient.

BELOW: exhibits inside and out at Pafos Archaeological Museum.

of the statues are the ones which come from the altar of Aphrodite in Palea Pafos, which display characteristics typical of Archaic sculpture. The Egyptian, Phoenician and Greek influences can be clearly recognised. The wonderful tomb relief in white marble, only parts of which have survived, is of Greek origin, whilst the tomb columns to the side come from Cyprus.

In the same room you can see a row of inscriptions in the Cypriot dialect, as well as the spelling of the Greek language used in Cyprus before the introduction of the Greek alphabet at the end of the 4th century BC. One of the glass display cases contains a collection of bronze and copper coins, most of which come from the mint in Pafos.

In the third hall there are glass and clay pots, along with sculptures and idols from the Hellenistic (325–58 BC) and Roman (58 BC to AD 330) periods. The two rectangular **sarcophagi** in the shape of a house are particularly impressive. Between them is a lion, another example of Attic work, which was found in Nea Pafos. Amongst the sculptures, the beautiful **head of the Egyptian Queen Isis**, with its characteristic locks of hair, is especially outstanding, as is the **statuette of Asklepios**, the god of medicine, which has survived in perfect condition. Among the lamps (or *lynchnas*) is a large lamp modelled in the shape of a ship from the House of Orpheus. It shows the embossed form of the Egyptian god Serapis. In another display cabinet are a number of clay "hot-water bottles", moulded to the shape of the feet, hands and other parts of the body that they might be required to warm.

In the fourth room objects from the Roman and Byzantine Periods (4th–10th centuries) are displayed. The local Roman pottery and the Byzantine amphora come from the House of Dionysos. Particularly worthy of mention are two

BELOW: covered market in Pafos.

Map on page 190

trapezophora made of marble; the first shows the drunken Hercules surrounded by the Erotidis and the other, which has only survived in part, shows Orpheus and the beasts. A number of Christian inscriptions in marble, and another in the form of a mosaic come from local basilicas. The columns with Arabic inscriptions come from the basilica of Limeniotissa, and are rare evidence of the Arabic presence in Cyprus.

In the last room are discoveries from the Frankish (1192–1489) and Venetian (1489–1571) periods, including a collection of handsome glazed ceramics. One display case contains examples of glazed Cypriot pottery, which was famous in its time. Another contains examples of imported ceramics from Syria, Italy, Spain and the Near and Far East.

Also from abroad is the **Group of Four Angels**, which was discovered during excavations of the Latin church near the church of Agia Kyriaki in Kato Pafos. The angels' bodies are made of limestone, whilst their wings are of terracotta and their decorations of multi-coloured marble. The Frankish **tombstones** are also highly important; their inscriptions reveal vital information about the nobles who died in Cyprus.

Ktima

On Leoforos Georgiou Griva Digeni are the particularly striking buildings of the **Gymnasium** (a grammar school built in 1960), the **Academy of Economics** (formerly a school and built in 1928) and the gateway to the stadium.

The school buildings – extraordinarily grand for a small town like Pafos – reflect the high value which Greek Cypriots continue to place on classical education. Educational institutions here have always been central to Hellenic

Ktima offers the quintessential charm of a Cypriot town. Its role as a commercial centre for the area ensures plenty of lively activity.

BELOW: the Pafos Gymnasium.

Exhibit at the Ethnographical Museum in Ktima.

BELOW AND RIGHT: a couple of local characters.

Map on page 190

dreams of liberation. One of the reliefs in the courtyard of the Gymnasium shows a schoolboy trying to kill a wild lion with a stone – which is symbolic of the heroic struggle of young Cypriots against the British colonialists towards the end of the 1950s.

If you turn off towards the town park and the town hall, you come to the **Bishop's Palace ®**. Archbishop Makarios fled here after the coup by Greek officers on 15 July 1974. It was from here, over the radio, that he denied the reports disseminated by the leaders of the coup that he was already dead. Pafos's **Byzantine Museum** (open Mon–Sat, to midday only on Sat; entrance fee) is within the grounds of the Bishopric. Although not greatly interesting to anyone who hasn't an abiding interest in religious icons, the museum's collection of icons is nevertheless the most impressive in the Pafos area, with works dating back to the 12th century.

Near the palace is the **Ethnographical Museum ⑤** (open Mon–Sun, to 1pm only on Sunday; entrance fee), housed in an interesting town-house. The rather eclectic collection of exhibits dates from the Stone Age right up to the present day. One highlight is the museum building's own **chapel** – in a Hellenistic rock tomb discovered in the basement. An 18th-century wooden bridal chest recalls just one folk tradition that was widespread even into recent times, but has now fallen into abeyance.

A little further to the north on a slope below a parking place is the newly renovated **Turkish Bath ⑦**. Until around 1955 this *hamam* was used by both Greek and Turkish Cypriots. In later years such peaceful coexistence was destroyed: on 7 March 1964 heavy fighting broke out between Greek and Turkish nationalists. There were deaths on both sides and hundreds of hostages were taken. As a result of the battle, the Turkish Cypriots were forced to withdraw to a heavily protected area. A mosque which stood on the square above the Turkish bath was pulled down by the Greeks after Turkish fighters had fired on civilians from the tower of its minaret.

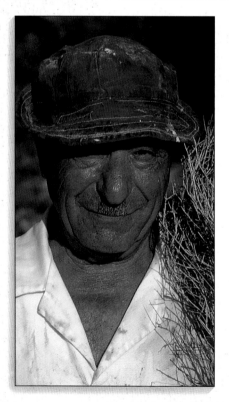

To the east of the **Covered Market ⓤ** you come into the new part of **Ktima**, with its main shopping street, **Leoforos Archiepiskopou Makariou III**. North and northwest of the market the Turkish street signs indicate the former Turkish area. The narrow streets, with their many nooks, crannies and cul de sacs, used to have a timeless appeal. However, the commercial centre of Pafos is changing rapidly, with burgeoning shops, shopping malls, workshops, restaurants and cafés occupying the former Turkish buildings (which probably would have collapsed through neglect if they had been left unoccupied). The streets are still narrow, so these days there is an almost constant traffic jam due to the stream of cars trying to move around the town.

Although some of the old atmosphere has been retained, particularly in the quieter side streets, Pafos is changing so fast and so furiously that it is too much to hope that it will long survive. At some time in the not far-distant future, it will probably be realised – too late – that Pafos has "developed" into another Limassol. ❏

OUTSIDE PAFOS

*Pafos provides an excellent jumping-off point for exploring the
"wild west" of Cyprus – towards Limassol via Palea Pafos, or
north to Cape Drepano, Polis and the Akamas peninsula*

Map
on page
188

Lefkosia/
Nicosia

● Pafos

T he road from Pafos to Limassol goes through the southern coastal plain,
now the most fertile region of the whole area. Fields of bananas, citrus
fruits, avocados, grapes, early potatoes, sesame and peanuts flank both
sides of the road. All these crops need considerable irrigation, and the water is
brought from a dam on the lower reaches of the Xeros Potamos to the west of
Kouklia, part of the Pafos Irrigation Project, one of the largest irrigation projects
on the island, covering 12,500 acres (5,000 hectares). This ambitious project was
completed in 1974. The profits from the area's production – devoted mainly to
export – have made a substantial improvement to the living standards in this formerly economically backward region.

Pafos to the Rock of Aphrodite

Beyond Pafos is the sign for **Geroskipou ❷**. The name means "Holy Grove".
What was once a tranquil garden on the pilgrimage route from Nea Pafos to
Aphrodite's shrine at Palea Pafos, is now a busy suburban village. Only a few
decades ago numerous mulberry trees and one of the largest silk-spinning mills
in Cyprus were here. Stools are still produced from the wild fennel in
Geroskipou. Other specialities of the area are the sweet *loukoumia*, which is
made from grape syrup, and *halloumi*, a cheese made
from the milk of sheep and goats, fed on the thyme-
rich pastures.

The church of Agia Paraskevi in Geroskipou is not
only a masterpiece of Byzantine sacred architecture,
but also one of the most important monuments from
the Iconoclastic period. The church, with its five
domes follows the same architectural pattern as
Peristerona, and is modelled on the multi-domed 6th-
century Justinian church of St John in Ephesus.

In the dome above the sanctuary rare frescoes with
Byzantine motifs have survived from the Iconoclastic
period (the first half of the 9th century). Only a few
fragments have survived from the frescoes of figures
from the end of the 12th century (for example the
head from the Assumption of the Virgin on the northern wall, centre aisle). Most of the works from this
epoch were painted over in the late 15th century.

Near **Acheleia ❸** a sign points the way to one of
the experimental farms run by the Cyprus Ministry
of Agriculture. Current projects centre on pig-rearing
and attempts to produce exotic fruits. The areas of
cultivation formerly belonged to a feudal estate dating
from the Lusignans. Later, in the middle of the 15th
century, a Venetian firm commandeered large areas
for growing cane sugar. According to one legend,
sweet-toothed buffalos swam here from Egypt,
attracted by the exquisite juice of the sugar cane.

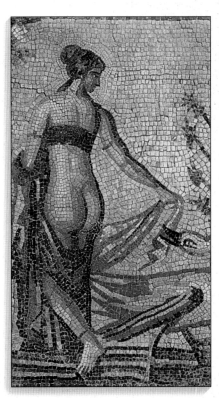

LEFT: icon in the
Agios Neofytos
monastery.
BELOW: mosaic in
Palea Pafos.

Palea Pafos

Palea Pafos ❹ is situated 10 miles (16 km) southeast of Nea Pafos. According to legend, the city was founded by King Agapenor from Tegea in the Peloponnese. The city owes much of its considerable fame to the Sanctuary of Aphrodite, which according to various writers – including Homer – was the most revered temple of the world.

The Sanctuary of Aphrodite

The present temple (tel: 06-432180; open daily; entrance fee) comprises a mixture of buildings from the Late Bronze Age and the Roman period. From the original buildings it is the enormous stone blocks in the southwestern corner which particularly catch the eye. Most of them have been drilled through at some time in the past by farmers from the surrounding area, searching for the mythical treasure of Aphrodite. A large part of the extant ruins and mosaics come from the construction which took place during the Roman period.

A number of Roman coins and cameos indicate what the temple could have looked like in its original form; it was in three parts, and in the middle there was probably a *baetylos* – an abstract representation of a goddess. According to ancient sources, the cult of Aphrodite was not represented by the statue of a woman. Indeed it is thought that the grey-green conical stone, now in the museum of Palea Pafos, was the symbol of the goddess. Between the temple and the medieval *kastron* (fortress), a path leads in a northwesterly direction into a small **Roman House**, only a small part of which – a room with floor mosaics, and a bath – has been excavated. In the centre of the geometrical mosaics is a picture of Leda and the Swan – a copy of the original mosaic, now kept in the museum

BELOW: the temple of Aphrodite, Palea Pafos.

Medieval manor house

During the Frankish Period, Cyprus became famous for its sugar production, and the area around Palea Pafos was one of the most important sugar cane and sugar-processing centres on the island. The medieval feudal **manor house** (open daily; entrance fee included with Sanctuary of Aphrodite ticket) was the headquarters of the district administration of the sugar-processing industry. It was built in the 13th century, and altered during the period of Ottoman rule. It consists of a large courtyard surrounded by four side buildings. On the eastern side, the large rectangular hall, half underground and surmounted by four small cross-vaulted domes, dominates the layout.

The small local museum consists of two rooms. On the ground floor is a mosaic brought here from a Roman building in Palea Pafos. In the upper floor, above the large rectangular hall, the discoveries from the area around Palea Pafos are arranged in chronological order.

In the area around the temple room, but above all in the neighbouring plain (local name Stavros), excavations have brought to light the remains of watermills which are still in good condition. These water mills were used to power the sugar-processing factory.

Rock of Aphrodite

A few miles after the turn to Palea Pafos the fertile coastal plain comes to an end. The road now runs through an area of deserted, barren land along the edge of an imposingly steep coast. A number of massive rocks appear below, as if tossed up by a raging sea. It is behind one of these rocks, **Petra tou Romiou** ❺ (Rock of the Romans, but better-known as Aphrodite's Rock), that Aphrodite, born

Map on page 188

Banana trees are a rather unexpected sight in the area around Pafos.

BELOW: birthplace of Aphrodite.

from the sea foam, is supposed to have stepped out of the waves. The view to Petra tou Romiou can be enjoyed from the tourist pavilion lying just inland.

Pafos to Cape Drepano

From Pafos roads lead northwards to the cove of Coral Bay and Pegeia. The villages of Chlorakas, Empa and Kissonerga, near the road going from Ktima, have already been swallowed up by the outskirts of Pafos. Extensive developments of holiday homes and apartments sprawl inland, their charms advertised to sun-hungry northern Europeans by means of massive hoardings. **Panagia Chryseleousa**, a domed cruciform church with a domed narthex extension, lies right in the middle of **Empa ❻** (the key is available from the village priest). It contains frescoes from the end of the 15th century and a valuable iconostasis from the 16th century.

Further uphill, beyond Tala village, is **Agios Neofytos monastery ❼**. In 1159 a 25-year-old monk by the name of Neofytos settled as a hermit to the north of Pafos. He cut a hermitage in the rock with his own hands, and by about 1200 a sizeable community had evolved around it. Even during his lifetime, people came on pilgrimages here. He was famous far and wide for denouncing the injustices of the Byzantine tax collectors. His bones, removed from his tomb in 1750, are in a wooden sarcophagus; his skull is preserved in a silver reliquary.

His rock grotto was painted in two distinct phases and styles at the end of the 12th century. In 1183 artists from Constantinople painted frescoes in the neoclassical style, and then in 1196 the "monastic" frescoes were painted, as was usual in monastic churches then. The paintings in the **Neofytos Rock-Grotto** are

Ancient texts at Agios Neofytos.

BELOW: Agios Neofytos monastery.

among the most important on the island. The few paintings from 1503 are in traditional rural character.

In the 16th century a large monastic development was built to the east of the rock-face (it is now inhabited by Orthodox monks). In the **northern aisle** of the monastic church some artistically valuable frescoes from the beginning of the 16th century have survived. In terms of their style and execution these are excellent examples of Italo-Byzantine art.

At **Lempa** ❽, a handsome little village overlooking the sea that has become something of an artist's haven, a **neolithic village** (open daily; free) has been excavated. Replicas of the kind of circular stone buildings in which the inhabitants lived have been built on the site. Beyond Kissonerga, the coast road passes through banana plantations.

The beautiful sandy cove of **Coral Bay** ❾ is likely to satisfy those disappointed by the quality of beaches near Pafos. However, you can't expect to find peace and tranquillity: Coral Bay is popular with locals and tourists alike, and is served by a public bus to and from Pafos. Indeed, Coral Bay is another place where a large tourist complex has been built, between the beach and the main road, with apartments, shops and restaurants, some of which are very good.

On the other side of Pegeia, around **Agios Georgios** ❿, you can find quieter beaches and tavernas, some of which have accommodation. At **Cape Drepano** ⓫ are the excavated ruins of a 6th-century Christian basilica with floor mosaics (there is no public access at present but they can be seen from behind the surrounding fence). You can, however, visit the nearby modern church of Agios Georgios, which stands on a clifftop overlooking the sea beside a tiny, and far older **Byzantine chapel** of the same name. Small strips of cloth hung on a nearby tree are an indication of the chapel's importance in the beliefs of local people. Lovers are supposed to come here to discover the outcome of their attachments. St George is also said to help shepherds and goatherds whose animals have gone astray.

Agios Georgios is a good starting point for a tour of the uninhabited **Akamas peninsula**. This journey is best undertaken on foot. A bumpy dust track leads along the coast as far as **Lara Bay** ⓬, home of the Lara Bay Project, which aims to ensure the survival of Cyprus's endangered green turtles.

Between Pafos and Polis

From Ktima the road winds upwards in a northerly direction, climbing into the wonderful landscape of the Pafian hill country. Wine is the main product of this area's light marlacious soil. Every turn-off to the left or right along the road to Polis produces its own special reward: there is nowhere better on Cyprus to see authentic rural life, which is now dying out. Be prepared, however, for a degree of adventure – some of the "roads" turn out to be no more than tracks strewn with pot-holes. Often the only alternative is to walk. The connecting road from Pafos to Polis wasn't built until the beginning of the 20th century when the British constructed a route for carts. Until then the only means of transport were donkeys, mules or, more usually, camels. The village of **Mesa Chorio** ⓭ (to

Map on page 188

BELOW: St George and the Dragon, church of Agios Georgios.

the east of the main road by the turn off to the monastery of St Neofytos) was famous for its camels. Wine and sultanas were transported to the coast and shipped to Egypt right up until World War II.

At the large village of **Stroumpi** ⑭ you reach the ridge of the range of hills separating Pafos from Polis. The wine from Stroumpi has a particularly good reputation and is mentioned in Lawrence Durrell's *Bitter Lemons*. Stroumpi was also near the epicentre of an earthquake which destroyed large parts of the Pafos district in September 1953. After the earthquake the British colonial administration erected simple prefabricated shacks for the homeless. In recent years the inhabitants who still remained in these huts were given detached family houses by the Cypriot government.

There are two possibilities for continuing to Polis; they can also be combined to make an interesting circular tour. The first variation is via the main road to Polis, which follows the fertile valley of the River Chrysochou, descending all the way. Adventurous travellers may want to make a detour from this route to the east in the direction of **Lysos** ⑮. In this area of barren but nevertheless dramatic-looking landscape you will come across a series of Turkish settlements which were abandoned by their inhabitants in 1975. Slowly but surely, the empty houses are falling into decay.

The second alternative leads from Stroumpi via Kathikas through mountain vineyards to the ridge of a further range of mountains with excellent views over the Akamas peninsula and the western foothills of the Troodos mountains. The beautiful village of **Arodes**, with its two communities (Kato and Pano), traces its name back to the medieval feudal rule of the Knights Hospitaller. They named the village after the island of Rhodes, the headquarters of the Order.

BELOW: countryside near Stroumpi.

The village of **Drouseia** ⓰ reflects on an even earlier history: the ancestors of the current inhabitants came here from Arcadia in the Greek Peloponnese. This wave of Arcadian immigrants is responsible for the remnants of Homeric Greek in the Pafian dialect. *Drouseia* is the dialect word for "cool, fresh", and indeed a cool wind from the Akamas blows almost constantly through the bizarre rock formations above the village. In the Droushia Heights Hotel it is possible to enjoy this rural idyll in comfortable accommodation.

Hikers are recommended to take the little stony road which winds its way from Drouseia into the eastern part of Akamas via the deserted Turkish villages of Fasli and Androlikou, and down to **Prodromi** ⓱ and **Polis** ⓲.

The villages which lie on the southern end of the Akamas peninsula have suffered a massive wave of emigration as a result of the meagre living conditions in the area. An "agro-tourist" project set up by Friends of the Earth is intended to open up new horizons for communities such as Kathikas, Kritou Terra, Theletra and Akourdaleia.

The aim of the project is to promote "gentle tourism". For example, the inhabitants of the villages have been given special low-interest loans to renovate their houses in traditional style so that one part of the renovated building can then be rented out to tourists. By such methods Friends of the Earth hopes, on the one hand, to encourage a form of tourism which will harmonise with the structure of the growing settlements, and, on the other, to ensure that the financial benefits of tourism are available to as many people as possible.

The village of **Pano Panagia** ⓳ and the nearby **monastery of Chrysorrogiatissa** ⓴ make enjoyable day excursions from Pafos or Polis. The journey ascends to more than 2,600 ft (800 m), to the western edge of the forest belt

Map on page 188

Carob tree.

BELOW: bindweed in the hedgerows.

encircling the Troodos mountains. Each of the possible routes to Pano Panagia passes through extraordinarily beautiful landscapes. The shortest way from Pafos is via Polemi and past the pretty village of Kannaviou. More impressive, however, is the road winding from the southern coastal plain in the direction of Timi. There are fantastic views over the Xeros Potamos valley, whose river is one of the few Cypriot rivers not to turn into a desiccated wadi in summer. The villages of **Nata**, **Axylou** and **Eledio** further to the north were destroyed by the devastating earthquake of 1953. Only a few old people are still living in the new settlements which the British erected following the disaster: the yields from the vineyards, carob trees and olive trees are too meagre to support much of a population.

Icons and vineyards

The founding of the monastery of Chrysorrogiatissa in 1182 followed the discovery of an icon – as in the case of many other monastic buildings in Cyprus. This one is reputed to have been painted by the Apostle Luke himself. The current monastery church was built in around 1770, and its splendidly carved iconostasis contains the reputedly miracle-working icon of *Panagia Chrysorrogiatissa*. This somewhat unpronounceable name means "Our Lady of the Golden Pomegranate" and symbolises the nurturing breast of the Virgin Mary. A large part of the monastery had to be rebuilt after a fire in 1966.

BELOW: Chrysorro-giatissa monastery, near the village of Pano Panagia.

One of the main reasons for visiting Chrysorrogiatissa, aside from its art-historical importance, is to enjoy the monastic grounds and their setting. The abbot here has his own vineyards, and the wine he produces is highly regarded by connoisseurs. You can buy it in the monastery itself or in the adjoining taverna.

BIRTH OF AN ARCHBISHOP

The village of Pano Panagia has a particular claim to fame. It was here in 1913 that a certain Michalis Mouskos was born, the eldest son of a simple farmer and goatherd. His entrance as a novice into the monastery of Kykkos was the first step in what was to be an extraordinary career, during which he was to become "Makarios III", Archbishop of Cyprus and, from 1960 until his death in 1977, the president of the island republic.

Metal signposts in the village point the way to the house of the parents of Makarios III. The traditional architecture of the house, characteristic of the area, makes a visit especially worthwhile. Both animals and people entered the house through the single door at the front. The whole family lived in the large front room, where you can see a collection of old furniture and ceramics. The smaller room at the rear was used as a stall for the animals. The reasoning behind this design was to make it more difficult for rustlers to steal livestock. A museum (open daily; free) and a larger-than-life sculpture of Makarios are further proof of the pride the inhabitants of Panagia feel for their famous son.

The important landmarks in the life of this charismatic church leader and statesman are documented with the aid of photographs, mementoes and insignia.

Polis to Akamas

Polis (meaning city) is the shortened version of **Polis Chrysochou**, which means "city of the golden land". There are a number of different interpretations of the origin of the eponym golden, all of which probably contain a degree of truth. One cites the extraordinary fertility of the land by virtue of the River Chrysochou, now augmented by water from a number of dams.

The main product of the Lusignans and Venetians was cotton, obtained from the large feudal estates. But the rich copper deposits in the area, which have been mined since ancient times, are another possible explanation for the name. And it is said that veins of gold really were discovered here during the Ottoman Period, though they were declared as vitriol for export purposes in order to evade Turkish tax laws.

Golden past

Certainly the region has experienced golden times during its history. The ancient city-kingdom of Marion, founded as a settlement by Ionian Greeks in the 7th century BC, was located just to the east of Polis. But by the time of the British takeover there was little sign of economic prosperity. A report of the District Commissioner of Pafos in 1879 castigated the activities of highwaymen, robbers and murderers in the region. Another type of robbery was also endemic at the end of the 19th century: many thousands of *necropoleis* were opened and robbed – their contents invariably taken abroad.

The English writer Colin Thubron, who visited Polis during his walking tour of the island in 1972, described it as a desolate spot: "I strolled among an unsmiling people down streets lined with deserted shops and houses with damaged roofs which were hanging down... It was the only town I saw in which the owls dared to come in at evening and cry from the rooftops."

Maybe it is precisely the charm of its shabbiness which has made Polis into what it is today: a last refuge in coastal Cyprus (at least in the south) for those whose idea of a fun time doesn't involve giant hotels. Polis is, however, building small hotels and holiday villas as fast as concrete can be trucked in, to cater for demand from "alternative" tourists and from Cypriots looking for a place to escape from wall-to-wall foreign tourists. Prices are getting higher, and although Polis retains some of the quaint good looks and laid-back attitudes that once made it an insider's tip for the rucksack set, there's no saying how long that can last.

Anyway, in Polis tourists can still find some of the things they know and love from Greece: cosy tavernas with candlelight, music from Theodorakis, and laid-back discotheques which look as though they have been plucked out of the 1960s. On the beach there is still room to move and the hinterland has something wildly romantic about it. Tourism has given the place prosperity, and a large proportion of the population has benefited from the purchasing power of the holiday-makers. Many people, for example, rent out private rooms. Polis sees its chance to catch up with the rest of Cyprus and is seizing it with both hands.

Map on page 188

A timeless scene of rural life near Pafos.

BELOW: Polis church.

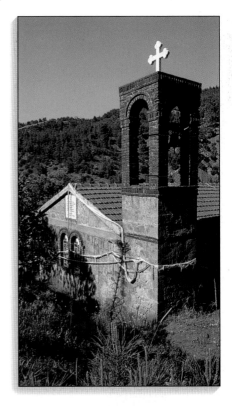

A few miles to the west of Polis is the Akamas peninsula, the most westerly part of Cyprus. This stretch of land is named after the mythical son of Theseus, and founder of the later city-kingdom of Soli. The wild landscape, with its steep slopes and deep gorges, is one of the last areas of Cyprus to remain untouched by human hand. Enthusiasts describe it as the last really Homeric landscape of the Hellenistic world.

Its lack of development has made the Akamas peninsula into an important haven for flora and fauna. However, today the Sleeping Beauty quality of the region is acutely threatened. Entrepreneurial Cypriots have long since recognised the potential for tourism – particularly the coastal area with its fantastic sandy bays – and are quickly acquiring the land.

That the further development and eventual destruction of the Akamas peninsula has so far failed to materialise is due solely to the indefatigable work of the Cypriot environmental campaigners. Conservation groups such as the Friends of the Earth have been campaigning for the Akamas, bringing to the attention of the Cypriot people the danger of further environmental destruction on the island. Other bodies are also concerned. The Council of the European Union has included the Akamas within its Mediterranean protection programme, and the Cypriot government has announced an intention to eventually turn the area into a national park.

Progress towards this goal is painfully slow, however, and "eventually" seems to recede ever further over the political horizon. In a case that acquired near scandalous proportions in 1997, planning regulations in the Akamas area were "relaxed" by the government to permit the building of a huge resort hotel by a company partly owned by the family of a government minister.

BELOW:
a lane in Polis.

One nature conservation project, with lessons for the entire Mediterranean area, has been underway since the middle of the 1970s: Lara Bay, which lies on the western coastal edge, serves as a breeding ground for two threatened species of turtle (the green turtle and the hawks-bill turtle). The Cypriot fishing authorities are collaborating with the World Wildlife Fund for Nature on the so-called "Lara Project". The aim of the project is to protect the spawning and newly-hatched young turtles – both from natural enemies and unthinking bathers.

Fish tavernas

From Polis the asphalt road runs in the direction of Akamas via the tranquil fishing village of **Latsi/Lakki** ㉑ where there are a number of good fish tavernas. Until recently Latsi was a commercial diving base, in particular for diving for sponges.

On both sides of Latsi there are beautiful sand and pebble beaches. Further to the west you come to the so-called **Baths of Aphrodite** ㉒. Under a rock overhang a cool spring emerges from the rocks and pours into a natural pool. It is here that Akamas is said to have caught Aphrodite unawares as she was bathing naked; the goddess is supposed to have fallen in love with the simple-minded voyeur. Others, however, say that the location of this mythical event was an altogether different spring in the far west of the peninsula. Whichever of the two the *fontana amoroza* is, those who drink from it are supposed to fall head over heels in love with the next person they see.

The asphalt road ends next to a tourist pavilion near the Baths of Aphrodite. If you happen to be travelling on a motorbike suitable for cross-country treks, you can drive on to **Cape Arnaoutis** ㉓. However, those who want to cherish

Map on page 188

A restaurant in Latsi advertises its menu.

BELOW: the harbour at Latsi.

the unspoilt quality of the Akamas should leave their vehicle here and proceed on foot. The scenery is particularly beautiful in spring when the slopes are covered with gorse and sage. For hikers, the Cyprus Tourism Organisation has designed nature trails, complete with information boards.

From Polis to Kato Pyrgos

The coast to the northeast of Polis, up to the demarcation line with the Turkish-occupied part of the island near Kato Pyrgos, is the most remote from the cities on the south coast.

Before the division of Cyprus it was possible to get to **Kato Pyrgos ㉔** relatively quickly from Nicosia via Morfou and Karavostasi, but since 1974 the area of northern Tilliria can be reached only via Polis. The border situation has prevented excessive tourist development – travellers can still find deserted pebble beaches. In Kato Pyrgos there is a small hotel, and in other places private rooms are let.

The coast road to Kato Pyrgos is blocked by the Turkish military enclave at **Kokkina ㉕**, and traffic is forced into the Tillirian hills to circle around it, with Greek Cypriot and UN military positions clearly visible on the bare heights. Just before here, at **Pachyammos ㉖**, the modern church of Agios Rafaelis has been built in a beautiful location overlooking the sea. Agios Rafaelis is notable for its interior covered with contemporary frescoes.

BELOW: beaches close to Pafos, like Coral Bay, are very popular.

From Polis you can drive past the now closed administrative buildings and the loading areas of the Limni mine. When, in 1979, the supplies of copper concentrates and pyrites were exhausted, the mines were closed down, thus ending a mining tradition that dates back to the Romans.

Map on page 188

The road, flanked by farmhouses, proceeds further along a small strip of irrigated land parallel to the coast. It is hard to imagine that the whole coastal area was virtually uninhabited at the beginning of this century. Until then it was mainly the domain of pirates and slave traders.

The local population preferred to settle further inland, in the area of the modern-day Pafos forest, living from their goats, charcoal burning and other types of forest farming. These ways of earning a living, destructive as they were for the forests, did not meet with the approval of the British Forestry Commission.

Whole villages were moved out, including the 14 families from the village of Dimmata. In 1953 they were given arable land and British-style brick houses in **Nea Dimmata** ㉗. These houses are still inhabited today.

Empty villages

The main road now goes in a large arc inland to the mountain region, skirting the village of Kokkina. This village was already a refuge for Turkish Cypriots from the Turkish villages of the surrounding area during the Greek-Turkish dispute of 1963–64. The inhabitants of the now empty villages of Alevga, Sellain t'Api and Agios Yeorgoudhi were evacuated to Kokkina by UN troops, to protect them from the attacks of General Grivas and his national guard. The Turks for their part launched bombing raids.

After the Turkish invasion of 1974 Turkish troops also held the area around Kokkina, even though it wasn't directly connected with the rest of the occupied north. Kokkina has remained a Turkish enclave, guarded by three different border posts of Greek, Turkish and UN soldiers, and the civilian population was evacuated to the North. ❑

TIP

The last part of the journey to Pyrgos is worth tackling but the border barricades that prevent visitors from travelling along the coast road beyond Pachyammos don't make it easy.

BELOW: the more remote Akamas coast is quieter.

AKAMAS PENINSULA – THE WILD WEST

The ruggedly beautiful Akamas Peninsula is one of the last truly natural places in Cyprus. Achieving National Park status would ensure its protection

Covering some 70 sq km (27 sq miles) the Akamas Peninsula juts out into the sea like a mighty bastion defending the natural riches within. Its coastline is jagged and treacherous, while inland forests of Aleppo pine mixed with juniper crown the rough range of hills that runs along the peninsula's spine. Some 530 plant species, almost one-third of Cyprus's indigenous total, grow in the Akamas, and in springtime the colours are those of a giant Expressionist palette. Some 168 species of birds have been observed in the area, and butterflies, snakes and other reptiles are abundant too.

There are those who ply their way wimpishly through this exhilarating landscape by four-wheel drive vehicle, but only your own legs will give you a real taste of the Akamas.

The most popular walks are along two sign-posted trails known as the Aphrodite and Adonis trails, which begin at the Baths of Aphrodite. There are also various unmarked trails, which you can pick up at the Baths, or at Neon Chorion village or Lara Bay, on the west coast. The longest of these take you along the east coast or over the hills past the Fontana Amoroza to Cape Arnaoutis: these are 20–30-km (12–19 mile) round trips so are for the serious walker only. Make sure you take plenty of water and a hat, and be prepared to sweat a great deal.

SOFT OPTIONS

The virtually unfrequented beaches of the Akamas, although mostly composed of pebbles or rock, are among the best places in Cyprus for sunbathing and swimming, but beware of razor-sharp rocks. For the laziest Akamas experience of all, consider hiring a powerboat at Latsi.

▷ **UNSPOILT CHARACTER**
Untouched – so far – by the developer's hand, the Akamas offers spectacular views and a remarkable diversity of vegetation, wildlife and geology.

△ **HAVE A BANANA**
The warm, well-irrigated and relatively sheltered hinterland of the Akamas makes it an ideal place for the cultivation of bananas.

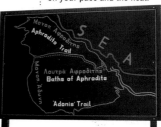

▽ **NATURAL AVENUES**
The Adonis and Aphrodite nature trails are both about 8 km (5 miles) long. The going is fairly easy and will take 2–3 hours depending on your pace and the heat.

DEVELOPMENT THE LAONA WAY

The Laona Project was conceived by the Cyprus branch of Friends of the Earth to demonstrate the feasibility of ecologically sound development in the Akamas Peninsula and the nearby Laona plateau.

Increasingly vocal and increasingly desperate – given the runaway environmental destruction which has washed over much of the coastline in a concrete tidal wave – Cypriot environmentalists and their international supporters are trying to draw a line in the sand around the Akamas. Securing the interests, above all the economic interests, of the local people is essential to the successful protection of this region, so the project aims to revitalise the declining economies of area's villages. Technical and financial assistance are offered to restore traditional properties for visitor accommodation and small-scale industry. Pictured above is one such restored house.

There is powerful opposition to any attempt to slow the development juggernaut, but this project is one of the area's last and best chances.

◁ **TURNING TURTLES**
The continued protection of the beach at Lara Bay, the last refuge for endangered green and loggerhead turtles, is a *cause célèbre*.

▽ **BATH TIME**
It is forbidden to dip in the Baths of Aphrodite, where the goddess is said to have bathed and which are said to be a source of eternal youth.

▷ **JUST VISITING**
The hoopoe (*Upupa epops*), a migrant visitor to Cyprus's shores, is just one of the many winged attractions in the Akamas. Its colourful plumage and distinctive call announce its arrival. If you're lucky, you might also see kestrels, falcons or vultures wheeling overhead.

THE TROODOS MOUNTAINS

Map on page 224

The Troodos mountains rise up like a gentle giant over the western part of Cyprus. Some of the island's most stunning scenery is here, together with a treasure trove of masterpieces of Byzantine art

Lefkosia/
Nicosia

The remoteness of the Troodos mountains, together with careful forestry policies, have ensured the preservation of a large forest area in the central part of the Troodos. This forest once extended to the plains, and is unique in the eastern Mediterranean both in terms of its extent and its beauty. The dominant tree in the Troodos mountains is the Aleppo pine, which accounts for 90 percent of the total stock. It is only in the upper reaches, above 4,900 ft (1,500 m), that the bizarre silhouettes of the black pine predominate.

Place of refuge

The inaccessible nature of the mountain area has made it a place of refuge since early times. Byzantine churches and monasteries here survived the period of Ottoman rule more or less undamaged. It is therefore possible to find a wealth of Byzantine art treasures in the Troodos.

In the 20th century the Troodos area has become a refuge of another sort: first as a summer destination for well-off foreign guests and now as a holiday and weekend retreat for the Cypriots themselves. The average temperature on Mount Olympus is around 15°C lower than in Nicosia. In July the maximum temperature is just 27°C (80°F).

Every year in August whole convoys of cars snake into the Troodos mountains to escape from the sticky heat of the cities. Camping and picnic spots are often jam-packed – it would appear that the Cypriots tend to take a substantial part of their household equipment with them on any outing.

Because it acts as a cloud trap for the prevailing westerly winds, the Troodos area receives a relatively high level of precipitation of between 31 and 39 inches (800–1,000 mm) – three times as much as on the plains. In the middle of winter the areas over 4,600 ft (1,400 m) above sea-level are covered with snow, which in some years can reach a depth of more than 10 ft (3 m). Between January and March skiers flit about on the slopes of Mount Olympus. Indeed, even in Ottoman times people knew how to take advantage of the snow, which they transported to Nicosia to sell as a cooling agent.

On the right track

The Cypriot Forestry Commission maintains a network of good (although not always asphalted) roads throughout the forest area, most of which are also suitable for walking tours. Those who drive into the remote forest areas (for example the Pafos Forest) in winter and spring should enquire at the local forestry stations about the state of individual roads. Roadworks, landslides or high water level can make even

PRECEDING PAGES: members of Kykkos monastery.
LEFT: rich interior of Asinou church.
BELOW: icon inside Kykkos monastery.

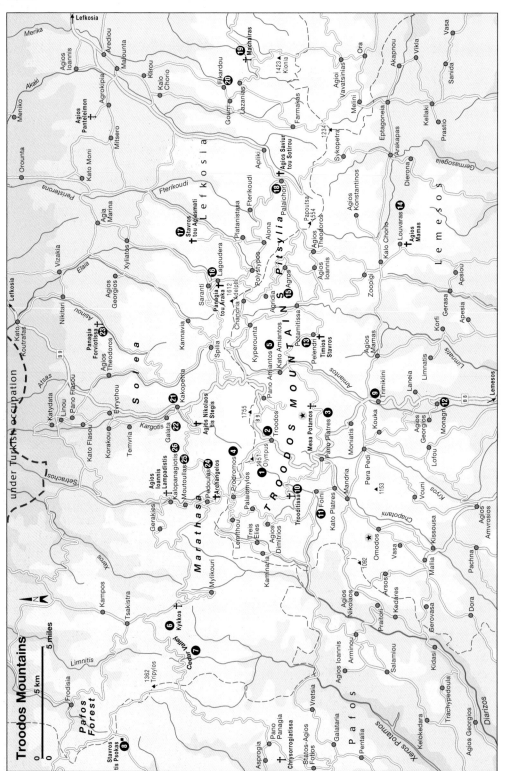

Troodos Mountains

some of the best roads impassable. Among the particular attractions of the landscape are the cultivated valleys and hills surrounding the high forests. In the middle of the vineyards, orchards, and olive and carob plantations, nestle quiet, unspoilt villages.

Map on page 224

Around Mount Olympus

The highest peak of this range is also the highest mountain in Cyprus. At 6,433 ft (1,951 m), **Mount Olympus ❶** takes its name from the famous home of the gods in northern Greece. The Cypriots use the more modest name of *Chionistra*, which is a reference to the snow (*chioni*) that lies here in winter. Apart from a fine view on a clear day, the mountain has little to offer. The large white "golf ball" of the British military radar station near the peak, visible for miles around, has virtually become a symbol of the area.

The unmissable golf ball atop Mount Olympus.

The village of **Troodos ❷**, at the foot of Mount Olympus, is not a particularly attractive place, unlike the mountains with which it shares a name. Without a settled resident population, it is just a loose conglomerate of tavernas, souvenir shops, accommodation for visitors and places where the Cypriot civil servants and British soldiers come to enjoy themselves. During the short winter season, from January to March, this is the main centre for skiing in Cyprus, with four ski runs, a ski school and places to hire out the necessary equipment.

Nearly 2 miles (3 km) from Troodos, in the direction of Platres, is the summer residence of the president of Cyprus. The main building was constructed in 1880 under the supervision of the 26-year-old French poet, Arthur Rimbaud (still unknown at the time), and was designed as the summer residence for the British governor.

BELOW: workmates.

For nature-lovers

With the aim of providing genuine nature-lovers with more than just holiday camps and fast-food snack bars, the Cypriot tourist authorities, together with the Forestry Commission, have laid out a number of nature trails in the upper reaches of the Troodos mountains.

The paths are easy to follow and provide the most vivid and impressive information about the flora and fauna of the area, and also the damage which has been done to the natural habitat.The paths take you past strawberry plants and junipers and various evidence of forestry practices and features: places where there have been forest fires, evidence of reafforestation, scarred trees from which resin has been extracted, disused quarries, strange rock formations and impressive views across the mountains, villages and coast.

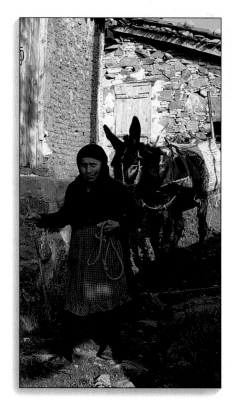

Hill resorts

The villages of **Pano Platres ❸** (Platres for short) and **Prodromos ❹** near the summer palace of the British governor were the most salubrious of all the so-called "hill resorts" of the 1940s and '50s (they were modelled on the hill stations in India, which were built as summer retreats for the British colonial administration). When the British departed, the upper social classes of the Near East started to spend their summers in the comfortable, but expensive, hotels here. Rich traders of Greek origin from Alexandria and Cairo frequented the area, and King Farouk of Egypt once owned a summer villa near Prodromos. Wealthy Israelis also congregated here. At that time, when beach tourism had yet to become popular and mass tourism was unknown, the hill resorts were among the most important tourists centres in Cyprus, in terms of the number of visitors, and the number of nights they stayed.

Coming to Platres and Prodromos today, you will see only a few reminders of the old days. The colonial rulers have long since disappeared from the island, and the development of air travel has opened up other destinations to the upper-crust of the Levant. The once noble hotels are now showing distinct signs of wear and tear, and attract only a run-of-the-mill clientèle during the short summer season.

Devastation

A very different, less glittering history can be found in **Pano Amiantos** ❺, on the eastern slopes of the upper Troodos. *Amiant* is the local name for asbestos, which was mined here in ancient times. In the past 80 years the mountain has been extensively levelled, first by pick-axes and then by bulldozers, in order to extract the fireproof material. The 10,000 men who worked here have turned the mountain into a barren lunar landscape.

The terrible conditions endured by the people who worked in constant contact with the dangerous asbestos fibres was in marked contrast to the luxurious idleness which the visitors to nearby Platres enjoyed. In the end asbestos became as outmoded as summer holidays in Platres: at the end of the 1980s the quarrying was brought to a halt, but the mountainside at this point remains a scene of

BELOW: helping to keep you on the right track.

TROODOS NATURE TRAILS

The four Troodos nature trails are all in an important state forest classified as a National Forest Park (a map of trails is given on the inside back cover of the book):
• **Atalante Trail** (6 miles/10 km): This begins at Troodos. After 2 miles (3 km) there is a spring with drinking water. The destination is the main road from Troodos to Prodromos, near a disused copper mine.
• **Persephone Trail** (2 miles/3 km): The starting point is Café Meli on the southern side of the main square in Troodos. The end of the trail has a good view.
• **Kaledonia Trail** (1¼ miles/2 km): Begins near the summer palace of the president, and follows the route of a river to a small but beautiful waterfall. It continues along a small forest road to the Psilodendro restaurant above Pano Platres. The restaurant is popular with tourists (its trout is recommended). This trail gives the best impression of the upper reaches of the forest vegetation.
• **Artemis Trail** (3 miles/7 km): The beginning and end of this trail is on the Troodos–Prodromos road, just above the turning which leads to Mount Olympus.
Information about flora and fauna is provided in a small brochure, *Nature Trails of the Troodos*, which is available free of charge in the offices of the tourist authorities.

devastation, and there are fears about carcinogenic asbestos fibres being blown around on the wind and infiltrating water supplies.

Map on page 224

Madonna worship

The most famous of all the monasteries in Cyprus is **Kykkos** ❻ (Panagia tou Kykkou; Our Lady of Kykkos), which is revered all over the Orthodox world. The iconostasis of the monastery church contains an icon of the Madonna, which is supposed to have been hand-painted by Saint Luke. The monk who founded the monastery received this icon in the 12th century from the Byzantine emperor Alexius I Comnenos, after he had cured the emperor's daughter of a severe illness.

Over the course of the centuries the monastery has been destroyed by fire on several occasions; the current building dates from the 19th century at the earliest. There is little historical art to be found here; the monastery is none the less worth a visit on account of the showy extravagance of its church and its grounds. That said, the dazzling marble and gold-plate are no more than modest expressions of the true wealth of the monastery.

At the beginning of the 19th century, when the tax burden on the Orthodox population was particularly excessive, many farmers donated their property to the church to relieve themselves of the tax burden which the land represented. Such donations even brought Kykkos property in Russia and Asia Minor. Enormous expanses of expensive land in modern-day Nicosia, which could be used to build on, belong to Kykkos.

Numerous pilgrims visit the monastery, particularly at weekends. They come to worship the icon of Luke and to pay their respects at the tomb of Archbishop

Mosaic detail from inside Kykkos monastery.

BELOW:
Kykkos courtyard.

Makarios III. Makarios entered the monastery as a 12-year-old novice in 1926 and was later to become its abbot. After his death in 1977 his mortal remains were buried on Throni Hill, above the monastery. In recent years the monastery authorities have added a series of buildings in which Cypriot visitors (but not foreigners) can stay overnight free of charge.

Cedar Valley

The mass of rock which makes up the central upper Troodos arose some 100 million years ago. The oldest part of the mountains is surrounded by a ring of younger rocks.

The monastery of Kykkos is also the starting point for a trip to the famous **Cedar Valley** ❼, at the foot of Mount Tripylos in the heart of the Pafos Forest. The area was named after a type of *cedrus brevifolia*, which is larger and more beautiful than the Lebanese cedar, itself a symbol of the Levant state. This type of cedar grows only in Cyprus, and it is only in Cedar Valley that the majestic tree is found in significant numbers.

With a bit of luck you may also come across a moufflon in or around Cedar Valley. This Cypriot species of Mediterranean wild sheep is both extremely rare and shy. Just as the species was on the point of extinction, successful attempts were made to breed it in captivity; a small boost to this noble campaign has been provided by the national airline, Cyprus Airways, which has adopted the moufflon as its emblem. For a virtually guaranteed sighting of one of these charming animals you should visit the reserve in the idyllically located Forest Station of **Stavros tis Psokas** ❽ in Cedar Valley. Stavros tis Psokas, the headquarters of the largest forest division of the Pafos Forest, was the first of the Cypriot forestry stations to be set up in 1882. It has a resident population of around 60 moufflons.

BELOW:
Cedar Valley.

There are two possible ways of proceeding from Pafos or Polis to Stavros tis

Psokas and into Cedar Valley: from Pafos, via the village of Kannaviou, and from Polis via Pomos on the north coast to a turn-off called the Lorovouno Junction, south of the Turkish enclave of Kokkina.

Map on page 224

The southern foothills

On the way from Limassol to Platres or the monastery of Kykkos you should take time to explore the southern foothills of the Troodos mountains, with their wide variety of landscapes and pretty villages. Here you can find peace and tranquillity in a shady *kentron*, such as near the famous Royal Oak, an ancient oak tree growing near **Trimiklini ❾**. On the side of the roads fresh fruits, nuts and figs are sold, all produced in the fertile land of the area.

On the way you can visit rustic **Trooditissa monastery ❿**, in a beautiful location amid pine forests at the top of a steep gorge near Platres. Although founded in the 13th century, the monastery's existing buildings date mostly from the 18th century, and house a silver icon of the Virgin. Trooditissa's treasures also include a leather belt with silver medallions, which is said to be an infallible charm against infertility.

A wide variety of wines and spirits are made in the Troodos mountains. As well as producing the excellent local wine and distilling the fiery *Zivania*, the local people also make a range of grape-based liqueurs such as *Palouzé*, *Sudjuko* and *Loukoumi*.

Fresh *loukoumades*, small doughnuts dipped in syrup, can be purchased in **Foini ⓫** (Phini), a pretty village which is worth visiting on a number of counts. In the local **Folk Art Museum of Phanis Pilavakis** (dedicated to Cypriot folk art), for example, you can find information about the production and use of the

BELOW: moufflons

large clay *pithoi*. The potters of Foini used to be famous for their skill in producing these storage containers.

On the direct road to Limassol from Platres you can visit the church of **Panagia Amasgou monastery**. This barrel-vaulted one-roomed chapel, which also has the additional protection of a barn roof, lies about 2 miles (3 km) outside the village of **Monagri ⓬**. The key to the church is looked after by the village priest. Inside are fragments of frescoes with very high quality paintings from the 12th and 13th centuries. On a more easterly route southwards off the Troodos, passing through **Pelendri ⓭**, is the church of **Timios Stavros**. Dating from the 14th century, the church is embellished with a fine suite of religious frescoes. Still further east, at **Louvaras ⓮**, the one-roomed chapel of **Agios Mamas** has a complete cycle of frescoes by Philippos Goul (1495).

The eastern foothills

Pitsylia is the name given to the slopes of the long eastern Troodos chain with its many forested peaks, the highest being Papoutsa which towers to a height of 5,098 ft (1,554 m). A total of around 21,000 people live in 49 villages, some of which are tiny. The area has always been inhabited by Greek Cypriots; many originally came here to flee from the Ottoman invaders. Like other remote areas, Pitsilia suffers from the emigration of its younger working population. Nevertheless a number of serious attempts have been made to reduce the exodus, and to prevent the decline of the houses and meadows.

In 1977 the Cypriot government started the Pitsylia Integrated Rural Development Project as a way of improving living conditions in the region. The World Bank, which helped finance the project and acted as a consultant, would

BELOW:
Troodos foothills.

like it to be regarded as a model for the whole of the eastern Mediterranean. At considerable expense and with great technical expertise new, wide arable terraces were laid out, small dams, reservoirs and water supply systems were built, and the road network was improved considerably. The farmers were given loans so that they could invest in the rural economy. A grammar school was built in **Agros ⓰**, a gymnasium and a health centre in **Kyperounta**. New life has since returned to the area, particularly in larger villages such as Agros and Pelendri. Many of the inhabitants, however, work in Nicosia or Limassol, as shown by the convoys of cars every morning and evening.

Agros offers visitors a special treat in the months of May and June, when local farmers unload vast baskets of rose petals in the village, for in an inconspicuous-looking factory on the outskirts rose-water is distilled. This makes an excellent souvenir to take home.

Byzantine masterpiece

Several of the finest Byzantine churches in Cyprus lie in the broadly defined area of the eastern Troodos, including the church that is widely considered to be the masterpiece of Byzantine art on Cyprus: **Panagia tou Araka**, with its frescoes from 1192, at the village of **Lagoudera ⓰**.

The church lies just outside the village to the west and looks more like a barn than a traditional church. This is typical of the Troodos churches where the mountain weather, particularly the heavy snow in winter, led to the construction of barn-like gable roofs for extra protection. The iconographic cycles of frescoes, traditionally painted in the dome, were housed on the raised long walls and on the surfaces of the gables.

Map on page 224

Troodos cherries.

BELOW: Panagia tou Araka church at Lagoudera.

Christ Pantokrator inside Panagia tou Araka church, Lagoudera.

The simple cruciform domed church contains works of the neo-classical style painted by artists from Constantinople. The name of a painter, Leon Authentou, is included in the donor's inscription. The most important iconographic themes are represented: in the **sanctuary**, with its semi-circular apse, is the Virgin Mary in majesty with child, flanked by the two archangels, Gabriel and Michael. Below this are seven medallions with the busts of saints (the third from the right is the Cypriot saint Irakleidios).

In the vertical section of the apse are the 12 Early Fathers, including the Cypriot St Barnabas to the right of the middle window, and (under the window on the left), the bust of the Cypriot St Spyridon, who became the patron saint of Corfu at the end of the 15th century. In the vault above the sanctuary is Christ's Ascension, on the northern wall below are St Simeon Stylites Thaumaturge and St Onufrios; on the southern wall is a portrayal of St Simeon Stylites Archimandrite.

On the eastern pendentives of the dome (the triangular supporting vaults between the piers and the drum of the dome) is a scene of the Annunciation with the Archangel Gabriel and Mary, whilst between them hangs a medallion depicting the beardless Christ Emmanuel. The western pendentives show the Evangelists Mark and Matthew (left) and John and Luke (right). On the piers of the drum are 12 life-sized figures of the prophets from the Old Testament, while the dome itself is filled with an impressive *Christ Pantokrator* (Christ as the judge of the world) surrounded by medallions with angels; on the east side is a medallion with the "empty throne" ready for Christ's rule over the world after the Day of Judgement.

In the vertex of the vault are four medallions decorated with the busts of

BELOW: many churches in the Troodos look more like barns than places of worship.

martyrs, below an *Anastasis* (Christ's descent into Hell following the Crucifixion) and the Baptism of Christ. On the lunette is a mural of the Virgin's Presentation in the Temple, below which are life-sized depictions of saints whose
expressive faces are unusually realistic for this kind of art: Sabbas, Nicholas,
Simeon with the baby Jesus, John the Baptist, *Panagia Eleousa* (Mary with
the Angels). A beautiful Assumption of the Virgin can be seen on the lunette of
the southern recess: Below is the *Panagia Arakiotissa*, which as *Panagia
Amolyntos*, the Mother of God with the Instruments of the Passion, has become
a model for numerous portrayals of icons.

Next to this on the right is a larger than life portrayal of the Archangel
Michael, and on the underside of the arches are excellent representations of
saints (for example St Antonios on the right). On the south side of the west
vault is a portrayal of the Nativity, and below St Peter and various other saints.

Frescoes and icons

Stavros tou Agiasmati ⓱ church is situated about 3 miles (5 km) north of the
village of **Platanistasa**, in a remote mountain area. Its gable roof has a cycle of
frescoes by Philippos Goul from 1494 which is well worth seeing. (Before visiting the church be sure to collect the key from the *kafeneion* in the village.) One
special iconographic feature in the church is the fresco-cycle entitled *The Discovery of the Holy Cross* (in the arched recess of the north wall).

The small chapel of **Agios Saviur tou Sotirou**, with just one room, in the village of **Palaichori** ⓲, 4 miles (6 km) southeast of Platanistasa, contains a number of frescoes from the first half of the 16th century. In particular, a detailed
iconographic cycle portrays the life of Christ.

Map on page 224

BELOW: monastery of Machairas.

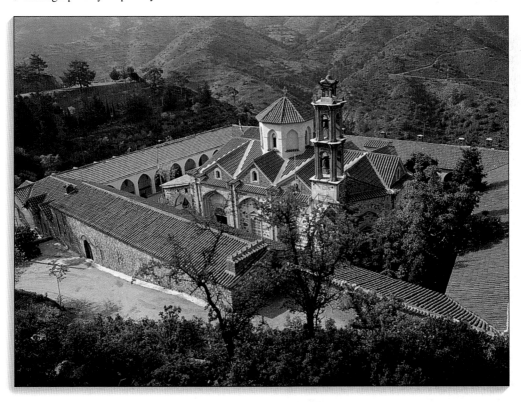

On the eastern edge of Pitsylia is the **monastery of Machairas** , a popular outing destination for the Cypriots themselves during the summer months, not least because of its shady location. Like so many Cypriot monasteries, the 12th-century building is supposed to mark the site where a miraculous icon was found. Under the gallery on the upper floor, the history of the monastery is recorded in illustrated texts.

The undisputed hero of the monastery is not, however, a devout man of the church, but Grigori Afxentiou, a secular rebel. Afxentiou, one of the leaders of EOKA at the time of the struggle for independence, was tracked down by British soldiers to a hide-out in a cave just below the monastery in March 1957. He put up bitter resistance against his enemies, but was killed when his refuge was set on fire. The place where Afxentiou died is now decorated with wreaths and the Greek flag. It has become almost as important a place of pilgrimage as the grave of Archbishop Makarios at the monastery of Kykkos. In the monastery of Machairas a little museum has been set up in memory of the heroic fighter. Visitors with a taste for the macabre can even see his partly charred remains.

Conservation

On the road just north of Machairas is a cluster of restored "conservation" villages. **Fikardou** ⊘ is the "official" one, its folk architecture coming under the auspices of the Department of Antiquities to ensure that its wooden-balconied Ottoman-period houses are not replaced with nondescript modern villas.

Nearby **Gourri** is equally rustic and unspoiled, while **Lazanias**, between Gourri and Machairas monastery, is not only rustic and unspoiled but so tranquil as to make it seem that its inhabitants have all tiptoed away.

BELOW: Fikardou.

The Solea and Marathasa Valleys

These valleys cut into the northern slopes of the Troodos mountains run parallel to each other. Without doubt, they comprise one of the most beautiful areas on the island, even though the lower reaches of the valley and the local connections to the sea have been cut off by the demarcation line and cannot be reached from southern Cyprus. The patchwork landscape, dotted by tightly-packed gabled houses, is enchanting. Each season has its own particular appeal: in spring, for example, the upper Marathasa Valley becomes a white sea of cherry blossom. Not least of the region's attractions, concealed under the rather inconspicuous "barn roofs" of local churches, are the most important religious art treasures of the Byzantine era.

Kakopetria ㉑ in the Solea Valley is a particularly popular Sunday destination for citizens of Nicosia, who come specially to eat its famous trout. Parts of the village have been undergoing extensive restoration in recent years in a successful attempt to preserve the traditional local building style.

Village of springs and Byzantine art

Further out on the Nicosia road, past Kakopetria, is **Galata ㉒**. This mountain village boasts plentiful springs and no fewer than four Byzantine churches. All are worth visiting, but two are particularly impressive. (Again, the keys can be obtained from the priest; the best place to find him is in the *kafeneion* near the bridge with the plane trees.) **Panagia Theotokos** is also known as the Archangelos Michail church, after a larger-than-life statue of the archangel which keeps guard over the main portal. The church houses a detailed cycle of Christian works, and the quality of the paintings is impressive. The frescoes,

Local priest, guardian of his church's treasures.

BELOW: decorative panels in Panagia Theotokos, Galata.

which were painted in 1514, are the work of the Cypriot artist Symeon Axenti.

Panagia tis Podythou church has a number of Italo-Byzantine frescoes from 1502. The influence of the Venetian epoch (1489–1571) is noticeable in the case of the portrayals of the Mother of God and the Communion of the Apostles in the apse. The dramatic portrayal of the Crucifixion in the western gable is very moving, although there is nothing Byzantine about it.

Northern constellation

A constellation of Byzantine churches is to be seen off the northern face of the Troodos mountains.

Taking the right fork from Troodos village (the Nicosia road) you come first to **Agios Nikolaos tis Stegis** (Saint Nicholas of the Roof), which lies some 2 miles (3 km) outside the village of Kakopetria, and contains important Byzantine paintings from the 11th to the 17th centuries. The examples from the 11th century include Christ's Entry into Jerusalem and the Transfiguration, which is portrayed in one large composition together with the Raising of Lazarus. The Comnenian style of the 12th century is represented by the Virgin Mary's Presentation in the Temple, the 40 martyrs, the Day of Judgement and so on. Examples from the 14th century include various excellent works in the nave, particularly the Nativity and the two soldier saints, Theodoros and Georgios.

A good 10 miles (16 km) further along the Nicosia road, via a diversion through **Nikitari** village, is the Byzantine church of **Panagia Forviotissa ㉓**, also known as **Panagia tou Asinou**. The church is a veritable museum of Byzantine art. The quality of the paintings from various epochs gives a very good impression of the art of Byzantine Cyprus. The key for the church is obtained

BELOW: the raising of Lazarus depicted in Agios Nikolaos tis Stegis near Kakopetria.

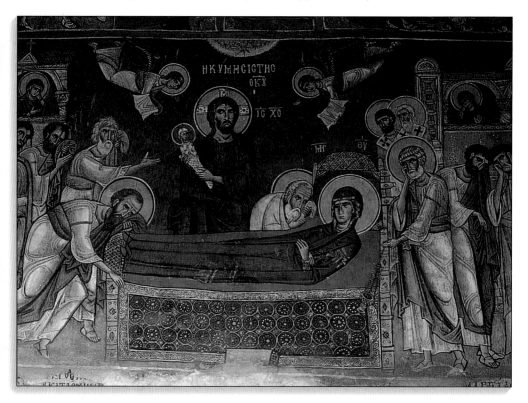

from the village priest in Nikitari. He accompanies visitors to the church, so a small gratuity is always welcomed.

The little one-roomed chapel, dating from the turn of the 12th century, was adorned with Comnenian paintings by artists from Constantinople in the years 1105–06, in accordance with the style of the capital.

At the end of the 12th century a **western narthex** (entrance hall) was added with semi-circular apses to the north and south. After the narthex had been built, the **southern portal** was walled up, and towards the end of the 12th century or beginning of the 13th century a picture of St George on his horse was painted on the inside of the portal.

All in all there are five different layers of paintings in the Asinou church, from four different epochs. Some paintings from 1105–06 are in the sanctuary, for example the Communion of the Apostles and Christ's Ascension. In the nave and on the western wall are portrayals of Christ's Entry into Jerusalem, the Last Supper and the death of the Virgin Mary. The 40 martyrs and various saints are depicted on the north wall. St George in the southern apse of the narthex dates from the end of the 12th century and the beginning of the 13th century. All the other paintings date from 1332–33, including the Mother of God in the apse and the patron's picture with St Anastasia in the narthex (to the right of St George). A booklet explaining the frescoes is available.

Back at Troodos village, and taking the left fork towards the Marathasa Valley and Pedoulas, you can visit the **Archangelos church**. The gable roofed church of the Archangel Michael is situated in the lower part of **Pedoulas ㉔**, The frescoes in the nave are the work of a certain "Adam" from 1474. The cycle depicts rarer themes such as Pilate, and Peter's denial of Christ.

Map on page 224

Archangelos church in Pedoulas.

BELOW: the fine interior of Panagia Forviotissa, also known as Panagia tou Asinou.

Map
on page
224

Preserved traditions

In the Marathasa Valley, which until a few decades ago was extremely remote, a number of interesting traditions have been preserved. You can still sample the valley's traditional speciality – wonderful aromatic dried cherries, once enjoyed as far away as Egypt.

In **Moutoullas ㉕** the mineral water of the same name is bottled, and *sanidhes* and *vournes* are produced from sandalwood. Sanidhes are long planks with hollows (usually 11), in which the bread dough was placed to rise in traditional farming homes. *Vournes* are wooden bowls also used in bread-making. Just a few decades ago such items could be found in every Cypriot kitchen. Only selected parts of pine trunks were used, and the carpenters' demand for wood was so great that they were regarded by the British forestry officials as one of the biggest threats to the Troodos forests.

Moutoullas and beyond

On the western edge of Moutoullas, (to the left of the road when you are coming from Pedoulas) is the tiny church of **Panagia Moutoullas**. Steps lead up from the road to the caretaker's house just below the church. This is the oldest known church with a gable roof in Cyprus. Its frescoes date from 1280. Some are not in very good condition, but the most interesting is the fresco of the donors; the carved doors are also worth closer inspection.

A mile or so (2 km) beyond Moutoullas is **Kalopanagiotis ㉖**, a Marathasa Valley town noted for its Byzantine monastery of **Agios Ioannis Lampadistis**. The monastery, which is no longer inhabited by monks, is situated in the valley on the opposite side of the river to the village (key from the village priest, who can usually be found at the church or in the nearby *kafeneion*).

Its colossal barn roof incorporates a collection of sacred Byzantine architecture spread over three centuries (from the 13th century to around 1500).

The extraordinary paintings in the domed Orthodox church of **Agios Irakleidos** have survived from the first half of the 13th century, from the Early Comnenian Period. Their expressiveness, lines and colours seem to indicate that they were painted by artists from Constantinople. The Entry into Jerusalem is particularly outstanding. Equally accomplished are the Raising of Lazarus, the Crucifixion, and the Ascension in the southern recess.

The scenes in the main church date from the period around 1400 and show good examples of traditional painting. The **narthex**, which was built later, was decorated with frescoes in the style of Constantinople, before the city was conquered by the Ottomans in 1453. According to one of the inscriptions, the painter was a refugee from Constantinople who painted this part of the church shortly after the fall of the city.

The 15th-century **Latin chapel** in the north of the complex is the work of a Venetian. Its frescoes of the Acathist Hymn were painted in 1500 and show strong Western influences in terms of their style, although iconographically they follow in the footsteps of the Byzantine tradition. ❑

RIGHT: local people are often kindly and helpful.
BELOW: enjoying a closer look at the mountains.

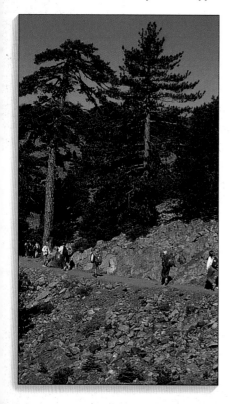

BYZANTINE LANDMARKS AND PROUD TRADITIONS

Cyprus's churches and monasteries are among the island's foremost tourist attractions – nowhere more so than in the Troodos mountains

Cyprus's Orthodox priests and monks climbed into the Troodos mountains to flee the coast with its invaders and worldly towns. Tourism and UNESCO have followed them there, and nine Byzantine churches have been designated as World Cultural Heritage Sites.

Looking more like barns than churches, none appears very promising from the outside. Their true glory lies in the magnificent interior frescoes, dating from the 11th to 14th centuries. The creators of these paintings may have been influenced by the style of now-vanished frescoes in the churches of the distant capital, Constantinople, and other religious centres, but it seems that Cyprus's own creative energies were the primary impulse. To these can be added influences from Christian churches from the Levantine mainland, including from what is now Lebanon.

KEYS OF THE KINGDOM

It used to be well nigh impossible to get into the churches, since the key-holding priest was almost invariably absent. But nowadays there is often a keyholder on site from dawn to dusk. Doing a tour of the churches is another matter. A few, such as those at Galata, are close together, while others are at the end of long and dusty trails. If you are keen to see all nine UNESCO churches you need at least two days, beginning at the central axis of the Troodos: the road from Platres to Kakopetria and Kalopanagiotis.

▷ **BULWARK OF FAITH**
Agios Neofytos monastery is a popular outing from Pafos – as it has been since the 1100s, when the monk Neofytos (*see page 208*) retreated to his cave here.

△ **BAPTISM OF CHRIST**
The frescoes in the Michail Arkhangelos church, Pedoulas, are credited to a fifteenth-century artist known only as "Adam".

△ **LAZARUS RISING**
Under the twin roofs of Agios Nikolaos tis Stegis, near Kakopetria, is a suite of superb murals including this *Raising of Lazarus*.

▷ **CAVE PAINTINGS**
High up on a cliffside near Pafos, the murals of Agios Neofytos illuminate the interior of the cave which was the saint's refuge.

MAGNIFICENT INTERIORS

The nine UNESCO churches in the Troodos are:
- *Agios Ioannis Lampadistis, Kalopanagiotis* – three churches in one, from the 11th to 18th centuries.
- *Panagia Theotokos, Galata (Archangelos)* – a timber-roofed church with post-Byzantine frescoes.
- *Panagia Forviotissa, Nikitari* – arguably the most unmissable of the nine.
- *Panagia tis Podythou, Galata* – with exquisite frescoes of the Crucifixion and Our Lady.
- *Panagia tou Araka, Lagoudera* – a 12th-century church with fine frescoes including the Last Supper.
- *Panagia tou Moutallas* – tiny church full of murals.
- *Stavros tou Agiasmati, Platanistasa* – with fine 15th-century frescoes.
- *Timios Stavros, Pelendri* – biblical murals in a 14th-century church.
- *Agios Nikolaos tis Stegis, Kakopetria.* An 11th-century church with frescoes and a double roof.

▷ **HEAVENLY VIEW**
An image of Christ Pantocrator (Lord of the Universe), gazing down from inside the dome – as if from Heaven itself – is characteristic of many Byzantine churches.

▽ **ACROBATIC ARTISTS**
The frescoes in Agios Mamas church at Louvaras, many by the renowned Lebanese fresco painter Philippos Goul, show how artists skilfully used even the most awkward spaces.

▷ **UNLIKELY BEAUTY**
Pictured here and top right is Panagia Forviotissa, also known as Panagia tou Asinou, which has perhaps the most beautiful frescoes in all the UNESCO-recognised churches in the Troodos mountains.

NICOSIA AND AROUND

*Nicosia is a divided city, split into two utterly separate communities
by the buffer zone known as the Green Line. Despite its status as
a capital city, South Nicosia sees relatively few tourists*

Map
Area 256
City 246

I n 1873 Ludwig Salvator, the Archbishop of Austria, described the city in
Lefkosia, the Capital of Cyprus: "When, having climbed up the gentle hills,
you first catch sight of Lefkosia, with its slender palms and minarets, and the
picturesque mountain range in the background on the scorched plains of Cyprus,
it is reminiscent of a scene out of the *Arabian Nights*. A jewel of orange gardens
and palm trees in an area otherwise devoid of trees, an oasis (by dint of its em-
bankments) – created by human hand. And in the same way that the contrast
between the city and its surroundings stands out clear and harsh, the spirit of
contradiction can also be felt within the city. Venetian fortifications and Gothic
buildings crowned by the half-moon of Turkey; Turks, Greeks and Armenians
mingling together colourfully on this ancient land, each other's enemies but
united in their love of this piece of earth which is their common home."

A divided capital

Today, however, **Nicosia** ❶ bears little resemblance to this description. The
Ledra Palace Hotel is damaged from shelling, and surrounded by barbed-wire.
To the right of Leoforos Markou Drakou are the remains of a burnt-out villa, just
100 yards from the Venetian Walls of the old city.

The walls are still functioning as a bulwark, 400
years after they were built. They are now part of a
heavily guarded border. And for many years the Ledra
Palace has served as the barracks for the units of the
UN peace-keeping troops. Leoforos Markou Drakou
is blocked by barbed wire, and blue-and-white painted
concrete walls. Ramps in the road near the Republic
of Cyprus guard post force the traffic to slow to walking pace. The UN guard in his shelter greets people
casually. There are no special incidents to report from
the only crossing between north and south Nicosia in
the buffer zone.

In Nicosia the Cypriot equivalent of formerly
divided Berlin's Checkpoint Charlie looks as though
it is here to stay. In fact very few people are allowed
to pass the Ledra Palace checkpoint; usually only
diplomats, UN soldiers and foreigners may cross the
border. Depending on the current state of relations
between the two parts of Cyprus, tourists holidaying
in southern Cyprus are allowed to go north of the
Green Line until sunset. The only Cypriots for whom
the barrier is open from time to time, and under controlled conditions, are members of the tiny minorities
– Greeks, Turks and Maronites – who live in the
"wrong" part of the island.

At first sight, the two halves of the city appear to
have virtually nothing in common. Greek Cypriot and
Turkish Cypriot soldiers irreconcilably face each other

PRECEDING PAGES:
Nicosia, ancient
and modern.
LEFT: Laiki Geitonia,
a restored district
popular with visitors.
BELOW: at the
Green Line.

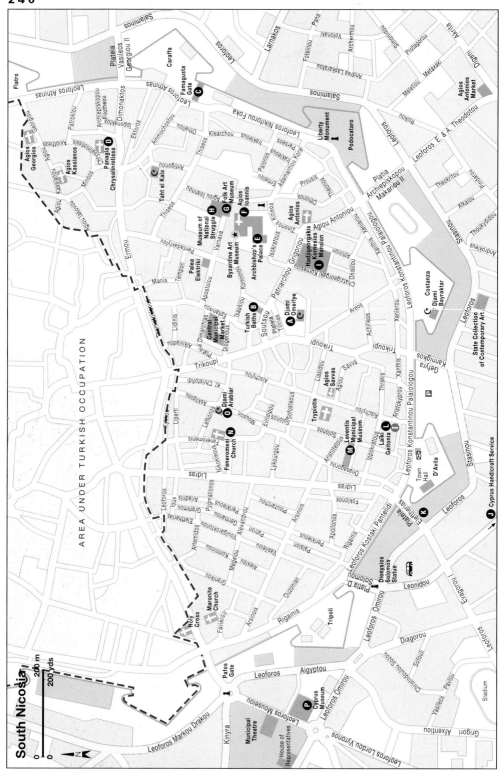

South Nicosia

AREA UNDER TURKISH OCCUPATION

in primitive shelters. The Green Line cuts the streets and water pipelines in two, has put the former international airport out of action, and divides the capital of the island into two parts. It is the job of the blue-helmeted soldiers of the UN to ensure that armed conflicts do not arise.

Map on page 246

Past glories

At the entrance to Odos Hermes in the old city, you can recognise the faded victory slogans of the Olympiakos football team, which once had its home here. *Olympiakos 3 Omonia 2* has been painted on the wall with an unsteady hand, along with the date – 8 June 1961. A hundred yards further on, near a post of the Cyprus National Guard, the buffer zone begins. Unlike in the rest of the island, the division of Nicosia didn't start with the Turkish invasion of 1974, but in 1964. On Christmas Eve 1963 civil violence broke out in the city. The Greek Cypriots demanded that the newly formed Republic become part of Greece, the so-called *enosis*. The Turks, on the other hand, fought for *taksim*, the division of the island. Neither of the two demands could be realised at the time, and yet the common state divided along ethnic lines.

The capital of Cyprus is called Lefkosia by the Greeks and Lefkosha by the Turks. Nicosia is the old name given to the city by the European conquerors.

The prosperous Greek Cypriot majority live in large apartment blocks or in their own detached houses in the new part of the city. In the old city centre the houses become more dilapidated every year. First the plaster crumbles away, then the roof begins to leak. The inhabitants have no money for the repairs, and the owners no longer care. Many valuable buildings from the Ottoman era now stand empty. In some, only the ground floor is inhabited, because the upper floor is in danger of collapsing.

The city authorities have renovated a small area of the city: Laiki Geitonia,

BELOW: a quiet backstreet of Nicosia.

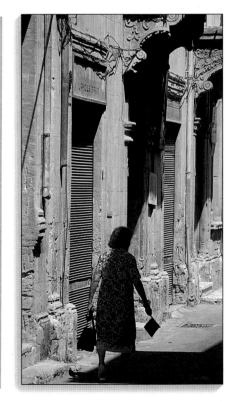

CROSSING THE GREEN LINE

In Nicosia it is particularly and painfully clear that the border dividing north from south cracks open a unity that was centuries in the making. The Green Line, created by the United Nations, is so called not because of the grass and wild flowers that now grow through the asphalt surfaces of no-man's-land, but because it was drawn with a green pen on a map in UN peacekeeping missions's headquarters. Everything must remain exactly as it was then. UN patrols check regularly that the opposing troops do not change the position of their sandbags or dug-outs, and no-one has ever been allowed to remove their belongings from the area in between.

Visitors to the Republic of Cyprus are not encouraged to cross to the north for a daytrip, but they can do so as long as they're back by 5pm. Three separate halts are required at the Ledra Palace crossing. First you fill in a form at the Greek Cypriot post, then pass the sometimes-manned UN barrier and on to the Turkish Cypriot checkpoint where you buy a day pass. Make sure the pass is issued on a separate sheet and not stamped in your passport, or you won't be allowed back into south Nicosia. There can be insurance problems and other obstacles to taking a hire car over but there are lots of (expensive) taxis waiting on the other side.

the "popular neighbourhood", could be a model for the restoration of the old city. The only problem is that virtually nobody lives there: it has been turned into an enclave of expensive restaurants and souvenir shops. However, the process of restoring the living spaces of the old city has begun, particularly in the zone around the Archbishop's Palace. Although for some of the old Ottoman architecture it is too late – some buildings have literally bitten the dust – the calm beauty of those parts that have had the treatment shows what is still possible if the will and the money stay on the table.

Most of the streets are narrow, the shutters of the houses pulled down. From the outside there is little indication of the beauty of the old buildings. Life here has always gone on in those parts of the buildings hidden from the outside. The traditional houses of the Levant face inwards, with arcades and inner courtyards, in which palms or orange trees grow.

Minarets and church towers rise above the mainly one or two-storey houses of the old city. And palm trees too, hundreds of them, either standing in line along the city walls, or in groups of twos and threes, casting their flat shadow on the narrow streets and courtyards.

From the Selimiye mosque in the north, the wind blows the *muezzin*'s call to prayer as far as Odos Patroclos. For the inhabitants of this area, the minarets of the cathedral of St Sophia, the coronation church of the Middle Ages, visible from a long distance, are an infinite distance away.

Daily life

BELOW:
drinking partners.

Although the citizens in the two halves of Nicosia are not allowed to visit each other, have two different religions, and speak different languages, they have

more in common than most of them would like to admit. In the south as in the north the men invariably spend their spare time in one of the small coffee-houses. All Nicosians – like all Cypriots in general – have a passion for extensive company. In the gestures that are used, in the customs of daily life, in the strong sense of family identity – life is much the same everywhere in the narrow streets of old Nicosia. In both north and south the carpenters are busy in their open work-places, and you can watch the chair-makers as they go about their business. Owners sit in front of their small shops and wait for customers, cats patrol their territories. It would be wrong to say that time has stood still in old Nicosia, but the clocks certainly seem to go slower than elsewhere.

City history

Nicosia was founded in AD 965 under Byzantine rule although the area was settled well before that. In the 7th century BC the city of Ledra, one of the Cypriot city kingdoms, was sited here. Under Greek and Roman rule Nicosia – which at that time had the name *Leukos* – was an important trading centre. Its upswing from the 9th century onwards was largely due to the fact that the coasts were plagued by pirates. Nicosia had the advantage of lying inland and so remained protected from such attacks.

Under the Lusignans (1192–1489) the city became the seat of residence of the Catholic archbishop and capital of the crusader state of Cyprus. At that time there were around 20,000 people in Nicosia, a considerable number for the time. The population was a colourful mixture: along with the Greek Orthodox majority and the Catholic feudal lords, there were Nestorians, Copts, Armenians and Jews. Gothic churches and cathedrals were built at this time.

Map on page 246

Drinks on the hoof: a man delivers coffee by bike in Nicosia.

BELOW: Venetian fortified walls.

Greek sculpture known to everyone in Cyprus as the head on the CY £5 note.

A large palace, built in the 14th century, served as the seat of government for the French nobles. Unfortunately little is known about its architecture, not even its exact location. Like many other buildings, the palace fell victim to the Venetian military planners. Between 1567 and 1570 they built a circular fortified wall with 11 bastions. To maintain a free field of fire all the buildings outside the new city boundaries had to be erased. Churches and palaces, cemeteries, domestic dwellings and monasteries were all burned to the ground. The engineers responsible for the wall also diverted the River Pedieios (which had previously flowed straight through the city) around the new city wall. The only entrance to the city was through one of the three heavily fortified gates.

The purpose of this bulwark was to repel the Ottomans. Yet this hastily erected fortification, praised as being of the most perfect design, proved to be no serious obstacle at all for the Sultan's troops: after a two-week siege they conquered Nicosia. The Venetians and the Catholic feudal lords were either killed or driven out, and the Ottoman soldiers and settlers from Anatolia moved in.

Favourable impressions

"Nicosia is the capital of Cyprus and lies under the mountains in the middle of a wide plain with a wonderful, healthy climate. As a result of the perfect air temperature and the healthy climate, the King of Cyprus and all the bishops and prelates of the Kingdom live in this city. A large number of the other princes, counts, nobles, barons, and knights also live here. They busy themselves each day with spear-throwing, tournaments and, above all, with hunting." Thus wrote the pilgrim Ludolf von Suchen in 1340.

BELOW: the Archbishop's Palace.

The walls have been maintained as a symbol of the city. On the bastions,

which are named after influential Italian families, the cannons of the defenders once stood. One of them, *Flatro*, remains a prohibited military zone up until today. The Greek and Turkish posts now stand facing each other at this point, separated only by a small UN building in the middle. In all other respects, however, the walls have lost their purpose; during the period of British colonial rule, gaps were cut in the wall, so that streets could connect the old and new parts of the city.

Map on page 246

Religious buildings

It is only a few steps from the Greek Orthodox Archbishop's Palace in the Agios Ioannis quarter to Taht el Kala with its mosque. The Faneromeni church is just a few yards from another tiny mosque. And from the church of the Armenians to the Arab Ahmet mosque is also not far. Yet nowadays the mosque in Taht el Kala is closed and the Armenian church lies in the middle of the Turkish military no-go area. The Armenians were driven out of their traditional area and now live outside the city wall in the new city.

The **Djami Omeriye** Ⓐ or Omeriye mosque (open daily; free, although a donation is appreciated) is the only place in the Greek Cypriot south of the city where the *muezzin* still calls the faithful to prayer five times a day – for the benefit of the Arabian tourists and the few remaining Lebanese refugees. The Agios Loukas church in the north has been turned into a secular cultural centre. Nevertheless, the intricate patchwork of churches and mosques shows just how closely integrated the Christian and Muslim communities used to be. There are 18 mosques and 13 churches in the 24 districts of the old city. Hardly any of these districts had an ethnically homogeneous population before the invasion.

BELOW:
the main square.

Sunni Muslims, Greek Orthodox and the small Armenian and Maronite minorities all lived together peacefully.

The Omeriye mosque, like several other mosques in the city, has a Christian past. The former Augustinian church was dedicated to John de Montfort, who accompanied St Louis on the Fourth Crusade but died here in 1249. It was destroyed by Mustapha Paşa during the Ottoman conquest, and a mosque dedicated to the prophet Omar, whose final resting place Mustapha Paşa thought it occupied, was erected on the site. It is sometimes possible to climb to the *muezzin's* platform of the minaret, from where there is a superb view clear across the roofs of the divided city. On one side, opposite the old **Turkish Baths** **Ⓑ**, it is still possible to trace elements of Gothic style. The tiny Djami Arablar or Arablar mosque, encircled by flowers near the Greek Orthodox Faneromeni church, was formerly a chapel.

Ottoman *caravanserais*, churches built by the Lusignans, the Greek Orthodox Panagia Chrysaliniotissa church in Byzantine style – Nicosia is a vast open-air museum, now divided and threatened with decline.

Foreign conquerors have left their mark all over the city and even in the 1950s and 1960s, certain cardinal sins were still being committed by builders – ghastly concrete buildings were put up in a number of streets and a tower-block was erected in the middle of the old city.

City gates

Two of the three former city gates have survived. In the north the smaller Keryneia Gate (formerly the Porta del Provveditore) spans a major roadway through the city wall. In the south the massive **Famagusta Gate Ⓒ** (formerly

TIP

Art exhibitions, concerts and lectures take place at the restored Famagusta Gate in the old city walls.

BELOW: the Famagusta Gate.

the Porta Giuliana) has been restored in the most exemplary fashion. The Pafos Gate – known by the Venetians as the Porta Domenica – has been reduced to a simple pedestrian gateway through the city wall.

Map on page 246

Churches and palaces

When the Ottomans conquered Nicosia, they changed only the Gothic churches of the Venetians into mosques. The Orthodox places of worship remained untouched: some of the churches of the Orthodox Greeks still survive virtually unaltered.

The most beautiful church of all is **Panagia Chrysaliniotissa** **D** (open daily; free), in an area that is being extensively renovated near the Famagusta Gate in the carpenters' quarter.

In the middle of this dilapidated area is the unexpectedly grandiose **Archbishop's Palace** **E** (occasional guided tours; entrance fee), a modern building completed in 1961. Directly in front of it stands the **statue of the Archbishop and President Makarios** in solitary splendour, measuring around 20 ft (6 m) high. The statue of the guiding father of all Greek Cypriots was erected a few years ago and was the subject of some controversy. Near the Archbishop's Palace is a smaller predecessor – the **Agios Ioannis church** **F**, the cathedral of Nicosia, also known as the Cathedral of St John the Evangelist (open Mon–Sat; free). Completed in 1662 on the site of a Benedictine abbey church destroyed by Egyptian raiders in 1426, Agios Ioannis is ornately decorated with murals, icons, chandeliers, the archbishop's throne, and a lectern in the shape of the Byzantine double-headed eagle. In the **Old Palace**, part of the former Benedictine monastery, is the small **Folk Art Museum** **G** (open Mon–Sat; entrance

BELOW: the interior of Agios Ioannis church.

fee), whose exhibits comprise mainly everyday items. Also in this building complex is the **Museum of National Struggle** (open Mon–Fri; entrance fee), which provides a reminder of the Greek Cypriot guerrilla struggle against the British. Photographs, mementoes, pistols and even a gallows are displayed. The right-hand section of the New Palace houses the **Byzantine Museum**, in which around 150 icons illustrate the development of 1,000 years of icon-painting, from the 8th to the 18th century.

The **Hadjigeorgakis Kornesios Mansion** ❶, or the House of the Dragoman Georgakis Kornesios (open Mon–Sat; entrance fee), documents the life of the upper classes during the Ottoman Period. Kornesios was one of the tax collectors appointed by the Sublime Porte. The inside of this building, which has been restored with old furniture and carpets, is a testimony to the comfortable life style which Kornesios enjoyed. But the splendour didn't help Kornesios in the end: in 1804 he was executed in Istanbul on account of his various intrigues.

Preserving crafts and forests

On the southern edge of the city, close to the start of the motorway to Larnaka and Limassol, is the **Cyprus Handicraft Service** ❶ (tel: (02) 305024; open Mon–Sat; free), at 186 Leoforos Athalassis. This is the main workshop of the government-owned foundation that aims to preserve Cyprus's endangered folk crafts. You can watch pottery, woodwork, embroidery and a range of other skills, and buy the excellent finished products at the CHS shop. Just across busy Leoforos Lemesou from here is the **Athalassa Forest** (open permanently; free), a piece of Cyprus's recreated forest right on the city's doorstep and a great place for fresh-air picnics.

BELOW: lunching in Laiki Geitonia.

A walk round Greek Nicosia

Begin this tour at **Plateia Eleftherias** Ⓚ near the centre of the old city, where the small Town Hall stands on one of the bastions of the city wall. From here it is only a few steps to Leoforos Konstantinou Palaiologou. Opposite the main post office is a small street to the left, and here you will find yourself in **Laiki Geitonia** Ⓛ, a reconstructed area of the old city with shady cafés, good restaurants and many souvenir shops. If you want to know more about the history of Nicosia, visit the new **Leventis Municipal Museum** Ⓜ (open Tues–Sun; entrance fee), which is nearby in Odos Ippokratous.

A little further to the west you come to Odos Lidras. This was once the most important area for shopping, although it wasn't always as busy as it is today: during the Greek Cypriot guerrilla struggle it was given the name"murder mile" by the British, because numerous soldiers were ambushed and murdered here. Nowadays, in terms of shopping, the street has been surpassed by Leoforos Archiepiskopou Makariou III in the new city. Odos Lidras ends abruptly at the Green Line after a few hundred yards.

Shortly before the Green Line, on the right, you come to the Greek Orthodox **Faneromeni** church Ⓝ, where Archbishop Kyprianou, executed in 1821 by the Ottoman authorities, lies buried. The small **Djami Arablar** Ⓞ, or Arablar mosque, is situated directly behind the church.

If you follow the Green Line to the east at a suitable distance (taking photographs is strictly forbidden) and go past the indoor market, you will come to a confusing maze of tiny streets, where you can watch various craftsmen at their trade. Continuing further, you come to the Archbishop's Palace. (The House of the Dragoman is situated a short distance away, in Odos Patriarchou

A piece of Greek memorabilia.

BELOW:
admiring glances.

Grigoriou to the south.) If you follow the street to the west you will arrive at the Omeriye mosque and the Turkish bath.

When you want to go back to the beginning of this tour, follow Odos Trikoupi to the city wall, and then go in a westerly direction along a palm-lined avenue. To the east, the way leads along the wall to the Famagusta Gate. After a further 100 yards you come to Odos Ektoros on the left and then turn right into Odos Chrysaliniotissa, which leads to the small church of the same name, a domed building in Byzantine style. (The whole walk lasts 2 to 3 hours.)

The oldest treasures on the island are in the **Cyprus Museum** ❿ (tel: 02-302189; open daily, to 1pm only on Sunday; entrance fee), a house built in classical style by the British in Leoforos Mouseiou. A representative selection of archaeological discoveries is on display in 14 separate rooms, stretching from the Stone Age (around 7,000 BC) to the time of the Roman Empire. Mycenaean ceramics and tomb monuments, larger than life bronze statues, furnishings fitted with ivory decorations, and coins and jewellery from over 5,000 years give an insight into the island's rich history. One of the most impressive exhibits is the collection of around 2,000 votive figures from the **Sanctuary of Agia Eirini**. Also on display is the famous **Aphrodite of Soli**, which has become a symbol of Cyprus, and a larger-than-life bronze nude statue of Roman Emperor Septimus Severus.

What is missing, however, are the discoveries which the Europeans made in the 19th century and at the beginning of the 20th century. These were taken off the island and now adorn museums all over the world, including the Metropolitan Museum of Modern Art in New York. Opposite the museum building is the City Garden and the Theatre of Nicosia.

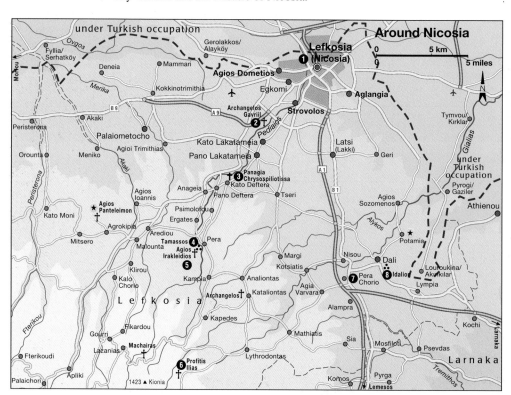

Outer Districts

Outside the centre, the city is growing in a more or less uncontrolled fashion (with the exception of the Turkish-occupied sector). What were previously independent villages have been swallowed up by the sprawling suburbs. In the outer districts, the Republic of Cyprus has built large settlements for refugees from the war in 1974. Banks, businesses and the subsidiaries of many European firms have been particularly drawn to Cyprus and Nicosia since the demise of Beirut as a business centre.

Collaboration

There are no official relations between the Republic of Cyprus and the Turkish Republic of North Cyprus. Nevertheless the city fathers have proved that a form of practical collaboration is possible across the Green Line. In the mid-1980s they began co-operation on a project to develop a joint sewage system which is now finished and fully operational.

Now the restoration of the valuable, beautiful buildings in the old city has also begun. It is a race against time, in which the decline of the city is currently going faster.

Money is also in short supply, despite help from international sources such as the European Union and the World Bank. With the help of the UN development plan (UNDP) a common city development plan has been drawn up to avoid planning catastrophes, for example to make sure a situation can't arise where a park is spoilt by the construction of a new factory just over the border. The plan contains alternatives for each eventuality: one with the Green Line firmly in place, and one without.

Map on page 256

Exterior detail, Agios Irakleidios.

BELOW: landscape near Tamassos.

Map on page 256

Around Nicosia

This subheading is, of course, a contradiction in terms: there can be no "around" Nicosia while the city is sliced in two and the two halves are all but inaccessible to each other.

Nevertheless there are a few places within easy striking distance by car that are well worth seeing. Nicosia International Airport, for a start, although as it is now UNFICYP headquarters you can't actually get there. In 1974 the Cyprus National Guard successfully defended it against élite Turkish paratroops, and wrecked aircraft can be seen as you skirt its edge.

Take the road through Strovolos towards the eastern Troodos mountains, and you will come to the monastery of **Archangelos Gavriil ❷** (Archangel Gabriel), whose 17th-century church has a noted fresco of the archangel.

Further out, near the village of Kato Deftera, you come to **Panagia Chrysospiliotissa ❸** (Our Lady of the Golden Cave). The church is in a natural cavern halfway up a cliff face, in a location that may have been used by early Christians. The faithful still climb up to leave votive offerings to the Virgin – wedding dresses seem especially popular.

Still further out on this road are the ruins of ancient **Tamassos ❹** (open daily, closes 3pm; entrance fee). There isn't a lot left of a city whose wealth was mentioned by Homer, and which won favourable reviews from Ovid and Strabo. Two Archaic tombs dating from the 7th century BC (a third was apparently appropriated by local villagers in the 19th century for building materials), a jumble of low walls, and that's about it.

Near Tamassos, the nuns of **Agios Irakleidios monastery ❺** look after the skull and handbones of Saint Heraclides, keeping them safe for posterity in ornate reliquaries. In a more user-friendly activity, they make honey and icons and sell them to visitors to their tranquil, flower-bedecked cloister.

RIGHT: Tripioti church, Nicosia.
BELOW: a market vendor.

Continuing on this road, in the general direction but slightly to the southeast of Agios Machairas, is another monastery, or in this case former monastery. **Profitis Ilias ❻** lies amid countryside so rugged that it seems hardly surprising that its monks gave up and pulled out. The Cyprus Forestry Department inherited the monastery's buildings and now runs it as a Forest Station, a great place for picnics and hikes in the woods.

A third direction to take from Nicosia is along the Nicosia-Larnaka motorway, turning off at junction 7 or 8 towards the village of Dali. You will pass **Pera Chorio ❼**, where the frescoes in the cemetery chapel of **Agii Apostoloi**, although not in good condition, are important because of their age and artistic quality. They were painted between 1160 and 1180 and are examples of the classic Comnenian style.

South of Dali is an archaeological site whose minimalist character marks it as being for enthusiasts only. **Idalion ❽** (open permanently; free) was an important Bronze-Age city linked to the myth of Aphrodite and Adonis, and which has the scattered remains of temples to Aphrodite and Athena. A statue of Sargon II found here lends weight to Assyrian claims of domination over Cyprus in the 8th century BC. ❑

NORTHERN CYPRUS

*Day trips to Northern Cyprus are made complicated by
bureaucratic hurdles and military no-go areas, but it is worth
making the effort to visit this very scenic part of the island*

Map
City 266
Area 268

Lefkosia/
Nicosia

Your picture of Cyprus will not be complete without a glimpse of the northern part of the island. It is also useful to see first-hand how this part has fared since 1974, and to draw your own conclusions about the truth of the various assertions made by each side.

Some Turkish Cypriots claim that the Turkish military presence is still essential to protect the area and its population; others believe they are kept on primarily for economic reasons. Matters are futher aggravated by chronic tension – officially denied, but universally acknowledged – between the indigenous population and Anatolian civilian settlers brought in after 1974. Many native Turkish Cypriots feel discriminated against in comparison to the "new Cypriots", and their numbers are steadily declining with emigration.

Visits to the north from the south are limited to the hours between 8am and 6pm. Bearing this in mind, there is really a choice of only two tours: one in a westerly direction, and the other going east, following a brief walking itinerary through northern Nicosia.

Taxi-drivers and money-changers cluster just beyond the checkpoints, though it's unwise to purchase too many Turkish lira, as they're worthless elsewhere, and most people in the north are happy to be paid in hard currency – though change may be given in Turkish lira.

Northern Nicosia/Lefkosia

Before engaging a taxi for your whirlwind tour of the north, you might spend a couple of hours taking in the medieval monuments and backwater atmosphere of northern Nicosia within the walls. Immediately past the Zahra (Mula) bastion, one of the five under Turkish-Cypriot control, a minor breach in the walls allows you to slip inside and follow quieter Tanzimat Sokak to the **Keryneia Gate Ⓐ** at the top of Girne Caddesi, logical start-point of a walkabout. The British left the gate isolated when they demolished the walls to either side in 1931 as a traffic-easing measure.

A few steps south along Girne Caddesi, on the left, stands the **Ethnography Museum** (open Mon–Fri 8am–1pm and 2–5pm), housed in the former **Mevlevi Tekke Ⓑ**. The Mevlevi Dervish order was active here until 1953, long after it was supressed in Republican Turkey; the multi-domed hall on the street side shelters the tombs of the 16 sheikhs of the Cypriot order. Near the south end of Girne Caddesi, **Atatürk Meydani Ⓒ** has been the heart of the city since Ottoman times, and is still ringed by banks, the British-built post office and law courts and a baroque 19th-century mosque.

From Atatürk Meydani, Asmaalti Sokak leads southwest past a functioning *hamam* or Turkish bath towards a pair of *hans* or medieval inns for travellers.

PRECEDING PAGES:
Salamis; Keryneia/
Girne harbour.
LEFT: children take
part in a Turkish
Cypriot festival.
BELOW: Atatürk
Meydani.

The smaller **Kumarcilar Hani** is more typically Cypriot with its pointed-arch colonnade; the larger **Büyük Han** is adheres more to Anatolian proto-types with its free-standing ablutions fountain, perched on six columns in the central courtyard. The Büyük Han has been slowly restored as funds permit and may have already opened as a museum.

Still further southwest from here is the bazaar district, mostly pedestrianised to match the same process in South Nicosia as part of the overall masterplan. In the **Belediye Pazari** , or covered market, by the Green Line, there are a few stalls selling crafts or antiques, more interesting than the cheap jeans outside pitched at Turkish soldiers.

Immediately north, past the locked **Bedesten**, looms the **Djami Selimiye** , formerly the Lusignan cathedral of Agia Sofia, begun in 1209 but still unfinished 150 years later. It is sometimes possible to climb one of the pair of 160-ft (50-metre) minarets added after the Ottoman conquest. Inside the west facade with its sculpted portal and giant rose window, inspired by French prototypes, the coronation of the Lusignan kings of Cyprus took place.

Directly east of the Selimiye stands the **Sultan Mahmut library** , with its collection of precious manuscripts and books – and a warden with the key to the **Lapidary Museum** across the meydan, essentially a warehouse for archaeological masonry established by the British. Star exhibit is the Gothic tracery window, rescued from a Lusignan palace at Atatürk Meydani, demolished by the British (who have at least as much as the modern Turks to answer for in the way of vandalism).

Just north of here rises the **Djami Haydarpaşa** , originally the 14th-century church of St Katherine, perhaps the most underrated Gothic structure in town;

TIP

If you're tempted to make purchases at the Belediye Pazari, or anywhere else in the north, bear in mind that the goods are liable to confiscation when you return to the south.

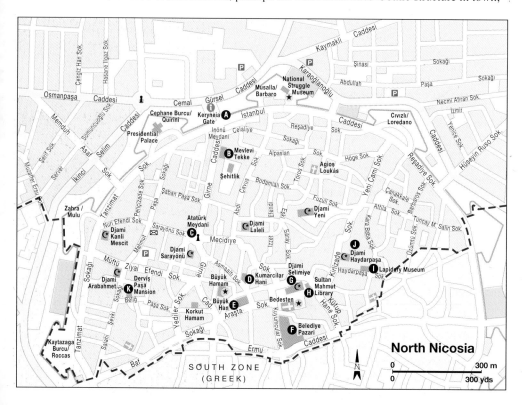

it now serves as an art gallery (open Mon–Fri 9am–1pm and 2–5pm, Sat 9am–1pm) and merits a look inside for its architectural details.

From the **Selimiye Meydani**, head west towards the minor gate near the **Zahra bastion**, admiring as you go the fine Ottoman houses of the Arabahmet district around the eponymous mosque. One of the oldest, the **Dervis Paşa mansion** ❻, once home to a local worthy who founded the first Cypriot Turkish-language newspaper, is now a minor ethnographic museum (open daily 9am–1pm and 2–5pm).

Western tour – Nicosia-Keryneia-Vouni

Heading northeast out of **Nicosia/Lefkosia** ❶, the road runs towards Keryneia, signposted as "Girne". This initially crosses the **Mesaoria**, the fertile plain whose name means "between the mountain ranges": the two in question being the **Pentadaktylos (Besparmak)**, the legendary "Five-Finger" mountains to the north, and the **Troodos mountains** on the south. During early spring this expanse becomes a vast carpet of flowers, quickly followed by golden corn or grain, reaped in June, leaving a brown, steppe-like landscape.

The unmistakable peak of Five-Finger mountain, northeast of Nicosia.

In 1191 a decisive battle took place on the Mesaoria which changed the historical course of the island. The fleet of Berengaria of Navarre, the fiancée of Richard the Lionheart, ran into a storm off the south coast of Cyprus, whilst her betrothed was fighting in the Crusades. Isaac Comnenos, the Byzantine despot of Cyprus, had taken Berengaria and Richard's sister prisoner, when Richard appeared to defend his kinswomen. Following his marriage to Berengaria in Limassol, the English king defeated the Byzantine army so decisively at Tremetousha, southeast of Nicosia, that the island remained under European Catholic rule for almost four hundred years.

BELOW:
the Mesaoria.

During the first three centuries of this era, under the Lusignan dynasty, various splendid public buildings were constructed. Many of these are still in good condition, including the Agios Nikolaos cathedral (Lala Mustafa Paşa mosque) in Famagusta and the beautiful Agia Sophia (Selimiye mosque) in Nicosia.

Three pre-existing Byzantine fortresses in the Pentadaktylos range were also reinforced during this period: the westernmost and best preserved of these, **Agios Ilarion** ❷, is reached after a short side-journey west from the main highway, through a Turkish military camp.

The present castle, on the site of a Byzantine monastery, is named after St Hilarion, a 7th-century Syrian hermit. The Lusignan nobility used it as a summer residence during the 13th and 14th centuries; magnificent jousting tournaments took place on the high plateau just below the castle pinnacle. It takes a good hour to scramble through the multi-levelled fortifications, from a Byzantine chapel near the bottom to the so-called royal apartments on the summit, with sweeping views over the north coast. The battlements and towers seem to grow naturally out of the steep limestone rocks of the mountains. The roof and modern plastered additions to the structure suffered heavy damage in a 1995 forest fire, but a snack bar/café should once again be operating inside.

Maps:
City 266
Area 268–9

Keryneia

Descending in wide, well-graded arcs from the Agios Ilarion saddle, you arrive at **Keryneia/Girne ❸**, built around a seaside fortress which was reinforced by the Lusignans. Those who knew this small coastal town before 1974, with its circular harbour, compactly picturesque town plan and cosmopolitan expatriate society, may not recognise it. Much of the town is an untidy sprawl of three- and four-storey buildings little different from anywhere else on the Mediterranean, especially the Turkish coast; little remains of Keryneia's Hellenic past, or the days when it could barely muster 2000 tourist beds. The visible architecture of the oft-painted old quarter curled around the harbour is Frankish-Byzantine, with Venetian and Ottoman additions. Much of the new construction is holiday accommodation, for Keryneia is the epicentre of such tourist industry that exists in the north. Only in the hillside village of **Karmi/Karaman ❹**, where foreigners have been issued long leases to renovate abandoned houses, is there a faint echo of the former post-colonial bohemianism.

There are a few small museums in the narrow alleys around Keryneia's port, such as the **Icon Museum** in the deconsecrated church of Archangelos, and the **Folk Art Museum** in a Venetian-vintage house, but with so little time available it's wisest to concentrate on the **castle** (open daily 8am–1pm and 2–5pm) on the eastern side of the old quarter. Its foundations were laid by the Byzantines after 7th-century Arab raids, but its present form is the work of Venetian military engineers. In addition to their dissimilar bastions and earlier Lusignan living quarters, one can tour the dungeons where rebellious nobles and knights starved to death in 1310; more recently, Greek Cypriot EOKA fighters were imprisoned here by the British.

Keryneia was founded by Greeks from Arcadia in the 10th century BC and numbered among the ten Classical city-Kingdoms of Cyprus, though little remains of this period.

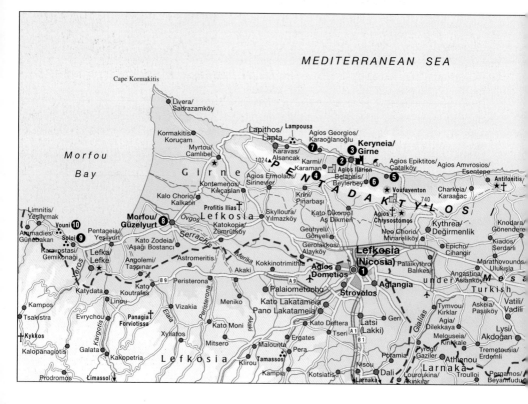

Highlight of the castle, however, is the **Shipwreck Museum** just off the courtyard, which features the oldest known wreck in the world: a Hellenistic cargo boat discovered at a depth of 108 ft (33 m) and salvaged, between 1968 and 1969, by a team from the University of Pennsylvania and the Cypriot Antiquities Service.

The wreck, 48 ft (15 m) long and 11 ft (3 m) wide, was a singled-masted boat travelling with a cargo of nearly 400 amphorae filled with wine, almonds and oil. The amphorae came from various potteries, indicating that the ship must have called at several ports en route. Radiocarbon analysis of the 10,000 almonds and the keel planks, along with the dating of two coins, indicate that the ship probably went down between 330 and 280 BC.

Around Keryneia: beaches and Belapais

By now you may have had lunch overlooking the harbour, and be ready to break the journey with a swim at one of the excellent beaches to the east of Keryneia.

In order of occurrence they are **Acapulco**, rather encroached on by the eponymous resort, and army installations; **Lara**, 2 miles (3 km) east, with a single restaurant; **Alagadi**, or "Turtle Bay" after the creatures which nest here; and best of all **Onucuncu Mil** (Thirteenth Mile), the stated distance east of town.

Acapulco lies next to the highway veering inland towards the second of the mountain castles, **Voufaventon**, but this is in poor condition and only open mornings for two days a week, since it falls within a Turkish military zone. From the high point of the bypass road to Famagusta via Kythrea/Degirmenlik, a rough, stony track leads west to the trailhead for the 45-minute ascent to the

Map on page 268–9

Sorting through the day's catch along the north coast.

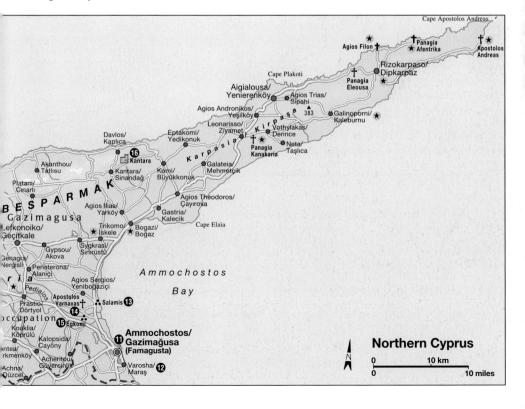

The ruined castle at Voufaventon is in a dramatic location.

BELOW: the landscape around Keryneia/Girne.

castle. This does add a two-hour diversion to a tightly scheduled day so, instead, you may prefer to backtrack slightly from the beach to a pair of sites prominently featured in Lawrence Durrell's classic *Bitter Lemons*, a portait of the area in the 1950s. Just seaward of **Agios Epiktitos/Catalkoy** ❺ stands the little shrine of **Hazreti Omer Turbesi** and, one cove west, Fortuna – the elaborate house built by Durrell's friend Marie; this is unfortunately now the residence of the Turkish military commander, and off-limits.

From Hazreti Omer a road leads inland to Agios Epiktitos (Catalkoy) and thence west to the abbey at **Belapais/Beylerbey** ❻, the third unmissable sight on this western tour, apart from the castles of Agios Ilarion and Kyernia. Lawrence Durrell put the village of Belapais on the touristic and literary map when he bought an old house here in 1953 and restored it, as related in *Bitter Lemons*; a plaque on the outer wall comemorates his stay, though the house has had several other owners since.

The abbey itself, at the north edge of the village, ranks as one of the more beautiful and atmospheric Gothic buildings on the entire island, despite vandalism by raiding Genoese, medieval villagers and even the British. Founded early in the 13th century by Augustinians fleeing Palestine, it changed its affiliation within a few years to the Premonstratensians, whose brethren wore white robes – giving rise to the epithet "the white abbey." Under the patronage of Lusignan King Hugh III (1267–1284), Belapais reached its zenith, with the existing monastic church built at this time, and the monks accorded numerous privileges, such as the right to travel on horseback, armed with gilded sword and spurs; other, less codified perks, such as the amassment of personal riches and the taking of (multiple) concubines, were overlooked so that the place soon

had a well-deserved reputation for luxury and scandal. Despite such goings-on, the palatial abbey was known as "L'Abbaie de la Paix", adapted under the Venetians to "de la Pais" – from which it was a short step to the present name. During the Genoese-Venetian period the abbey went into a physical decline to match its moral one; there were few monks left for the victorious Ottomans to drive out in 1570, after which the grounds were handed over to the Orthodox church.

The delicate 14th-century cloister is mostly intact; on its north side, perched at the edge of an escarpment, is the sumptuous refectory, where six bay windows look onto the sea, and (conditions permitting) the Taurus mountains in Turkey. Because Belapais sees plenty of foreign tourists, the 13th-century church here is undesecrated, and much as the local Greeks left it when they departed under duress in 1976, the last group around Keryneia to do so; perhaps their tenacity and loyalty to their parish church was owed to the legend that the village was originally populated by the bastard offspring of the monks.

West of Keryneia

Some 5 miles (8 km) west of Keryneia is **Agios Georgios/Karaoglanoglu** ❼, site of the Turkish amphibious landing on 20 July 1974. A cluster of hideous monuments – including a cement structure resembling an artillery piece – marks the spot; nearby is a "Peace and Freedom" Museum consisting of disabled Greek-Cypriot military equipment, and a wall-relief chronicle of atrocities perpetrated on Turkish-Cypriots by Greeks and Greek-Cypriots. For Turkey, the landing marked the start of the "Peace Operation" – the "invasion and occupation" in Greek-Cypriot eyes, the "intervention" for the studiously even-handed.

Map on page 268–9

BELOW: the ruined abbey at Belapais/Beylerbey.

The town of **Morfou/Güzelyurt** ❽, fourth largest settlement in the north, lies amidst extensive citrus groves; export of the fruit provides much-needed income to the unrecognized state of Northern Cyprust. In the years immediately after 1974, there was an insufficient population for the labour-intensive job of tending citrus; most of the Turkish Cypriots who settled nearby were from the grape-growing areas of Limassol and Pafos. Apart from the combined natural history and archaeological museum, the main sight is the originally Byzantine (but much altered) monastic church of **Agios Mamas**, where the venerated tomb of the saint is actually a Roman sarcophagus a few centuries too old to have housed his mortal remains. But at intervals a magic unguent oozed forth from holes bored in the tomb, the liquid a panacea for earache and stormy seas. Mamas is more renowned as the patron saint of tax evaders; he was a Byzantine hermit who successfully defied a Byzantine governor on the issue of head tax.

The town of Morfou/ Güzelyurt is famous for its citrus fruit.

A 30-minute drive west of Morfou brings you to the ruins of ancient **Soloi** ❾, just past the little modern port of **Karavostasi/Gemikonagi**. The name of Soloi is often spuriously derived from the Athenian statesman Solon, who supposedly urged King Philokypros to move the city from an inland site to this spot early in the 6th century BC; it seems almost certain, however, that there has been a settlement here since the late Bronze Age. One of the ten ancient city-kingdoms of Cyprus, it was the last holdout against the Persians during the 498 BC revolt against the Persians; later, under Roman rule, Soloi flourished again, courtesy of the rich copper mines just inland. The visible remains of Soloi (the site is unfenced and an admission is charged only sporadically) date from the Roman and Byzantine eras.

BELOW: floor mosaic in the basilica at Soloi.

The 2nd-century AD amphitheatre was dismantled by the British and its cut

stone sent to line the Suez Canal and the quay at Port Said, and the ugly concrete structure of today was a crude 1963 restoration. More worthwhile, perhaps, is a 5th-century basilica to the east, which features extensive floor mosaics including a swan and waterfowl with dolphins. To the west lies the ancient *agora*, which has been fenced off since Canadian excavations were suspended in 1974; here was uncovered the Roman statuette of Aphrodite, now in the Cyprus Museum in southern Nicosia.

Should time permit, you may want to continue 2 miles (3 km) west to the palace of **Vouni ⑩** (unrestricted foot access, though cars banned), located on a hill 820 ft (250 m) above the sea. Its history is shrouded in mystery – even the ancient name is unknown – but it was apparently founded early in the 5th century BC by the pro-Persian king Doxandros of Marion (modern Polis) to watch over pro-Hellenic Soloi in the wake of the recent revolt. Following Kimon of Athens' campaign on the island, a Greek dynasty seized control and remodelled the palace, which in the event lasted only a few decades before being burnt down early in the 4th century BC.

The mud-brick walls of the upper storey were unable to withstand the fire and many centuries of erosion, so only foundations remain. The most comprehensible structures are a monumental seven-stepped stairway, a guitar-shaped windlass serving as a deep cistern, and the low remains of two temples, one of which has what is obviously an altar; many votive offerings were recovered.

Map on page 268–9

Eastern tour: Nicosia–Famagusta–Salamis

A separate day-trip can be made to points of interest east of Nicosia, scattered along the east coast in the district of Famagusta. Unfortunately, the Karpasia/Kirpasa peninsula, with its undeveloped beaches and numerous Byzantine monuments, is beyond the scope of an eight-hour journey, especially if two hours have already been devoted to north Nicosia.

Of all the towns in Cyprus, **Famagusta (Ammochostos/Gazimagusa) ⑪** has been the worst affected by the events of 1974, but earlier in its history it was often hostage to fortune. A town of some sort existed here in Hellenistic and Roman times, but it first achieved prominence when Byzantine settlers arrived from Salamis, after it fell victim to the Arabs during the 7th century.

The Greek name subsequently bestowed on the city, and still used by Greeks today, is Ammochostos, "sunken in sand", after the shifting beaches and sandbars all around. Later, in 1136, Famagusta received an influx of Armenians compulsorily settled here by the Byzantine emperor.

Its golden age was kick-started, however, by the Saracen capture of Acre, the last Crusader stronghold in Palestine, in 1291. The population swelled dramatically with the influx of refugee Christians, and thanks to its strategic location, decent natural harbour and the Pope's ban on trade with the infidels of the Holy Land, the city became spectacularly wealthy from a monopoly in trans-shipping exotic oriental commodities.

A contemporary German traveller, Ludolf von

BELOW: fresh produce for sale, in the streets of Famagusta.

Suchen, left a vivid description of the splendour of Famagusta, then the richest – and most ostentatious – city in the world. According to him, the wedding jewellery of a Famagustan merchant's daughter was "worth more than that of the Queen of France"; one citizen, Frangiskos Lakhas, frequently entertained the upper echelons with banquets where precious stones were left on the tables as party favours; and the local loose women were "the most expensive in the world", and could earn a fortune "of at least 1,000,000 gold ducats" at the discreet drop of a handkerchief.

So much vulgarity and riches was naturally a source of envy and jostling for influence, particularly between the Genoese and their main rivals the Venetians. Matters came to a head in 1372, at the coronation of the Lusignan King Peter II, where a scuffle between the Genoese and Venetian escorts degenerated into anti-Genoese riots. The Genoese retaliated by landing troops to ravage the island in general, and Famagusta in particular; it took the Lusignans over 70 years to expel the Genoese, but the damage had been done and Famagusta never recovered its former prominence. The last Lusignan ruler, Queen Caterina Cornaro, abdicated in 1489 at the insistence of the Venetians, who instituted military rule, and decided to make Famagusta their most impregnable stronghold, in advance of the inevitable Ottoman attack.

This came in October 1570, after Keryneia and Nicosia had been taken with litte or no resistance. Famagusta proved different, however; the commander of its Venetian garrison, Marcantonio Bragadino, was ingenious and resolute, despite being outnumbered 25 to 1 by the Ottoman forces under Lala Mustafa Paşa. Finally, in August 1571, the 2,000 surviving, haggard defenders marched out to surrender to Lala Mustafa, who at first received them with all courtesy and promised them safe passage to Venetian-held Crete.

BELOW: backgammon behind the city walls.

But at some point the parley went sour, and the Ottoman commander – despite the disapproval of his own subordinates – hacked Bragadino's lieutenants to death, and then flayed Bragadino alive in front of St Nicholas cathedral. Thus ended one of the most celebrated campaigns of medieval times; had the promised Venetian relief fleet arrived in time, the outcome might have been different.

Despite the high cost of Famagusta's capture, the Ottomans had little use for the walled town, reserving it as a place of exile for disgraced notables, and repairing few of the many buildings damaged by artillery during the long siege. As elsewhere in Cyprus, Orthodox Christians were forbidden residence within the citadel, and were obliged to establish a new settlement outside the walls: **Varosha/Maras** ⓬, which in a few brief years after independence experienced both prosperity and catastrophe. With the emergence of mass tourism, an ugly hotel ghetto of some 4000 beds sprang up behind the sandy beaches fringing Varosha, making it one of the biggest foreign-currency earners in Cyprus. In mid-August 1974, the Turkish military bombarded Varosha, sending the 40,000 inhabitants into precipitous flight prior to capturing it and sealing most of it off with cordons. Since then this ghost town has remained empty and can only be entered by the Turkish army, and occasional UN patrols. Gardens

Map on page 268–9

grow wild, while the buildings slowly decay from the effects of the sun, wind and sand. A number of hotels just outside the dead zone, and north along the coast en route to Salamis, totalling about 2000 beds, were unaffected by the invasion and still operate under Turkish-Cypriot management. The original Greek-Cypriot owners have yet to receive any compensation.

In Old Famagusta several Gothic churches were converted into mosques following the Ottoman conquest, by the simple addition of minarets. These curious architectural chimeras are still attractive, but overall the walled town's medieval legacy is neglected. That which can't serve touristic purposes is used as car parks, football pitches, or for anchoring washing lines.

The formidable city walls total 2 miles (3 km) in length, and average 47 ft (15 m) in height and 25 ft (8 m) in thickness, with deep moats on the landward sides. Unhappily, much of them fall into Turkish military zones, so it's only possible to climb up the southwesterly Rivettina bastion, where the Venetians ran up the white flag of surrender, or visit the rather mediocre museum inside the southeasterly Canbulat bastion. As at Keryneia, every bastion or tower was designed differently by the Venetian military engineers, in accordance with the threats it was likely to face.

A stroll around Old Famagusta will reveal a series of architectural curiosities.

The most impressive single fortification is the northeasterly Citadel, frequently reckoned as the setting for Shakespeare's *Othello*, and therefore known as **Othello's tower**. It's uncertain whether the dark-haired vice-governor Christofero Moro (served 1506–08), who lost his wife here, was the role-model for the tragic figure, or whether it was one of his successors, Francesco de Sessa, known as "Il Capitano Moro", banished from here in 1544 with two subordinates – possibly the basis for the Iago and Casssio characters. Nevertheless, this originally Lusignan fort, redesigned in 1492 by the Venetian engineer Foscarini, remains a plausible and atmospheric venue, used frequently in the past as a film location.

BELOW: Othello's tower.

Elsewhere, in the centre of the old city, spare a glance for the scant remains of the **Palazzo del Proveditore**, the palace of the Venetian Governor in which the Turkish man of letters Namik Kemal was incarcerated for 38 months between 1873 and 1876 for writing a play critical of the sultan. Of the various surviving churches, the smaller among them normally closed, the 14th-century **Sinan Paşa mosque** (formerly the church of St Peter and St Paul) near the Venetian palace is the most substantial. It was built by a merchant, Simone Nostrano, from the profit of a single transaction with a Syrian friend. The building served the Ottomans as a mosque, the English as a potato store, and is now the municipal playhouse.

About 650 ft (200 m) east of the preceding two monuments towers the former cathedral of St Nicholas, now the **Lala Mustafa Paşa mosque.**

Salamis and the Royal Tombs

Leave Famagusta on the most northerly road, passing delightful sandy beaches such as Glapsides and "Silver". After about 5 miles (8 km) a turning heads east to the partially excavated remains of ancient **Salamis ⑬**. The ruins are extensive, scattered over

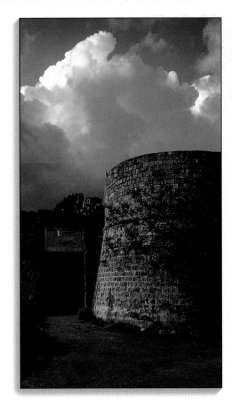

an area of about 2 sq miles (5 sq km), so with the limited time at your disposal you'll need your taxi driver to shuttle you between points of interest. The site is fringed by excellent beaches, and in spring splashed bright yellow with flowering mimosa; near the ticket-booth entrance (daily sunrise–sunset) is a beachfront restaurant well placed for lunch on this tour.

Legend has it that Salamis was founded by the Trojan War hero Tefkros, who was exiled by his father King Telamon from his native island Salamina, and brought along his homeland's name – and Bronze-Age culture. Thanks to its good natural harbour, the city was for several centuries one of the most important city-kingdoms on the island, until dominated by the Ptolemaic kings. During the Byzantine era, it was renamed Constantia, designated capital of the island and regained its former importance, before devastation by 4th-century earthquakes and 7th-century Arab raids.

Immediately southwest of the site entrance stands the most interesting excavation, the Roman *palaestra*, with its inner courtyards surrounded by columns, and the floors of its east portico tiled with variegated marble. Equally impressive are the monumental baths complex from the 3rd century AD, its various halls still decorated with fragments of mosaics. The best of these, in bays of the southernmost hall, show the river god Evrotas, and a fragmentary battle scene thought possibly to depict Apollo and Artemis fighting against the Niobids.

South of the *palaestra* and baths looms the Roman amphitheatre, dating from the reign of the emperor Augustus, though rebuilt in early Byzantine times. It originally held 15,000 spectators; the rows of seating have been well restored and eight of the eighteen are original. If you're ahead of schedule, direct your vehicle to the extreme southeast corner of the site, where the Kam-

BELOW: detail of the Lala Mustafa Pasa mosque (formerly St Nicholas Cathedral) in Famagusta.

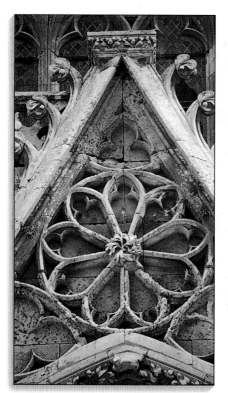

FROM CATHEDRAL TO MOSQUE

The former cathedral of St Nicholas, now the Lala Mustafa Pasa mosque, was erected by the Lusignans between 1298 and 1326 and is often regarded as the supreme Gothic masterpiece on the island.

Built in conscious imitation of the cathedral at Rheims, it lost its twin towers during the 1571 seige, and gained the single minaret afterwards. The west facade, with a huge rose window and gabled porticoes more impressive than those of Nicosia's Selimiye mosque, can be contemplated from the courtyard where a massive fig tree is believed to be as old as the building. The cathedral and its environs saw many crucial moments of medieval Famagusta. Here the Lusignan rulers underwent honorary coronation as kings of Jerusalem, having already received the crown of Cyprus in Nicosia; here the young widow of the last Lusignan king was forced to sign her abdication, and here too, lashed between the two granite columns pilfered from ancient Salamis, Bragadino was flayed.

Inside the building, two rows of columns support the magnificent vaulting, all is plain and whitewashed in accordance with Islamic doctrine, Koranic calligraphy hangs from the walls and prayer rugs cover old tombstones, the graves long since emptied by an enraged Lala Mustafa.

banopetra basilica retains its *synthronon* or bishop's seat, and also some small baths with a brilliant geometric mosaic floor.

To gain a fuller understanding of late Bronze Age culture, visit the nearby **Royal Tombs**, accessible via a side road starting opposite the disused western gate to Salamis. Most of the 150-plus tombs here were plundered in antiquity, but 1957 excavations here uncovered two (numbers 47 and 79) that yielded sensational artefacts confirming Homer's descriptions of Mycenaean funerary rites. These finds included three thrones, a magnificent wooden bed decorated with ivory and silver, pitchers and amphora containing food, jewellery and weapons, all intended to serve the deceased in the next world. Most of the tombs opened towards the east, and were approached by sloping *dhromoi* or ramps; here, archaeologists found chariots, which had carried the biers of dead kings or heroes, and the skeletons of various horses which had been sacrificed – as well as favourite human servants, some discovered bound hand and foot. It seems that these Homeric rituals were being observed as late as the 7th century BC, nearly 500 years after Bronze Age culture on the Greek mainland had faded away.

The findings from the tombs are in the Cyprus Museum in Nicosia, accompanied by photographs and reconstructions. There is also a small site museum, with more plans and photographs, as well as a reconstruction of one chariot.

St Barnabas and the Church of Cyprus

The monastery of the Apostle Barnabas, **Apostolos Varnavas** ⑭ (open daily 8am–sunset), 500 yds/m beyond the Royal Tombs on the same minor road, commemorates a saint who played a pivotal, and posthumous, role in the history of the Cypriot Orthodox Church. Born in Salamis and brought up in Jerusalem,

Map
on page
268–9

ABOVE AND BELOW: examining the headless statues in the *palaestra* at Salamis.

Richly gilded icon inside the monastery of Apostle Barnabas (Apostolos Varnavas).

where he became a follower of Jesus, Barnabas toured Cyprus and Asia Minor with the Apostle Paul, and again seven years later with his cousin Mark. He was stoned to death by the Jewish community of Salamis in about 75 AD, and buried at an undisclosed location by Mark. Some four centuries later Barnabas appeared in a dream to the archbishop of Salamis, then embroiled in a dispute with the archbishop of Antioch over ecclesiastical precedence, and revealed the location of his tomb. The good bishop dug, and found a catacomb with a skeleton inside, clutching a handwritten copy of St Matthew's Gospel. The authorities in Constantinople were sufficiently impressed by this miracle to declare the Cypriot church autocephalous, independent from Antioch, and divided it into several bishoprics of its own. To the present day, the archipishop of all Cyprus enjoys the the right to carry a sceptre, wear a purple coat and to sign his name in red ink, all in the manner of the Byzantine emperors.

A monastery was founded on the location of the tomb in the 5th century; its present building dates from 1756. It now serves as an ad hoc archaeological museum, most of the items probaby rescued from the looted district museum and Hadjiprodhromou collection in Famagusta. Just outside the gate is the entrance to the purported tomb of Barnabas; stairs lead down to a pair of very ancient rock-cut chambers, with space for several deceased.

Egkomi and Kantara

RIGHT: Salamis.
BELOW: the watch-tower at Kantara castle.

On the way back to Nicosia from the monastery, one more possible stop for archaeology enthusiasts is at the excavations of **Egkomi** ⑮. This early Bronze-Age city, later supplanted by Salamis, was a major copper-exporting port with links to Egypt and Asia before the arrival of migrant Myceneans in the 12th century BC. When archaeologists began excavations here in 1896, they thought they had found the necropolis of Salamis, as there was a skeleton buried under every structure. But this was merely a form of ancestor-worship in what turned out to be a real city, with a clear grid plan of rectangular houses. Today the site is of mainly specialist interest; its many treasures have been removed to the safety of the main museum in Nicosia.

If you would like a break from serious cultural sightseeing, you could finish the day by climbing from Salamis to **Kantara castle** ⑯, from where you can enjoy a simultaneous view of the north and the east coast. Kantara, the best preserved castle of the three in the Keryneia range, is where Isaac Comnenos surrendered to Richard the Lionheart after the debacle at Tremetousha in 1191; it also saw considerable action during the 13th-century wars between the Holy Roman Emperor and the Lusignan nobility.

From Bogazi/Bogaz a narrow road leads up to virtually abandoned Kantara village, from where another road leads a further 2½ miles (4 km) to the castle. A long flights of steps leads from the car park through the barbican, massive southeast bastion and barracks, all of which are relatively intact. Above and beyond, the castle is far more ruined; it was partially dismantled by the Venetians in the 16th century to render it useless to domestic rebels or the Ottomans. ❑

INSIGHT GUIDES
TRAVEL TIPS

Simply travelling safely

American Express Travellers Cheques

- are recognised as one of the safest and most convenient ways to protect your money when travelling abroad

- are more widely accepted than any other travellers cheque brand

- are available in eleven currencies

- are supported by a 24 hour worldwide refund service and

- a 24 hour Express Helpline service provides assistance and information when travelling abroad

- are accepted in millions of shops, hotels and restaurants throughout the world

Travellers Cheques

CONTENTS

Getting Acquainted

The Place

Situation The third biggest Mediterranean island, Cyprus is at 34°33–35°34N and 32°16–34°37E at the northeastern end of the Mediterranean.

Area 9,251 sq km (3,572 sq miles), with the south under the control of the internationally recognised Republic of Cyprus, and north under Turkish military occupation.

Capital Nicosia (Lefkosia/Lefkosha), with a population of around 225,000, with 190,000 living in the south and an estimated 35,000 in the north.

Population Of the estimated 775,000 people currently living on the island, approximately 616,000 are Greek Cypriots, 90–95,000 are Turkish Cypriots (including 60,000 immigrants from Turkey but not including the 35,000 Turkish occupation troops), 7,000 Armenians, Maronites and several Latin ("Western Christian") minorities.

Languages Greek (southern Cyprus) and Turkish (north).

Religion Greek Orthodox and Muslim.

Time Zone 2 hours ahead of GMT. The switch to Daylight Saving Time occurs at the same time as in other European countries. Darkness falls earlier and more quickly than in northern European countries; twilight lasts for only 30 minutes.

Currency Cyprus pound (CY£), divided into 100 cents.

Weights & Measures Metric.

Electricity 240 volts; flat three-pin plugs. Some hotel rooms have a 110-volt outlet for electric shavers.

International dialling code 357

The Climate

Cyprus has a long, hot and dry summer with relatively low humidity; a short spring and autumn; and a mild, wet winter when snow often falls in the Troodos Mountains (but even in December seawater temperatures remain at around 19°C). The average peak daytime temperature in July and August is 35°C, and 15°C in January. Maximum summer temperatures inland go above 40°C and minimum winter temperatures go below freezing in the mountains. Most rainfall is between November and February, when you can expect approximately 9–11 days of rain per month (winters since 1994–95 have been characterised by below-average precipitation, leading to water shortages).

Best Times to Visit

Cyprus is at its best in springtime, when the island is covered in a carpet of green vegetation and varicoloured flowers, and the air is fresh. While autumn temperatures are similar (you can still enjoy outdoor lunches, sunbathe and even swim), the intervening summer burns away much of the vegetation and flowers, and the air may be dry and dusty.

Many hotels offer reduced prices in off-peak seasons. In the popular swimming resorts the off-peak season runs from 1 November to 31 March (except Christmas holidays between 20 December and 6 January), and in the Troodos mountains from 1 October to 30 June.

Government

The Republic of Cyprus has a democratic constitution based on the Zurich Agreements of 1959 and 1960. It grants a great deal of authority to the country's president, who is chairman of the council of state and is directly elected by the Cyrpriot population for a term of five years.

Since 1960 Cyprus has been an independent republic. Previously the island was a British colony and it remains a member of the British

Public Holidays in Northern Cyprus

- **1 January** New Year's Day
- **23 April** National Sovereignty and Children's Day
- **1 May** Labour Day
- **19 May** Young People's and Sports Day
- **20 July** Peace and Freedom Day (the anniversary of the invasion of the northern part of the island)
- **1 August** Communal Resistance Day
- **30 August** Victory Day (Turkish victory over the Greeks in 1922)
- **29 October** Turkish National Day
- **15 November** Anniversary of the proclamation of "Turkish Republic of Northern Cyprus"

All museums are closed on 1 January, 19 May, 29 October and 15 November.

In northern Cyprus Islamic rather than Christian holidays are celebrated. The most prominent of these include the end of the month of fasting, Ramadan, referred to as the Sugar Festival (*Seker Bayram*); the sacrifice festival (*Kurban Bayram*), which takes place about two months after the end of Ramadan; the Muslim New Year Festival and the birthday of the Prophet. As these holidays are celebrated in accordance with the Islamic (lunar) calendar, their dates shift back 11 days each year.

Public Holidays in the Republic of Cyprus

- **1 January** New Year's Day
- **6 January** Epiphany
- **25 March** Greek Independence Day
- **1 April** Greek Cypriot National Day
- **1 May** Labour Day
- **15 August** Assumption
- **1 October** Cyprus Independence Day
- **28 October** Greek National Day, *Ochi* (No) Day
- **25 December** Christmas Day
- **26 December** Boxing Day

VARIABLE HOLIDAYS
The Orthodox Church usually celebrates Easter a week or two later than central Europe, so forthcoming dates include:
- **Green Monday** About 50 days before Greek Orthodox Easter: 22 Feb 1999; 13 Mar 2000
- **Greek Orthodox Good Friday** 9 Apr 1999, 28 Apr 2000
- **Greek Orthodox Easter Sunday** 11 Apr 1999, 30 Apr 2000
- **Greek Orthodox Easter Monday**

12 Apr 1999; 1 May 2000
- **Pentecost-Kataklysmos** (Festival of the Flood) 31 May 1999; 19 June 2000

ORTHODOX CHURCH HOLIDAYS
These have no effect on regular business hours and are often celebrated only in certain regions (these include name days of local holy figures and the patron saints of monasteries). They are always celebrated with processions and festivities:
- **6 January** Coastal regions hold the *Blessing of the Sea*. In the ceremony the bishop plunges a cross into the sea.
- **17 January** *St Anthony's Day*. Services in Nicosia and Limassol in honour of the Egyptian father of monasticism.
- **24 January** *St Neophytos's Day*. A massive procession ending at the cave of this hermit at Tala near Pafos.
- **1, 2 February** *Jesus's Presentation in the Temple.* Pilgrimage to Panagia Chrysorrogiatissa Monastery.

- **23 April** *St George's Day*. Services just about everywhere.
- **29 June** *SS Peter and Paul*. A large service is held in Kato Pafos, celebrated by the archbishop and other bishops.
- **15 August** *Death of the Virgin*. Celebrations conducted in the larger monasteries, with processions all over the island.
- **14 September** *Raising of the Holy Cross*. Large celebrations, particularly in the Stavrovouni Monastery and in Lefkara and Omodos.
- **4 October** *Ioannis Lampadistis* (St John). Service in the monastery at Pedoulas devoted to this local patron saint.
- **18 October** *St Luke's Day*. Celebrated in Nicosia and Palaichori in particular.

The following Orthodox holidays are also worth keeping an eye open for: the *Procession of the Lazarus Icon* through Larnaka, a week before Easter; and the *Festival of the Flood*, with celebrations in Larnaka at Whitsun.

Commonwealth. The Republic of Cyprus also belongs to the United Nations and the Council of Europe. It has been an associate member of the European Union since 1973 and in 1990 applied for full membership, being confirmed by the EU as a candidate member in 1997. In the 1998 presidential elections the conservative Glavkos Clerides narrowly won another term of office.

On 20 July 1974, the island was effectively split into two when Turkish troops invaded in response to a Greek-inspired coup against the government of Archbishop Makarios. Today the Republic of Cyprus controls about 63 per cent of the country in the south while the Turkish-occupied north consists of about 37 per cent.

In 1983, the north unilaterally declared itself to be the independent Turkish Republic of Northern Cyprus, but apart from Turkey no country recognises northern Cyprus as an independent state. In an international context, the "president" of northern Cyprus, Rauf Denktash, is known only as the "Leader of the Turkish Cypriot People". Around 35,000 soldiers from the Turkish mainland are stationed in northern Cyprus and a large number of mainland Turks are now resident there. All settlements in northern Cyprus have been given Turkish place-names. The Republic of Cyprus does not recognise these new names. In the main guide section of this book, the Turkish name is given in brackets after the Greek name.

This information is included only to help the traveller. It does not represent recognition of the renaming policy.

Numerous initiatives and rounds of negotiations under the auspices of the United Nations have so far yielded no solution to the Cyprus problem. New initiatives launched by the UN, with the support of the United States and European Union, were begun in 1997 and continued in 1998. Cyprus's pending accession to the European Union lends a degree of urgency to the search for a settlement, but entrenched positions on both sides have torpedoed all previous initiatives and there is no compelling indication that it will be any different this time. Greek Cypriots are prepared to concede a degree of autonomy to their Turkish Cypriot counterparts within a federal state consisting of two provinces but not with shared sovereignty. However, the leadership in the north will contemplate only a loose confederation with a significant degree of independence for their sector.

Business Hours

Republic of Cyprus
Shopping hours
● *Winter:*
Mon/Tues/Thur/Fri: til 6pm
Wed/Sat: til 2pm
● *Summer:*
Mon/Tues/Thur/Fri: til 7.30pm
Wed/Sat: til 2pm
Closing times may be slightly earlier in spring and autumn (about 7pm) and most shops take an afternoon recess some time between 1pm and 4pm in the summer.
Business hours
● *15 Sept–31 May:*
Mon–Fri: 8am–1pm, 3–6pm
● *1 June–14 Sept:*
Mon–Fri: 8am–1pm, 4–7pm
You will find that many businesses stay open longer than the official hours.

Place Names

After the 1974 partition of Cyprus into the Republic in the south and Turkish sector in the north, southern Cyprus changed many of its place names and streets in a bid to emphasise its Greek roots. For example, the capital of Nicosia is referred to as Lefkosia, Limassol has changed to Lemesos and the transliteration of Larnaca is now Larnaka and Paphos has become Pafos.

All literature and sign-posting in southern Cyprus or from tourist offices uses the new names.

Northern Cyprus
Between 15 May and 14 Sept most businesses are open 8am–1pm and 4–7pm Mon–Sat. From 15 Sept to 14 May shops remain open all day, 8am–6pm.

Although banks, shops and businesses are closed on public holidays, in resort and coastal areas shops and certain services may remain open.

Planning the Trip

Passports and Visas

Visas are not required by, among others, nationals of Australia, Canada, Denmark, France, Germany, Ireland, Italy, The Netherlands, New Zealand, Spain, the UK and the US.

Passports must be valid for at least three months beyond the date of entry into the Republic of Cyprus; a personal identification card is not sufficient. Children and minors must have their own passports if their names are not entered in their parents' passports.

Any kind of stamp issued in the Turkish Republic of Northern Cyprus found among your travel documents constitutes grounds for denying you entry to the southern part of Cyprus. Although it is possible to enter Turkish-occupied Cyprus directly from Turkey, visitors using this route will be prohibited from entering the southern part of the island. The Republic of Cyprus regards direct entry into the occupied territory as an illegal act. A stamp from the Turkish Republic of Northern Cyprus may even cause you difficulties when trying to enter Greece.

If you plan a future holiday in Greece or southern Cyprus, ask customs officials to stamp a loose sheet of paper instead of your passport – they're used to such requests at Ercan Airport!

Visiting Turkish-Occupied Cyprus
Currently the only way to visit both the southern and the northern part of the island

during the same holiday is to arrive in the former and take a day's excursion into the north. It's impossible to manage this the other way around as officials in the south refuse to recognise entry documents issued in northern Cyprus.

The only border-crossing is located at the Green Line in Nicosia (taking photographs here is strictly prohibited). The crossing lies directly to the west of the Venetian Walls, not far from the Pafos Gate, at the old Ledra Palace Hotel. The Republic of Cyprus authorities keep a record of the date of passage and the place where the guest is staying. The Turkish checkpoint is approximately 150 metres (500 ft) away. All potential visitors must apply here for a day visa. This costs CY£1 and is speedily obtained. Passports are not stamped in this procedure. You will be asked to name the destination of your excursion. The Turkish-Cypriot authorities' visa office usually has copies of the free brochure *Kibris* (written in English), containing useful travel tips.

The border-crossing is open after about 8am. The Republic of Cyprus requires visitors to return by 6pm at the latest, which means that time is limited. You are not allowed to spend the night in northern Cyprus if you've entered through this border. Bringing goods acquired in the north into the south is also prohibited.

The northern section of Nicosia can easily be explored on foot; but for destinations outside the city the only real option is to take a taxi. There are cabs ready and waiting at the border-crossing itself, as well as at Atatürk Square, distinguished by a Venetian column. It is also possible to rent a car from one of the travel agencies at the Keryneia Gate. Communal taxis operate throughout the day between Nicosia, Famagusta, Keryneia

and Morphou. Rental and ticket prices are cheaper in the north than in the south.

Under normal circumstances the southern authorities permit tourists one excursion to the northern part of the island per stay. But if you can manage to convince the appropriate officials of a passionate artistic and/or historical interest in the monuments in the occupied territory, chances are good that they'll allow you more than one.

Money Matters

REPUBLIC The unit of currency in the Republic of Cyprus is the Cyprus pound (CY£), called the lira in Greek. The pound is divided into 100 cents. Cypriot banknotes come in denominations of 1, 2, 5, 10 and 20 pounds, coins in 1, 2, 5, 10, 20 and 50 cents.

While there are no limitations restricting the importing of foreign currency, sums of US$1,000/£650 (or equivalent) or more should be declared upon entering the country. The import or export of Cypriot money is limited to CY£50. It is usually more advantageous to exchange money in Cyprus than in your own country.
NORTH In the northern part of the island the Turkish lira – the same money in circulation in Turkey – is the official currency.

Exchange Facilities

REPUBLIC In addition to banks, most hotel receptions will exchange cash, traveller's cheques and Eurocheques. Many banks have automated cash dispensers which you can use for withdrawing cash using Eurocheque cards, credit cards and cards linked to the Plus and Cirrus networks.

As a rule, banks are open 8.30am–12.30pm Mon–Fri and 3.15–4.45pm on Mon; in July and August opening hours are 8.15am–12.30pm Mon–Fri only; in tourist centres, however,

banks frequently operate a special Tourist Afternoon Service between 3.30pm and 5.30pm (Oct–Apr) and 4–6pm (May–Sept) except Monday. Some banks open on Saturday morning. Currency exchange counters at Larnaka and Pafos airports are open following the arrival of foreign flights. All banks are closed on public holidays (including Easter Tuesday) but not 24 December.

If you lose your credit card, you should inform your own bank, but you can also contact JCC Payment Services in Nicosia on (02) 360820.

NORTH For a visit to the north, you are best off taking one of the main international currencies, such as dollars or pounds sterling, as exchanging money can be less straight-forward than in the south. Banks operate only limited hours (generally 8.30am–noon), but there are money exchange houses in all the major centres. These are open longer hours (8am–6pm Mon–Fri with a lunch

Tourist Offices Abroad

UK Cyprus Tourist Office, 213 Regent Street, London W1R 8DA, tel: (0171) 734 9822/734 2593, fax: (0171) 287 6534, e-mail: ctolon@ctolon.demon.co.uk Northern Region of Cyprus Tourist Information Office, 29 Bedford Square, London WC1B 3EG, tel: (0171) 631 1930, fax: (0171) 631 1873.
USA Cyprus Tourism Organisation, 13 E 40th Street, New York, NY 10016, tel: (212) 683 5280, fax: (212) 683 5282, e-mail: gocyprus@aol.com Northern Region of Cyprus Tourist Information Office, 1667 K Street, Suite 690, Washington DC 200006, tel: (202) 887 6198, fax: (202) 467 0685.

break, and Saturday mornings), offer a fast, reliable service and do not charge commission.

Foreign money can also be exchanged in many shops (and often for a better rate than at the bank). But it is usually possible to pay for hotel bills, taxis from the airport, souvenirs and meals in overseas cash. Eurocheques must be issued in a hard currency in return for Turkish lire. Most hotels and shops accept credit cards.

Customs

In addition to limitations on the import and export of Cypriot money (*see Money Matters, page 285*), duty-free goods brought into the country are restricted to:

REPUBLIC 2 litres of fortified wines, champagne and aperitifs, plus 2 litres of other wines; 1 litre of spirits (for visitors over 17 years of age); 50 cigars or 200 cigarettes or 250g tobacco (over 17s only); 0.6 litres perfume; 0.31 litres eau de toilette. The total value of other imported goods, such as electronic wares, may not exceed CY£100 (items such as cameras, binoculars and cassette players for personal use, will not normally be subjected to duty).

NORTH 1.5 litres of wine; 1.5 litres of spirits; 400 cigarettes

or 100 cigars or 500g tobacco; 100ml perfume; 100ml eau de toilette.

All animals must be quarantined for six months on entering the country, so it is practically impossible for a tourist to bring along a pet.

Health

There are no specific vaccinations required by visitors to Cyprus. Medical care, dentists and chemists are on a par with central Europe.

In all cities there are hospitals with English-speaking doctors. It is advisable to take out health insurance, but even tourists who are covered by such insurance (check before your journey whether or not you'll need to take out an additional travel policy) will initially have to pay for doctor's fees and medication and be reimbursed later; but these sums are fairly low owing to a glut of doctors. Be sure to ask for and keep all receipts and bills for any medical treatment and medicine.

It is important to compensate for fluid, electrolyte and salt lost through sweating by drinking plenty of bottled water or soft drinks. Generally speaking, most Cypriot dishes are prepared with sufficient salt.

What to Pack

For summer visits to Cyprus, visitors should pack lightweight, cotton clothing and sun protection (*see Health*). It is also wise to take mosquito repellent. Those planning to spend time exploring the mountainous interior should bear in mind that even in summer temperatures can drop considerably after dark or during storms; and it is advisable to pack a warm sweater, long trousers and rain gear.

Generally, during the winter months you should take warm clothes (and bear in mind the likelihood of snow in the Troodos Mountains). However, even in winter the sun's rays can be strong enough to warrant wearing sun cream, a hat and sunglasses.

A torch is a good idea for sightseeing, as many monasteries, churches and church ruins are poorly lit and northern Cyprus is prone to power cuts.

Few basins or baths have plugs, so be sure to pack a 37mm or 44mm plug.

Specialist Holidays and Packages

● **Cruises (Cyprus to Egypt)**
Argo Holidays, 100 Wigmore Street, London W1H 9DR, tel: (0171) 331 7070.
Magnum Travel, 747 Green Lanes, London N21 3SA, tel: (0181) 360 5353.
● **Fishing**
Cyprus Angling Holidays, 3 The Drive, Sevenoaks, Kent TN13 3AB, tel: (01732) 450749.
● **Golf**
Cyprus Golf Resorts, PO Box 2290, Pafos,

tel: (06) 642774/5, fax: (06) 642776.
Exclusive Golf Tours, 132 Green Lanes, London N13 5UN, tel: (0181) 882 7153.
● **Hiking**
Pafos and Troodos Mountains: Waymark Holidays, 44 Windsor Road, Slough SL1 2EG, tel: (01753) 516477.
● **Off the beaten track**
Villas and village houses in quiet, rural western Cyprus: Sunvil Holidays, Sunvil House, Upper Square, Old Isleworth,

Middlesex TW7 7BJ, tel: (0181) 568 4499.
● **Outward bound**
Jeep, canyoning and walking safaris to remote, unspoiled parts of the Pafos district: Exalt, PO Box 337, Kato Pafos, tel: (06) 243803.
● **Scuba-diving**
Diving holidays in Keryneia in north Cyprus: Scuba Cyprus, 533a Kingsland Road, London E8 4AR, tel: (0171) 923 2085.

Getting There

By Air

REPUBLIC The two main airports in the south are at Larnaka and Pafos. Until the Turkish invasion Cyprus's main airport was Nicosia International Airport (it is currently closed and occupied by the United Nations Force in Cyprus, although its re-opening is always a possibility). Now Larnaka International Airport has taken over Nicosia's role.
• **Larnaka International Airport**, tel: (04) 643000.
• **Pafos International Airport**, tel: (06) 422833.

The national airline, Cyprus Airways, operates direct flights between Larnaka and London, Birmingham, Manchester, and major continental and Middle East cities. Most major European and Middle Eastern airlines fly to Cyprus (usually only to Larnaka), although some, such as KLM and Sabena, have route-sharing agreements with Cyprus Airways. Since the liberalisation of air travel to and from Cyprus, the number of operators offering flights between Europe and the Middle East has greatly increased.

The two main airlines to serve Cyprus from the UK are:
• **British Airways**, 52a Leoforos Archiepiskopou Makariou III, Nicosia, tel: (02) 442188.
• **Cyprus Airways**, 21 Odos Alkaiou, Nicosia, tel: (02) 443054.

NORTH There are two airports in northern Cyprus: Ercan, 16 miles (25 km) east of Nicosia/Lefkosia and Lefkonoiko/Gecitkale (20 miles (30 km) northwest of Ammochostos/Gazimagusa (Famagusta).

At the moment the Turkish national airline, Turkish Airlines, flies into northern Cyprus from Istanbul, Ankara, Izmir and Adana. Istanbul Airlines, Kibris Turkish Airlines and Noble Airlines also operate services to Cyprus from Istanbul and Ankara.

• **Turkish Airlines** Mehmet Akif Cadesi 52, Kösklüçıftlik-Dereboyou, Lefkosha/Nicosia, (tel: 227 1382/227 1061 and 227 7124; fax: 228 7341). The airline also has countless offices in Turkey.

European charter companies do not fly into the northern part of Cyprus. It is important to remember that those who enter Cyprus via the north cannot extend their journey into the southern part of the island. The Republic of Cyprus treats direct entry into the occupied territory as an illegal act (*see Passports and Visas*).

By Boat

REPUBLIC Mediterranean cruise ships often call at Limassol. Boat traffic between Europe and Cyprus is also conducted from the harbour here; there are connections to the island of Rhodes, to Heraklion in Crete and to Piraeus. The crossing to Piraeus takes about 48 hours. Ticket prices vary, depending upon whether you are travelling during the peak or off-peak tourist seasons.

Those going to Cyprus who prefer not to travel long distances to Piraeus overland can use one of the boat connections to Greece. There are direct passages from Ancona and Venice to Piraeus, and in summer a ferry connects Bari and Brindisi in Italy with Igoumenitsa and Patras in Greece. (The final leg of the journey to Piraeus from the latter two cities is overland.)

During the main tourist season boat passages are offered, according to demand, direct from Italy. They depart from Ancona or Venice and include a stopover in Limassol, where the Cyprus Tourist Office can provide an up-to-date schedule of boat arrivals and departures.

Other shipping lines connect Limassol with Port Said in Egypt and Haifa in Israel. The tourist

board has an office for boat passengers in Limassol harbour.

For information about car ferry services on the Piraeus (Athens)–Rhodes–Limassol–Haifa routes, contact:
• **Poseidon Lines**, tel: (05) 355555.
• **Salamis Lines**, tel: (05) 341043.

NORTH Famagusta is the most important port, with boat connections to Syria and Turkey. The main service is to Mersin on the southern coast of Turkey.

In addition to these, shipping lines operate between the southern coast of Turkey and Keryneia/Girne on the northern coast of Cyprus. The quickest way to cross is by Hovercraft. Between May and October a Hovercraft service operates three times a week, departing from Tasucu, about 7 miles (11km) southwest of Silifke, Turkey. This passage, usually conducted overnight and usually offered at a 20 percent discount to students, takes about 8 hours.

The main boat operator is:
• **Turkish Maritime Lines** 3 Bulent Ecevit Bulvari, Famagusta, tel: (366) 4557, fax: (366) 7840; or just right of the harbour gate at Keryneia/Girne, tel: (815) 7885, fax: (815) 7884.

By Car

As a rule, the aforementioned shipping lines also transport motor vehicles (most international boat services are by car ferry). Prices vary considerably, depending on whether it is the peak or off-peak season.

If you and your car do not remain in the country for more than three months, you will not be required to pay any additional tax or duties; should three months be too short a time for you, it is possible to apply at the main customs office in Nicosia for permission to stay in Cyprus for a period of up to 12 months.

Practical Tips

Medical Treatment

Pharmacies are well trained for minor ailments and sell almost all brands of medicines, plus many over-the-counter drugs that are prescription-only elsewhere. To find out where the nearest pharmacy is open after hours, ask the reception desk at your hotel, or phone the emergency number below. There are also listings in local papers.

In case of accidents, hospital casualty departments in Cyprus will deal with minor wounds (such as cuts needing stitches or broken bones) free of charge.

If you need to see a doctor, most hotels have access to names and addresses of those who speak English. Most private doctors operate visiting hours of 9am–1pm and 4–7pm Mon–Fri. For information on doctors on call during weekends or holidays, there are listings in local newspapers or you can call the following numbers:

Limassol	1425
Larnaka	1424
Nicosia	1422
Pafos	1426
Famagusta	1423

Media

Newspapers and magazines

Foreign publications and other sources of information can be purchased in bookstores, hotels and at newspaper kiosks in both parts of Cyprus. Most UK newspapers are on sale a day after the day of issue.

Two English-language papers are regularly available in southern Cyprus: the *Cyprus*

Embassies and Consulates

REPUBLIC
Australia High Commission, corner of Leoforos Stasinou and 4 Odos Annis Komninis, 2nd Floor, 1060 Nicosia, tel: (02) 473001, fax: (02) 366486.
Canada Consulate, Margarita House, 15 Odos Themistokli Dervi, Nicosia, tel: (02) 451630, fax: (02) 459096.
Ireland Consulate, Leoforos Armenias & Kalypso, Flat 301, PO Box 523, 1660 Nicosia, tel: (02) 333985, fax: (02) 331580.
New Zealand Consulate, 35 Odos Agiou Nicolaou, Egkomi, PO Box 4676, 1302 Nicosia, tel: (02) 476100, fax: (02) 590048.
South Africa Consulate, 101 Leoforos Archiepiskopou Makariou III, 1071 Nicosia, tel: (02) 476100, fax: (02) 377011.
UK High Commission, Odos Alexandrou Palli, PO Box 1978, 1587 Nicosia,

tel: (02) 473131, fax: (02) 367198.
USA Embassy, corner of Metochiou and Ploutarchou, Egkomi, 2406 Nicosia, tel: (02) 476100, fax: (02) 465944.

NORTH
Because northern Cyprus is not recognised as an independent country, no official reciprocal exchange exists between ambassadors or consuls. But representatives can be found at the following offices:
American Centre Guner Turkmen Sokak, Ksoklu Ciftlik area, Nicosia, tel: (22) 72443.
Australian Respresentation Division Saray Hotel, Nicosia, tel: (22) 77332. Tues/Thur 9am–12.30pm only.
British Council former embassy chancellery, near the Green Line off Mehmet Akif, Nicosia, tel: (22) 83861. Mainly mornings only.

Mail (daily) and the *Cyprus Weekly*. There are two English magazines, *Seven Days in Cyprus* and *Nicosia this Month,* which cater to tourists and contain an extensive calendar of events; look for them in hotel receptions or tourist offices.

In north Cyprus there is a weekly English-language newspaper, the *Cyprus Times,* and a monthly, *Kibris Monthly.*

Television

In the south, the CyBC 2 television network broadcasts a daily news summary in English at 9pm, and carries Euronews from about midnight to 5pm. All television networks in the south (CyBC 1 and 2, Logos, Sigma, Antena, and Greece's ET1) often broadcast programmes and films in English with Greek subtitles. British Forces

Broadcasting Service (BFBS) television programmes can no longer be accessed outside the British Sovereign Base Areas.

Many hotels and some bars have satellite television, receiving among others CNN International, BBC World Television and Sky Television.

Radio

CyBC Radio 1 has daily news broadcasts in English, while Radio 2 (91–1MHz FM) features programmes in English at 10am (weather, currency rates and cultural events), 1.30–3pm (magazine programme with interviews, short talks on Cyprus and music) and 8pm–midnight (starting with news). From June to September the information programme *Welcome to Cyprus* is broadcast between 7pm and 8pm.

When you're
bitten by the travel bug,
make sure you're protected.

Check into a British Airways Travel Clinic.

British Airways Travel Clinics provide travellers with:
- A complete vaccination service and essential travel health-care items
- Up-dated travel health information and advice

Call **01276 685040** for details of your nearest Travel Clinic.

**BRITISH AIRWAYS
TRAVEL CLINICS**

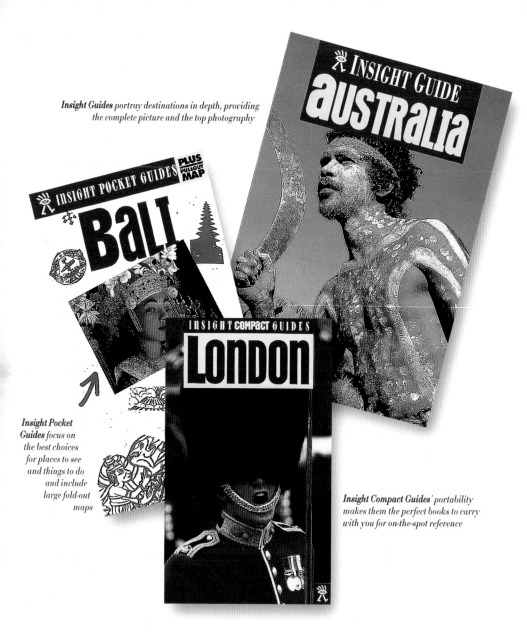

Insight Guides portray destinations in depth, providing the complete picture and the top photography

INSIGHT POCKET GUIDES PLUS PULLOUT MAP

Bali

INSIGHT GUIDE australia

INSIGHT COMPACT GUIDES

London

Insight Pocket Guides focus on the best choices for places to see and things to do and include large fold-out maps

Insight Compact Guides' portability makes them the perfect books to carry with you for on-the-spot reference

Three types of guide for all types of travel

INSIGHT GUIDES Different people need different kinds of information. Some want *background information* to help them prepare for the trip. Others seek *personal recommendations* from someone who knows the destination well. And others look for *compactly presented data* for on-the-spot reference. With three carefully designed series, Insight Guides offer readers the perfect choice. Insight Guides will turn your visit into an experience.

The world's largest collection of visual travel guides

The Voice of America and BBC World Service Radio can also be picked up. British Forces Broadcasting Service radio is on the air 24 hours a day, with a diet of music, magazine programmes and news.

Bayrak Radio and Television in north Cyprus have occasional English-language programmes.

Postal Services

REPUBLIC Post offices in southern Cyprus are open from 7.30am to 1.30pm Mon–Fri and 3–6pm Thur. The main post offices in Nicosia, Larnaka, Limassol and Pafos stay open in the afternoon (except Wed and Sat) 3–6pm.

A letter sent by airmail to a European country takes about five days to arrive. Stamps can be purchased from hotels, news-stands and some shops as well as post offices.

NORTH Post offices open daily 7.30am–2pm, Mon also 3.30–6pm, and Sat 9am–noon. Because northern Cyprus is not recognised as an independent country, postal authorities in other countries are not permitted to recognise stamps issued by this "country". All mail destined for northern Cyprus must first make a detour through Turkey. In practice this means that, in addition to the address in northern Cyprus, you must write Mersin-10, Turkey on the envelope. This does not affect outgoing post, however.

Telecommunications

Telephone
The Cyprus Telecommunications Authority (CYTA) has area administrative offices in the larger towns and cities, but calls cannot be made from them or from post offices. There are a great many CYTA public telephone booths, however, in the centre of towns and villages and in tourist areas. Most of

these accept only telecards (CY£3, CY£5 and CY£10 from CYTA offices, banks, post offices, souvenir shops and newspaper vendors), although a few still take 2, 5, 10 and 20 cent coins.

More than 200 countries worldwide can be dialled direct from southern Cyprus. Calls made from hotels cost well in excess of the standard charge. Reduced rates for international calls are from 10pm to 8am Monday to Saturday and all day on Sundays.

Mobile phones can operate in the Republic provided your service provider has a roaming agreement with CYTA. For details phone CYTA's customer service department on 132.

Collect Calls To reverse charges, Call Direct puts you through to the operator in your own country, who will connect you once the person at the other end accepts the call. This service is cheaper than collect calls, and you do not need to go through the operator in Cyprus. Numbers to ring are:

● **Australia** 080-90061 (Telstra) 080-90002 (Optus)
● **Canada** 080-90012
● **Ireland** 080-90053
● **UK** 080-90044 (BT) 080-90004 (Mercury)
● **USA** 080-90010 (AT&T) 080-90000 (MCI) 080-90001 (Sprint)

Emergency Numbers

Emergency services are on these numbers. Operators usually speak good English.
REPUBLIC
Ambulance **199**
Police **199**
Fire brigade **199, 112**
Night pharmacies **192**
NORTH
Ambulance **112**
Police **155**
Fire brigade **199**

Dialling Codes

● **Republic of Cyprus** 357
● **Area codes**
Nicosia 02
Agia Napa/Protaras 03
Larnaka 04
Limassol/Troodos 05
Pafos/Polis 06
If phoning from abroad, delete the initial 0.
● **Country codes**
Australia 61
Canada 1
Ireland 353
New Zealand 64
South Africa 27
United Kingdom 44
United States 1
To telephone from Cyprus, dial 00 + country code + area code (minus the initial 0) + subscriber number.

Faxes/telexes
There are no public fax or telex facilities in Cyprus, but most hotels will send be willing to send a fax for you.

For further enquiries about transmitting within Cyprus phone 192, for overseas 134.

Telegrams
CYTA offices will send telegrams, or you can phone through a message on 196 from 7am to 7pm daily including public holidays.

NORTH Telephone connections to northern Cyprus are conducted via Turkey. Because of this you must first dial the Turkish dialling code 00 (90), followed by 392 (the direct number for northern Cyprus), then the seven-digit number of the person you are trying to reach.

Religious Services

During the summer, some religious services are held in English in the Republic of Cyprus.
Agia Napa
Ecumenical Centre, Agia Napa

Monastery.
Larnaka
Anglican: St Helena's Church,
Leoforos Grigori Afxentiou &
Agia Elenis,
tel: (04) 651327.
Catholic: Terra Santa Church,
Terra Santa,
tel: (04) 652858.
Limassol
Anglican: St Barnabas Church,
177a Leoforos Archiepiskopou
Leontiou I,
tel: (05) 362713.
Catholic: St Catherine's Church,
259 Odos 28 Oktovriou,
tel: (05) 362946.
Nicosia
Anglican: St Paul's Church,
Leoforos Vyronos,
tel: (02) 442241.
Catholic: Holy Cross Church,
Pyli Pafou (Pafos gate),
tel: (02) 462132.
Pafos
Anglican: Chrysopolitissa
Church, Kato Pafos,
tel: (06) 252486.
Catholic: Chrysopolitissa
Church, Kato Pafos,
tel: (06) 238856.
   There are also services of the
Seventh Day Adventist Church,
the Church of God of Prophecy,
the Apostolic Church of Jesus
Christ, the International
Christian Fellowship, the Grace
Church and the International
Evangelical Church. These are in
addition to Greek Orthodox,
Armenian, Maronite, and Coptic
churches, as well as mosques in
Nicosia, Larnaka and Limassol.

Photography

Cyprus provides plenty of
interesting subject matter for
photographers. Basic rules of
courtesy should be observed
when photographing people –
always ask permission. Film
and video camera cassettes
may be more expensive in
Cyprus than at home.
   Photography is strictly prohibited in the areas surrounding
military facilities and security
zones. These include but are
not limited to the British military
bases at Akrotiri/Episkopi and
Dhekaleia; UN Peacekeeping
Force in Cyprus (UNFICYP) positions and bases; military
installations associated with the
Inner-Cypriot Line of Demarcation. Even in the interior, and
in seemingly unlikely places,
photography may be forbidden
because of the existence of a
military base or training area,
radar or communications sites,
even dams.
   As a rule, visitors are not
allowed to take pictures inside
museums. However, you can
take snaps in the museums'
gardens and at outdoor
archaeological sites if no
excavations are under way.
   Apart from at Stavrovouni,
visitors are allowed to take
photographs inside
monasteries, though usually
without flash. Photography is
forbidden inside the church at
Kykkos Monastery, a rule that is

energetically enforced. The
same rules of courtesy apply at
religious sites as anywhere
else: ask permission before
snapping pictures of monks or
nuns. Keep in mind that these
sacred buildings with their
wealth of frescoes and icons
are considered holy places, and
that the frescoes and icons can
be damaged by flash photography. Discretion should be
employed at all times.

Security and Crime

Cyprus is one of the safest
places to visit in the
Mediterranean. Crime is low,
and in both north and south
people are generally relaxed
and hospitable. As society is
still centred around the family,
children are particularly
welcomed and catered for. Lone
women are rarely harrassed
even in tourist areas, and are
likely to be given royal treatment
in rural villages.
   Cyprus police are also
hospitable and helpful, and
tourists are unlikely to
experience anything but the
warmest of treatment from the
island and is people unless they
are foolhardy enough to cross
the Green Line dividing the
north and south sectors; stray
near military zones; take
photographs in any prohibited
places (see above); or drive on
roads marked as no-go areas
on a map.

Tourist Offices in Cyprus

REPUBLIC
19 Leoforos Lemesou, PO Box
4535, Nicosia, Cyprus, tel: (02)
337715, fax: (02) 331644.
Agia Napa 12 Leoforos Kryou
Nerou, tel: (03) 721796.
Larnaka Larnaka International
Airport, tel: (04) 643000.
Plateia Vasileos Pavlou,
tel: (04) 654322.
Limassol 15 Odos Spyrou
Araouzou, tel: (05) 362756.

35 Odos A Georgiou A',
Germasogeia, tel: (05)
323211. And Limassol Harbour
Passenger Terminal, tel: (05)
343868.
Nicosia 35 Odos Aristokyprou,
Laïki Geitonia, tel: (02)
444264.
Pafos 3 Odos Gladstonos,
tel: (06) 232841.
Airport, tel: (06) 422833.
Polis 2 Odos Agiou Nikolaou,

tel: (06) 322468.
Platres Village Plateia,
tel: (05) 421316.
NORTH
Famagusta
Fevzı Cakmak Bulvari, tel:
366 2864.
Keryneia Kordon Boyu
(Harbour), tel: 815 2145.
Nicosia Sht Tegmen Idris
Dogan Sokak B Block,
Lefkosha, tel: 228 9629.

Tipping

As a 10 percent service charge is levied in hotels and restaurants, a tip is not obligatory, although small change is always welcomed. If service is not included a 10 per cent tip is standard in restaurants. It is traditional to give taxi drivers 10 per cent extra, and porters, tour guides, hairdressers and cloakroom attendants a few cents.

Etiquette

Cyprus is a relaxed holiday country, so few strict codes of conduct apply.

If you are staying at a luxury hotel, it's wise to wear elegant clothes in the evening as Cypriots are likely to be dressed up to the nines.

When you visit a monastery you should take care to be appropriately attired: people wearing shorts, no shirts, backless tops, very short dresses and swimwear are not admitted (sometimes even women in trousers).

Shoes should be removed before entering a mosque. Make sure a service is not in progress, and don't walk in front of someone who is praying.

Bartering is not really a feature of shopping in Cyprus. You may get small reductions in prices for souvenirs, but if the cost is clearly marked you're unlikely to be able to bargain. In the south hotel prices are generally posted, with little room for reductions, but you may have more luck in the north.

There is not wide social acceptance of gay people in Cyprus, and open displays of affection are not recommended. Recognised gay venues are scarce, and word of mouth is usually the best way to find out where gay people tend to gather.

Getting Around

If you want to travel around within Cyprus, you are probably best off driving. There are no trains in the south or north. A reasonable bus service, which is frequent and inexpensive, links the major towns and sites in both south and north. One of the more characterful ways of seeing Cyprus is by "communal" taxis (called service taxis in the south and *dolmus* in the north), which take 4–7 people on main routes – though the driving can be hair-raising!

But if you'd like to venture even slightly off the beaten track, the car is the best way of getting about since public transport is non-existent in remote areas. The major towns are linked by fairly good roads, and four-lane motorways connect Nicosia with Larnaka, Limassol and Keryneia. The Limassol–Pafos road can be a nightmare for congestion, and driving at night in the north is hazardous as you're likely to encounter unlit military trucks.

Minor roads and forest routes are usually unsurfaced, varying from the passable (provided you take care in wet weather) to tracks only fit for four-wheel drive vehicles.

Drivers are advised to wear good sunglasses as glare from the Mediterranean sun can be intense.

Driving

All you need to drive in Cyprus is a valid international or national driving licence, plus Green Card insurance.

Distances are marked in kilometres in the south, whereas in the north signs are in kilometres on major routes and miles (or not at all) on minor roads and forest tracks.

All road traffic signs in the south are written in both Greek and English.

Petrol in the south costs about the same as in central Europe, but is cheaper in the north. All types of petrol and diesel are readily available in the south, but in the north there is no unleaded.

In the south petrol stations are open 6am–7pm in summer and 6am–6pm in winter Mon–Fri, and until 3pm on Saturday. Early closing (2pm) is on Wednesday in the Nicosia district, and Tuesday in Limassol, Larnaka, Pafos and Ammochostos. A few petrol stations in Nicosia and in the coastal regions are open 24 hours. Several in Nicosia and all coastal areas are equipped with vending machines that take bank notes and credit cards and operate out of working hours, at weekends and during holidays.

In the north petrol stations open until 9 or 10pm, and regular working hours on Sundays.

Traffic Regulations

In both parts of Cyprus vehicles are driven on the left side of the road – a practice dating back to when the island was a British colony. Despite this, vehicles approaching from the right always have the right of way, provided there isn't a sign in the vicinity stating otherwise.

Seat belts are compulsory in the front of cars and in the back in cars where they are fitted. Children under five must not sit in the front, and five to 10-year-olds are permitted in the passenger seat only if a child's seat belt is fitted.

Drink-driving laws are similar to those in the UK and North America, with the limit of alcohol

Breakdown Service

If you break down in south
Cyprus, a 24-hour towing
service is offered by the
Cyprus Automobile
Association in Nicosia. The
association is a member of
the Alliance Internationale de
Tourisme and Fédération
Internationale de
L'Automobile, to which all
nationally recognised
motoring associations belong.
**Cyprus Automobile
Association** tel: (02)
313233, fax: (02) 313482.
**Cyprus AA Breakdown
Service** (24 hours) tel: (02)
313131.

in the breath 39mcg and in the
blood 90mcg per 100ml. Police
operate random breath tests.
   When you are going around
bends, where visibility is limited,
it is common practice to warn
any oncoming vehicle by tooting
the horn.

Car Rental

Hire cars are often called Z
cars because their registration
numbers, on distinctive red
plates, begin with Z. They can
be in a dreadful state (particularly the brakes), so it's worth
taking a spin round the block
before commiting yourself.
   All it takes to hire a car in
Cyprus is a valid national
driver's licence. The person
renting the car, plus any other
driver, must be at least 21 years
of age. Drivers under the age of
25 require additional insurance.
   In the south there are car
rental agencies at the airport
and in all main towns and resorts.
Many hotel receptions can provide access to an agency. If you
choose one of the international
car rental companies that
maintains an office on Cyprus,
reservations can be made in
advance from home. The extensive annual hotel guide available

from all CTO offices also contains
a list of car rental agencies.
   Hiring a car for several days
will ensure a better rate; the
longer you keep the car, the
less you'll have to pay per day.
Vehicles are rented out
grudgingly – if at all – for one
day at a time. Rates are
generally calculated per day and
without any mileage limitations.
   Some major car hire
companies in the south are:
• **Astra/Eurodollar** (02)
775800
• **Budget** (04) 629170.
• **Europcar** (05) 371441.
• **Hertz** (02) 477411.
• **Petsas** (02) 462650.
   In the north, there are none
of the internationally recognised
car hire operators, so you are
probably best off arranging hire
from home.

Public transport

Buses

In the Republic of Cyprus
buses run infrequently on
Sundays. During the rest of the
week, however, the inner city
buses in the larger cities
operate between 5.30am and
7pm (approxi-mately), with
hours occasionally extended
throughout the peak tourist
season. Long-distance buses
also connect all major city
centres, departing at roughly
one-hour intervals.
   In addition, there are
numerous small, private "village
buses" which transport
passengers between country
villages and the nearest main
town (usually at the start and
end of the working day).
   For intercity bus information,
contact:
• **Nicosia–Limassol** Kemek
Transport, tel: (02) 463989 or
(05) 747532.
• **Nicosia–Pafos** Costas,
tel: (02) 464636.
• **Nicosia–Larnaka** Kallenos
Buses, tel: (04) 654890.
• **Limassol–Larnaka** Kallenos
Buses, tel: (04) 654890.

Bike Hire

Rental agencies in the south
often lease motorcycles and
sometimes even bicycles too,
as well as cars. For
information on bike tours
through the island, contact:
Cyprus Cycling Federation
PO Box 4572, 1301 Nicosia,
tel: (02) 456344,
fax: (02) 360150.

Taxis

Communal (Service) Taxis
Service taxis are an inexpensive
way of travelling between the
larger towns in the south. Usually
a minivan, they can take 4–7
people and cost little more than
double bus fares. Each person
pays a fixed amount which is not
contingent upon how many
people are actually in the vehicle.
   Service taxis connect the
cities of Nicosia, Larnaka,
Limassol and Pafos, departing
approximately every half hour
between 5.45am and 6.30pm
(in summer 7.30pm) on
weekdays and 7am–5.30pm (in
summer 6.30pm) Sundays and
public holidays.
   As is the case with regular
taxis, they will pick up from your
apartment or hotel if you are
within the city limits and if the

Speed Limits

REPUBLIC
• Motorways/dual carriageways
100 kmh (60 mph)
65 kmh (39 mph) minimum
• Cities and towns
50 kmh (30 mph)
• Country roads (unless
otherwise marked)
80 kmh (48 mph)
NORTH
• Motorways/dual carriageways
100 kmh (60 mph)
• Cities and towns
50 kmh (30 mph)
• Country roads (unless
otherwise marked)
60 kmh (36 mph)

taxi has been summoned via the taxi control office. Likewise, on reaching the destination, drivers usually deposit passengers at their front doors.

Service taxis operate only between the four main towns, not to and from either of the airports or between towns and villages. At the airports, new arrivals must use the private taxis found outside the airport terminal. Unfortunately, their rates are higher than those of the much cheaper and almost as speedy group taxis.

The biggest service taxi companies include Akropolis, Karydas, Kypros, Kyriakos and Makris. For service taxi information, contact:

Nicosia–Larnaka–Nicosia
• Acropolis Taxis, tel: (02) 472525; (04) 655555.
• Kyriakos Taxis, tel: (02) 444141; (04) 655100.
• Makris Taxis, tel: (02) 466201; (04) 652929.

Nicosia–Limassol–Nicosia
• Karydas Taxis, tel: (02) 462269; (05) 361114.
• Kypros Taxis, tel: (02) 464811; (05) 363979.
• Kyriakos Taxis, tel: (02) 444141; (05) 361114.
• Makris Taxis, tel: (02) 466201; (05) 365550.

Limassol–Larnaka–Limassol
• Acropolis Taxis, tel: (04) 655555; (05) 366766.
• Makris Taxis, tel: (04) 652929; (05) 365550.

Limassol–Pafos–Limassol
• Karydas Taxis, tel: (05) 361114; (06) 361114.
• Kyriakos Taxis, tel: (05) 361114; (06) 361114.
• Makris Taxis, tel: (05) 365550.
• Nea Pafos Taxis, tel: (05) 355355.

Private Taxis

If you're interested in taking a sightseeing tour by taxi, it's advisable to choose a private one and come to an agreement beforehand as to how much it will cost, how long it will last,

and exactly which sights you will be visiting. At the end of such a private tour the driver will expect to receive a tip. There are set rates for uninterrupted long-distance trips. Currently the base fare is 65 cents, with an additional 22 cents reckoned per kilometre; having the taxi wait for you costs about CY£4 per hour. There is an extra charge of 22 cents for every piece of luggage (weighing more than 12 kg); for each additional piece you'll be expected to pay

22 cents more. Between 10.30pm and 6am passengers pay an extra "night-rate charge".

Hitching

You won't get great mileage from hitching in Cyprus. People in the south will be welcoming though hitching is not a regular pastime, and in the north there are so few cars that you could stand for hours in the heat.

Sightseeing Tours in the Republic of Cyprus

Tour operators offer sightseeing tours out of Agia Napa, Larnaka, Limassol, Pafos, Paralimni and Polis. Excursions are half or full-day trips to major places of interest (entrance fees included) in air-conditioned coaches with qualified guides. They can also arrange night tours, dinner at a local restaurant and often folk dancing/music, or boat trips.

● AGIA NAPA
Eman Leoforos Makariou III 32, PO Box 73, CY 5340 Agia Napia, tel: (03) 721321, fax (03) 722190.

● LIMASSOL
Amathus Plateia Syntagmatos 2, PO Box 3023, CY 3300, Limassol, tel: (05) 369122, fax: (05) 358354.
EAL Dromos Lemesou-Ypsona, PO Box 1117, CY 3501, Limassol, tel: (05) 390044, fax: (05) 392046.
Fame Azur Court 105, Potamos tis Germasogeias, PO Box 6113, CY 3304, Limassol, tel: (05) 322866, fax: (05) 322165.
GTA Travel Georgiades Travel Agency, Georgiou A', Lordos Beach Gardens, Block C, PO Box 1132, CY 3501 Limassol, tel: (05) 323522), fax: (05) 314956).
Heatwave Riga Fereou 8, PO Box 6763, CY 3310 Limassol, tel: (05) 355343, fax: (05) 372664.

Paradis Island Mitropolitou Kitiou Kyprianou 52, PO Box 157, CY 3601 Limassol, tel: (05) 357604, fax: (05) 370298.
Salamis Chr Hatzipavlou, Salamis House, PO Box 157, CY 3601 Limassol, tel: (05) 355555, fax: (05) 364410.
Sea Island Ithakis, Neapolis Centre G1, PO Box 4256, CY 3607 Limassol, tel: (05) 374725, fax: (05) 369992.
True-Blue Americanes 2, Athina Court, Flat 22, Patamos tis Germasogeias, PO Box 6832, CY 3310 Limassol, tel: (05) 311353, fax: (05) 311352.

● NICOSIA
Aeolos Zinas Kanther 6, PO Box 1236, CY 1504 Nicosia, tel: (02) 445222, fax: (02) 447222.
Airtour-Cyprus Airtour CTA, Naxou 4, PO Box 5108, CY 1307 Nicosia, tel: (02) 374282, fax: (02) 375220.
National Louis Tourist Agency, Leoforos Evagorou 54–8 PO Box 1301, CY 1506 Nicosia, tel: (02) 442114, fax: (02) 461894.

● POLIS
Century 21 PO Box 34, CY 8830 Polis, tel: (06) 322011, fax: (06) 321693.

● PAFOS
Exalt Tours Odos Agias Kyriakis 24, Pafos, tel: (06) 243803.

Where to Stay

Hotels

The best guide to hotels in the Republic of Cyprus is the annually up-dated hotel guide issued by the Cyprus Tourist Office, available free at all tourist information centres. The room rates listed in this guide have been determined by the official authorities and hotels that try to demand more than the prices quoted from their guests will be reprimanded (if caught). Moreover, each room must be furnished with a list of rates for overnight accommodation and extra services.

The price for an overnight stay in a simple hotel room is the equivalent to about £15/US$25 per person. During the off-peak season (see Best Times to Visit) many hotels offer price reductions.

Because official control of overnight lodging is fairly tight, private pensions are almost non-existent. This situation is irksome in smaller villages where there are no hotels. (It is no longer possible for tourists to get a room at one of the monasteries without prior arrangement.) This means that excursions must be planned beforehand and must end in larger towns or cities where hotels are available.

However, in a bid to spread some of the economic benefits of tourism away from the coast to the financially strapped villages and countryside, Cyprus is developing an Agrotourism/Rural Tourism initiative. To date, the Cyprus Agrotourism Company has converted for tourist accommodation some 30 traditional properties in picturesque village and country locations. The company's guide is available from CTO offices in Cyprus and abroad.

Before the Turkish invasion, beach tourism – and thus hotels – was mainly concentrated on the eastern coast south of Famagusta (Varosha) and by Keryneia. Today the hotel strip at Varosha lies inside the Turkish ceasefire line and has been abandoned.

The remaining hotels in the north have been taken over by Turkish Cypriot or Turkish management, even though the former Greek operators still claim ownership. In addition there are hotels that were run by Turkish Cypriot proprietors from the start and others that were built shortly after the invasion. Among these are the Saray in Nicosia, the Celebrity and Acapulco near Keryneia and the Altun Tabya and Kutup in Famagusta.

In the Northern Cypriot Tourist Information Agency brochure you'll find a complete list of hotels and pensions.

Hotel Listings

Larnaka
Harry's Inn
2 Odos Thermopyles, Larnaka.
Tel: (04) 654453.
There are only 9 rooms in this modestly priced hotel in a traditional house, and they fill up fast. $

Larco
Odos Umm Haram, Larnaka.
Tel: (04) 657006.
A swimming pool and an atmospheric location in the old Turkish Quarter make this mid-priced hotel a good deal for Larnaka. $$

Sun Hall
Leoforos Athinon, Larnaka.
Tel: (04) 653341.
This is a good resort hotel in the city, with 112 rooms and a sea view. $$

Limassol
Continental
137 Odos Spirou Araouzou, Limassol.
Tel: (05) 362530.
A sea view and good location compensate for the lack of a swimming pool. It has its own restaurant and 27 rooms. $

Le Village
242 Leoforos Archiepiskopou Leontiou I, Limassol.
Tel: (05) 368126.
A simple, family-owned downtown hotel with 32 rooms. It has a welcoming atmosphere and a reasonable degree of comfort. $

Nicosia
Classic
94 Odos Rigainis.
Tel: (02) 464006.
A modern, air-conditioned hotel with 57 rooms in the Old City, ideal for the main shopping and restaurant areas. $$

Cyprus Hilton
Leoforos Archiepiskopou Makariou III, Nicosia.
Tel: (02) 377777.
With 300 rooms, the Hilton is the biggest and also the best hotel in Nicosia. It has an indoor and a heated outdoor swimming pool, as well as other sports facilities and shops. $$$

Regina Palace
42 Odos Rigainis, Nicosia.
Tel: (02) 463051.
A good budget option in the Old City. None of the 30 rooms in the hotel are remotely luxurious but all are clean and comfortable. $

Venetian Walls
38 Odos Ouzounian, Nicosia.
Tel: (02) 450805.
With 48 rooms, the hotel offers a degree of comfort and a

Price Categories

Price categories are based on the cost of a double room for one night in the high season.
$ = under CY£30
$$ = CY£30–75
$$$ = CY75–100 and above

restaurant in the Old City for a reasonable price. $

Pafos–Polis
Agapinor
26 Odos Nikodemos Mylonos, Ktima (Nea Pafos).
Tel: (06) 233927.
If you want to be away from the coast and amid the action in the heart of Ktima, you can't get much closer than this central 37-room hotel. $

Coral Beach
Coral Bay, near Pegeia, 8 miles (12 km) north of Pafos.
Tel: (06) 621601.
A luxurious 5-star hotel with top-grade rooms, good restaurants, excellent sports and other facilities, and both indoor and outdoor swimming pools. With 304 rooms, it is also convenient for the beach at Coral Bay. $$$

Droushia Heights
Drouseia village, 22 miles (37 km) north of Pafos.
Tel: (06) 332351.
A different kind of Cyprus experience is on offer at this inland hotel, set within great walking country between Pafos and Polis. It benefits from 46 rooms and an outdoor swimming pool. $$

Kings
Leoforos Tafon ton Vasileion, Kato Pafos.
Tel: (06) 233497.
Popular with British travellers who don't want to stay at one of Pafos's big resort hotels. It has 27 rooms and a location convenient for the Tombs of the Kings archaeological site.

Park Mansions
16 Odos Pavlou Melas, Ktima (Nea Pafos).
Tel: (06) 245645.
One of Cyprus's accommodation gems, this is an old Venetian-style mansion now converted into a characterful hotel with 25 rooms. It also has a swimming pool.

Souli
Latsi–Neon Chorion Road, Pafos. Tel: (06) 321088.

This hotel overlooks the sea in a beautiful position within striking distance of the Akamas Peninsula. It has 19 comfortable rooms and a fine seafood restaurant. $

Troodos Mountains
Churchill Pinewood Valley
Outside Pedoulas on the Prodromos–Pedoulas road.
Tel: (02) 952211.
A rustic location among the mountain forests is enhanced by excellent service, good sports facilities and an outdoor swimming pool in this 49-room hotel. $$

Edelweiss
Pano Platres.
Tel: (05) 421335.
As its name implies, this hotel looks like a typical Austrian Alpine hotel, set down in the Troodos. With 22 rooms it stands on the main street in Platres. $

Forest Park
Pano Platres.
Tel: (05) 421751.
Set amid the forests outside Platres, this 137-bed hotel is considered to be the best in the mountains. It also has a heated outdoor swimming pool. $$$

Mountain Rose
Pedoulas.
Tel: (02) 952727.
A jovial and informal place with a popular restaurant, it has 20 rooms and is situated on the hilly main street in Pedoulas. $

Stavros tis Psokas Rest House
Stavros tis Psokas Forest Station, Pafos Forest, 6 miles (10 km) northwest of Panagia tou Kykkou Monastery.
Tel: (06) 722338.
This forest station is in a uniquely inaccessible spot and has just 7 rooms and a few chalets. Its location in the Pafos Forest near Cedar Valley is as rugged as Cyprus gets. Inevitably, it is very popular, and reservations must be made in advance. $

Youth Hostels
Access to youth hostels depends on possession of an International Youth Hostel Card. Currently the price for an overnight stay is between CY£3 and CY£5 per person. Reservations are recommended. For general information on hostels in Cyprus, contact the **Cyprus Youth Hostels Association** (PO Box 1328, 1506 Nicosia, Cyprus, tel: (02) 442027.

Youth Hostel Addresses
Agia Napa, 23 Odos Dionysiou Solomou, tel: (02) 442027 or (03) 723113.
Larnaka: 27 Odos Nikolaou Rossou, tel: (04) 621188.
Nicosia: 5 Odos Hadjidaki, tel: (02) 444808.
Pafos: 37 Leoforos Eleftheriou Venizelou, tel: (06) 232588.
Troodos: in a pine forest near Troodos, on the Troodos–Kakopetria road, tel: (05) 422400. Open Apr–Oct.

Camping
At present, there are seven licensed camp sites in the south of Cyprus. Rates are the same at all of them: currently CY£1–1.25 per person each day with an additional charge of CY£1–1.50 per caravan or tent.
Each camping area has its own sanitary facilities and a grocery shop or restaurant. With the exception of the camp site located in the Troodos Mountains, all sites are situated along the coast.

Agia Napa Camping
West of the town. Open: Apr–Oct, tel: (03) 721946.

Feggari Camping
Near Coral Bay, 7 miles (11 km) northwest of Pafos. Open: all year round, tel: (06) 621534.

Forest Beach
About 13 miles (8 km) east of Larnaka. Open: June–Oct, tel: (04) 644514.

Governor's Beach Camping
About 12 miles (20 km) east of Limassol. Open: all year round, tel: (05) 632300 or (05) 632878.

Polis Camping Along the town beach in a small stand of eucalyptus trees. Open: Mar until end-Nov; tent rental possible, tel: (06) 321526.

Troodos Camping About 2 miles (1 km) northeast of the town in the midst of a pine forest. Open: from May until end-Oct, tel: (05) 421624.

Zenon Gardens Camping
At Geroskipou about 3 miles (5 km) east of Pafos. Open: Mar–Oct, tel: (06) 242277.

Although it is illegal to camp anywhere you happen to find a suitable spot, during summer it is common – among tourists and natives alike.

In the northern part of the island there's a camp site near Famagusta. Camping in the wild is permitted.

Marinas

Yachting crews wanting to break their cruise across the Mediterranean Sea can take advantage of the marinas near Larnaka or Limassol. Both are equipped with repair facilities and supplies (petrol, diesel, electricity, drinking water, laundry and sanitary facilities).

Larnaka: Located in the bay of Larnaka (34° 55'N–30° 38'E) with 210 mooring slips, tel: (04) 653110/3; telex: 4500-CYTMAR; fax: (04) 624110.

Limassol: Located east of the city (34° 42'N–33° 11'E); operated by the St Raphael Hotel; 227 mooring slips, tel: (05) 321100; telex: 3229-SHERANT CY; fax: (05) 329208.

Radio Cyprus broadcasts the weather report on channels 15, 24, 26 and 27.

Where to Eat

Eating Out

In southern Cyprus there is a dearth of the kind of simple, traditional tavernas that are common in Greece, which serve memorably tasty local food and make eating out one of the highlights of a holiday. Just as much of Cyprus's tourism "product" is aimed squarely at the mass sector, with little consideration for independent travellers, so much of the food on offer takes a bland "international" approach, usually heaped up with that limp and greasy legacy of the British – the ubiquitous chip. Despite the fact that the markets are overflowing with a wide variety of vegetables, in nearly every restaurant the emphasis is on meat dishes. Vegetarians can opt for a range of vegetable-based side-dishes.

That's the downside, and since the downside represents most of what you will encounter, it is best to be armed and ready for it. The upside is that Cyprus does actually have a tradition of fine cuisine: a mix of Greek, Turkish and Middle Eastern influences. And the island really is that well-worn cliché: a cornucopia of fresh fruit and vegetables, which retain something that European supermarket shoppers may remember with wistful fondness, taste. Finally, there is a growing niche market of real tavernas dishing up the genuine cuisine of Cyprus at levels that range from homely to sophisticated.

Seafood represents a special case. Fish is relatively scarce in the eastern Mediterranean, due to a combination of naturally low populations in these nutrient-poor waters, and overfishing. It tends to be expensive and much of what you see is imported frozen. There are, however, fishing harbours dotted around the coast and the fish the boats catch often go straight onto the table of the nearest seafood restaurants. Watch out, however, for owners who display fresh fish for you to select, then take something from the freezer after you've gone back to your table, keeping the genuine items for their favoured regular customers!

Included in the prices listed on every menu is a 10 per cent service charge. It is customary to leave the waiter a little something extra too. The best place to eat if you're looking for a relatively authentic and inexpensive meal is in one of the aforementioned traditional tavernas, and the best introduction to Cypriot cuisine is the *meze* (see below). Washed down

Meze

You can't stay in Cyprus without sampling the traditional *meze*. Available in both south and north, it's served to two or more people – and worth starving yourself for the rest of the day. *Meze* is a cascade of as many as 30 little dishes (a good bet if you have small children as there's bound to be something they like!) that run the gamut of meat, vegetable, seafood and dessert items on the menu. The dishes come in wave after wave, usually in something like this order: Greek salad, *halloumi*, *loúntza*, *kalamári* rings, *sheftaliá* and *souvlákia* pieces, *afélia*, *stifado* and lamb chops served with olives, *tahíni*, *taramosalata* and *talattouri*.

with local barrel wine, a *meze* at the right time and place is a real delight.

Restaurants in the northern part of the island offer pretty much the same fare and national dishes – with the addition of a few specifically Turkish specialities. However, both the wine produced in the south as well as southern-brewed beers are not available in the north, where you'll have to choose from an assortment of imported Turkish brands.

In line with the predominance of Muslims on the northern part of the island, beef and lamb are eaten rather than pork.

What To Eat

National Specialities

Afélia: pork marinated with coriander.
Bread: an indispensable component of every meal.
Fish: usually deep-fried.
Fruit: apples, pears, little local bananas, grapes, figs, melon, citrus fruits, papaya, peaches, almonds, apricots, avocados, pomegranates and strawberries (usually very early in the year).
Greek salad (Horiátiki salata): salad composed of cabbage, lettuce, celery, cucumber, tomato, pepper, olives, feta cheese and herbs.
Güvec (Turkish): vegetable stew with meat.
Halloúmi: cheese made from either sheep's or cow's milk which tastes especially good when fried; spiced with peppermint (Turkish: *helim*).
Hiroméri: smoked ham.
Húmus: cold chickpea purée.
Keftedes: fried meatballs (Turkish: *köfte*).
Kléftiko: lamb simmered in foil.
Kolokási: root vegetables.
Kolokithákia: courgettes either stuffed or plain, as a side-dish.
Koukiá: broad beans, either as soup or raw in salad.
Koupépia (dolmadakia): stuffed vine leaves (Turkish: *dolma*).
Loúntza: ham, especially when

served in sandwiches and fried with *halloumi*.
Makarónia tou Fournou (pastítsio): macaroni casserole made with ground meat.
Oil: the local olive oil is especially tasty and used liberally – though not excessively – in the preparation of many foods.
Olives: marinated exquisitely with garlic, coriander, lemon and thyme.
Pastourmas: garlic sausage (Turkish: *sucuk*, but with the omission of pork).
Pilaf: coarsely ground wheat grains and vermicelli cooked in chicken broth and served with a selection of different vegetable side-dishes (Turkish: *bulgur*).
Pitta: flat, hollow rounds of bread filled with different *sheftaliá* or *souvláki* and vegetables.
Sheftaliá: grilled sausage made of ground meat.
Soúvla: lamb roasted on a spit, especially popular fare at family picnics.
Souvlakia: grilled meat kebabs (Turkish: *i kebab*).
Stifado: beef or rabbit prepared with lots of onions – reminiscent of goulash.
Tahíni: sesame sauce with lemon and garlic (Turkish: *terator*).
Talattouri: yogurt prepared with cucumber and peppermint, similar to *tzatziki* (Turkish: *cacik*).
Taramosalata: cods roe with

lemon, potato purée, onions and oil.
Trahanas: coarsely ground wheat grains dried with yogurt and added to soups together with *halloumi*.
Vegetables: artichokes, asparagus, various kinds of lettuce, potatoes, mushrooms, aubergine, courgettes and celery.

Desserts

Báklava: puff pastry filled with nuts and soaked in syrup.
Dáktila ("finger"): finger-shaped strudel pastry filled with a nut-cinnamon mixture and soaked in syrup.
Glykó toó koutalioó: fruit or walnuts marinated in syrup and served with a glass of water as a welcome titbit for guests.
Honey: very aromatic. Often served with yogurt and almonds.
Kourabiédes: *see* Wedding Meal; this delicacy also available in shops at Christmas.
Koulourákia: a ring-shaped cookie sprinkled with sesame seeds.
Loukoumádes: deep-fried balls of choux pastry served in syrup.
Loukoúmia: a famous culinary speciality from Geroskipou, near Pafos: cubes of gelatin flavoured with rose water and dusted with powdered sugar.
Paloúses: a kind of pudding made from grape juice and flour; it is the basis for *soutsouko* (see overleaf).

Popular Snacks

Street vendors aren't as prevalent in Cyprus as they are in Greece, so you're more likely to pick up snacks in a café. These are the most popular:

● *Eliópitta* Olive turnover
● *Takhinópitta* Sesame turnover
● *Kolokótes* Pastry triangle stuffed with pumpkin, cracked wheat and raisins
● *Soudzoúko* Almond strings

dipped in molasses
● *Pastelláki* Sesame, peanut and syrup bar
● *Börek* Meat/cheese turnover
● *Airáni (ayran* **in the north)** Refreshing herby yogurt drink with mint or oregano
● *Pide* The north's answer to pizza, usually served with soup (*çorba*). Standard toppings include cheese, egg, mince and sausage, or combinations of these.

Soutsoúko: a long chain of almonds strung together, dunked in *palouses* and then dried (very popular).
Sütlac (Turkish): a pudding made of milk, rice and rose water.

Restaurants

Agia Napa
Esperia
Agia Napa harbour.
Tel: (03) 721635.
Seafood is the natural speciality of this friendly taverna that stands right beside the fishing harbour. $$
Potamos
Harbour, Potamos Creek near Xylofagou, between Agia Napa and Larnaka (no telephone).
A simple family restaurant that makes its mark with tasty, no-frills seafood supplied direct from the fishing boats tied up alongside. $

Coral Bay
Golden Barrel
Coral Bay Road.
Tel: (06) 621790.
Classier than the usual taverna-fare, thanks to a Swiss-trained owner/chef who knows his international sauces but remains proficient at Cypriot dishes as well. $$
Saint George
Agios Georgios (north of Coral Bay).
Tel: (06) 621306.
A deceptively unattractive-looking restaurant that occupies a stunning location on the cliff above Agios Georgios harbour, and serves great seafood fresh off the boats. $$

Foini
Phini Taverna
Foini village.
Tel: (05) 421828.
A delightful village taverna in one of the prettiest mountain villages (although with a slightly stuffy image as an "artist's haven"), serving good traditional food. $

Kathikas
Araouzos
Main street.
Tel: (06) 632076.
This may well be the most authentic village taverna in Cyprus (Kathikas lies midway between Pafos and Polis). A wickerwork covering softens the stone floor, and there's no menu, just whatever the family feels like rustling up that day. $

Kakopetria
Maryland at the Mill
Kakopetria village.
Tel: (02) 922536.
You may get vertigo getting to the dining room of this astonishingly high, wood-built restaurant, and its fresh mountain trout and other dishes occupy a culinary pinnacle. $$

Price Categories

Prices are based on the cost of a meal for one person without drinks.
$ = under CY£8
$$ = CY£8–15
$$$ = CY15 and above

Larnaka
Archontiko
71 Leoforos Athinon.
Tel: (04) 655905.
Cypriot food in a picturesque old building beside the seafront Foinikoudes Promenade. Next door is the associated Archontissa steakhouse. $$
Monte Carlo
28 Odos Piyale Pasha.
Tel: (04) 653815.
In the old Turkish quarter of Larnaka, this is a stylish place with a balcony overlooking the sea. $$

Latsi
Porto Latchi
Main street.
Tel: (06) 321530.
Although it has an outside terrace facing the water, the romantic, cellar-like interior is maybe the best place to eat

the seafood served here. $$
Yiangos and Peter
Fishing Harbor, Latsi.
Tel: (06) 321411.
A legend in its own lunchtime (and dinnertime), Y&P is a breezy place beside the harbour. You're unlikely to eat better seafood in Cyprus, nor have a better dining experience. $$
Ttakkas Bay
Between Latsi and the Baths of Aphrodite.
Tel: (06) 321087.
Eat right on the beach at this excellent seafood restaurant, reached along a signposted side-road. $$

Limassol
Akti Olous
Galatex Beach Centre, Potamos Germasogeias.
Tel: (05) 314404.
With an outside terrace overlooking the sea, this is a great place to eat the house speciality: *meze*, either meat or seafood. There are other dishes as well, such as *stifado*, *kleftiko* and steak. $$
Blue Island
3 Leoforos Amathoundos.
Tel: (05) 321466.
One of Limassol's classiest restaurants, serving French and international cuisine in a formal setting, although there is also a vine-shaded patio for outdoor dining. $$$
Gallo de Oro
232 Odos 28 Oktovriou.
Tel: (05) 343382.
Tourist-orientated, yes, but still a taverna with good food where you are made to feel at home. $
Porta
17 Odos Genethliou Mitela.
Tel: (05) 360339.
Fancy eating in an atmospher-ically renovated donkey stable? Well, this is the place. Designer class and good taste have also been added at this restaurant in the old Turkish quarter. $$
Vassilikos
Odos Agiou Andreas.
Tel: (05) 375972.
A violinist accompanies you at

your meal at this fine Cypriot restaurant, specialising in *meze*. It also has a garden terrace. $$

Nicosia
Aegeon
40 Odos Ektoros.
Tel: (02) 433297.
The Famagusta Gate area has developed a reputation for being smart, stylish and pricy. Aegeon, however, has managed to keep to its simple family-taverna origins. $$

Arhondiko
27 Odos Aristokyprou Laïki Geitonia.
Tel: (02) 450080.
Laïki Geitonia can seem just a little too twee to be true. Yet it's undeniably romantic to eat here surrounded by lanterns and serenaded by Greek music. $$

Armenaki
15 Odos Sans Souci.
Tel: (02) 378383.
As its name implies, this is an Armenian restaurant and, although a simple place at heart, is popular with well-heeled Nicosians. $

Axiothea
14 Odos Axiotheas, Nicosia.
Tel: (02) 430787.
A superbly traditional restaurant jammed up against the barricades of the Green Line. The food is good and authentically Cypriot, and there is convivial seating in the narrow street outside. $

Erenia
64a Leoforos Archiepiskopou Kyprianou, Strovolos.
Tel: (02) 422860.
Strovolos is a little way out of town, but it is worth the trip to eat *meze* here in surroundings of unpretentious charm. $$

Konatzin
10 Odos Delfi.
Tel: (02) 446990.
Serves a great vegetarian *meze* in the fine setting of a converted mansion with a garden. $$

Plaka
Plateia Archiepiskopou Makariou III, Egkomi.
Tel: (02) 446498.
The restaurant occupies the centre of the old village square of now suburban Egkomi,

spreading its terrace among the flowers and bushes. $$

Xefoto
6 Odos Aeschylou, Laïki Geitonia.
Tel: (02) 477840.
Xefoto has three faces: a breezy outside terrace; a stylish café-restaurant on the ground floor; and a more intimate spot upstairs. It serves a well-considered interpretation of Cypriot cuisine. $$

Neon Chorion
Prengos Sea View
Outside Neo Chorion village.
Tel: (06) 321000.
Owned by a local fisherman, which means that seafood is popular here, especially when served on the terrace with a wonderful view of the Akamas Peninsula and the sea. $$

Pafos
Cavallini
Leoforos Poseidonou, Kato Pafos (near the Amathus Hotel).
Tel: (06) 246464.
With a relaxed environment, this

Drinking Notes

Visitors to Cyprus will find plenty of both alcoholic and non-alcoholic drinks to choose from. Coffee is prepared in the traditional Turkish way: boiled in a little pot with sugar added upon request and poured into a cup with the steeped coffee grounds. For those who prefer something a bit less fierce, Nescafé is usually available.

Tapwater is generally safe to drink, although it can be rather brackish in the north. Mineral water is readily available.

An especially delicious treat is a glass of freshly squeezed orange juice, sold by numerous street vendors.

In addition to beer, a number of excellent wines, local brandies and fruit liqueurs are offered. These are not only significantly cheaper than

other, imported spirits, but are often of very high quality. Alcohol is usually drunk only with meals by the locals, so late-night revelries in the steet are likely to be frowned upon.

WINE
In the south Arsinoe, Palomino and White Lady are palatable dry whites. Bellapais, a medium-dry sparkling white, comes in white or rosé. Aphrodite is a cheap medium white. For reds, Othello is a full-bodied, Cabernet Sauvignon type, while Hermes is a heartier dry wine. There are also several versions of Commandaria, a dessert red like Madeira. In villages, your best choice is definitely the cheap local barrel wine, which is often very good.

In the north most wine is

imported from Turkey, so the choice is less extensive. Play safe with Turasan and Peribacasi.

BEER
In the south KEO pilsener is a good all-day beer, though deceptively strong at 4.5 per cent (drink the bottle version as the draught is insipid in comparison). In the north the Turkish brands you're likely to encounter are Efes or the Austrian pilsener Gold Fassl.

SPIRITS
As well as ouzo (or, more likely, raki in the north), locals tend to go in for brandy, the best brand of which is Three Kings. A popular aperitif, both with Cypriots and holidaymakers, is brandy sour: brandy spiked with lime or lemon juice and Angostura bitters.

excellent Italian restaurant offers an upmarket approach and fine cooking. $$$

Demokritos
1 Odos Dionysou, Kato Pafos.
Tel: (06) 233371.
Prides itself on being Kato Pafos's oldest taverna, having opened in 1971. Traditional Greek and Cypriot dance accompanies dinner. $$

Dover
Leoforos Poseidonos, Kato Pafos.
Tel: (06) 248100.
An excellent seafood restaurant with an international approach. $$

Fettas Corner
33 Odos Ioannis Agrotis, Ktima.
Tel: (06) 237822.
A gem virtually untouched by tourists. An unpromising location and unforced atmosphere are the setting for genuinely great Cypriot food. $$

Nostalgia
8 Leoforos Tafon ton Vasileion, Kato Pafos.
Tel: (06) 247464.
A Russian restaurant that caters mostly, though not exclusively, to well-heeled Russian tourists and businessmen. $$$

Nicos Tyrimos
75 Odos Agapinor, Kato Pafos.
Tel: (03) 831386.

Festive Fare

Weddings *Réssi* (wheat with meat), *pastítsio, kleftiko*, cucumber, tomato, chips for each well-wisher and *kourabiedes* (shortcrust pastry filled with almonds).
Easter lamb *Soúvla*, Easter Soup (made of parts from the head of a calf or lamb and vegetables, served with garlic bread), eggs dyed red, and *flaoúnes* (turnover made from a yeast dough and filled with eggs, cheese and raisins).
Christmas *Vassilópitta* (cake made from yeast dough, spread with egg and generously strewn with sesame seeds and almonds).

Pafos's fishermen themselves come to eat at this excellent, family-owned seafood taverna, where airs and graces are left at the door. $$

Pelican
102 Leoforos Apostolou Pavlou (Pafos Harbor).
Tel: (06) 246886.
Probably the best of a line of harbour-front tavernas that are popular because of their atmosphere and location, but where quality is often indifferent. $$

Pedoulas

To Vrysi
Pedoulas Village Centre.
Tel: (02) 952240.
Otherwise known as Harry's Spring Water Restaurant, this unusual looking place is one of the best restaurants in the mountains. $$

Pegeia

Vineyard
Coral Bay Road.
Tel: (06) 621994.
The home-cooked food is of a high standard at this modern taverna set among scented fields outside Pegeia. $

Peyia Tavern
Pegeia village centre.
Tel: (06) 621077.
Grilled meats are the speciality here in this rustic place, accompanied by side dishes and village wine. $

Pissouri Bay

Simposio
Pissouri Beach.
Tel: (05) 221158.
All the restaurants at Pissouri Beach are more expensive than need be, and Simposio is no exception, but the Cyprus *meze* and the setting here are both well worth experiencing. $$

Platres

Kalidonia
Pano Platres.
Tel: (05) 421404.
Cypriot food tastes great on a summer evening when served in this unpretentious place. $

Price Categories

Prices are based on the cost of a meal for one person without drinks.
$ = under CY£8
$$ = CY£8–15
$$$ = CY15 and above

Polis

Finikas
9 Odos Louliou.
Tel: (06) 322373.
This is an attractive garden café-cum-restaurant which offers a range of vegetarian and Italian dishes in addition to standard Cypriot choices. $$

Old Town
Polis-Paphos Road.
Tel: (06) 322758.
Another of Polis's garden café-restaurants, with an extensive menu. There are both meat and vegetarian dishes. $$

Protaras

Spartiatis
Konnos Beach.
Tel: (03) 831386.
Serves seafood fresh from the nearby harbour, as well as a selection of traditional Greek dishes, amid a quiet, romantic atmosphere. $$

Anatolia
Agios Elias.
Tel: (03) 831533.
Despite the Turkish name this taverna specialises in Cypriot *meze*. $$

Troodos

Civic
Troodos village.
Tel: (05) 422102.
A scenically located little place just outside the village and away from the summer crowds. $

Zygi

Apovathra
Seafront, Zygi village.
Tel: (04) 332414.
Stands out for quality in a waterfront village where seafood tavernas are common, but not always good. $$

Attractions

Monasteries

There are 12 Greek Orthodox monasteries still in operation on the island today, all of them in southern Cyprus.

Generally speaking, the monasteries do not maintain specific visiting hours. However, prospective guests should respect the midday pause and plan their visits outside this time. Frequently the monks must unlock the churches, and when this is the case it's customary to leave a small donation for the monastery after you have completed your tour. The most courteous way to do this is not to hand your donation to the monk himself, but to leave it either on the plate left for this purpose at the entrance to the church or near the iconostasis.

Out of respect, visitors should avoid pointing to icons or standing with their backs turned towards them or with their hands clasped behind their back. (For further information regarding appropriate behaviour when visiting a monastery, refer to the section *Photography, page 290*.)

The most important monasteries are:

Agios Georgios Alamanos: 12 miles (20 km) northeast of Limassol, not far from the road to Larnaka, near Governor's Beach.

Agios Irakleidios: in the village of Politiko, about 24 km (15 miles) from Nicosia.

Agios Minas: near Lefkara.

Agios Neofytos: 6 miles (10 km) north of Pafos.

Kykkos: in the Troodos Mountains, northwest of Pedoulas.

Machairas: in the eastern foothills of the Troodos Mountains, about 25 miles (40 km) south of Nicosia.

Panagia Chrysorrogiatissa: 2 miles (3 km) south of Panagía village.

Stavrovouni: west of Larnaka; be warned that women are not permitted to enter.

Trooditissa: 3 miles (5 km) northwest of Platres. Open only to adherents to the Greek Orthodox church.

Churches

As many of the most beautiful Byzantine churches are situated in rather remote areas, only a few can be reached directly by public transport.

To minimise damage to their interior decorations and contents, most of the churches are kept closed; if you want to look around them you must first collect the key. Usually a local in the coffee house in the nearest village will help. After your visit, it is customary to give a small tip to the person responsible for the keys.

Over the past years nine churches of Troodos Mountains have been added to the UNESCO list of the buildings important to the cultural heritage of mankind. For a full list of these, turn to the Byzantine Landmarks feature on pages 240–41. Other important churches are:

Arkhángelos Mikhail In the village of Pedoulas.

Agia Paraskeví In the village of Geroskipou, about 2 miles (3 km) east of Pafos.

Agii Apostóloi In the village of Perachoria, 10 miles (17 km) from Nicosia.

Agioi Varnavas & Hilariou In the village of Peristerona, about 17 miles (27 km) west of Nicosia.

Agios Ioánnis In Nicosia, directly next to the new palace of the archbishop.

Panagia Angelóktisti In the village of Kiti, 7 miles (11 km) west of Larnaka.

There are also numerous Orthodox churches in the northern part of Cyprus that are worth visiting. Unfortunately, though, since the Turkish invasion of 1974 most of them have been vandalised, and priceless icons, frescoes and mosaics have been stolen or destroyed. Today, most of these churches are, with good reason, permanently closed; some have been converted into mosques and others are currently used as sheep-cotes. Churches and monasteries still open for public viewing include:

Arabahmet Mosque in Nicosia.

Barnabas Monastery near Famagusta.

Bellapais Monastery near Keryneia.

Agios Mámas Church near Morphou.

Cyprus's Flora

Of the 130 plants endemic to Cyprus, nearly half grow close to the peak of Mount Olympus. From February to April the Cyprus crocus pops its head through melting snow. By April lowland areas are a sea of wild flowers, from small blue irises, crocuses and tulips to poppies in red, yellow and purple. Roadsides are bright with buttercups, crown daisies, marigolds and huge wild fennel. Metre-high stems of white asphodel signal spring, and in June and July dense dwarf broom carpets the top of Olympus. After a lull in summer, the red of the vines in autumn is a glorious sight. There is a feature devoted to flowers on pages 100–101.

Fun for the Kids

Luna Parks These permanent fun fairs can be found in all major towns in the south. Most are open all year round until 8pm weekdays and later at the weekend. Admission is free, but rides can add up! For the best head for Tivoli Luna Park, Elia Papakyriakou 10, Egkomi.

For the more daring, Skycoasters at Agia Napa, just by the Luna Park, features some heart-stopping rides; and there's a go-karting track at Nicosia Luna Park.

Waterworld Agia Napa Water chutes galore, log rolling, river trips and geysers are just some of the delights of Waterworld. 3 miles (5 km) from Agia Napa along the Agia Thekla Road. Open daily 10am–7pm.

Agia Napa Marine Park Dolphin and seal displays, plus a miniature railway. Beach Road. Open mid-Feb until Oct.

Limassol Zoo Municipal Gardens, 28 Odos Aktovriou. Open daily 9am–1pm, 2.30–6.30pm.

Glass-bottomed boats A great way to see marine life at Agia Napa and Pafos harbours. Daily throughout the summer.

Ostrich Farm Park Said to be Europe's largest ostrich farm (with exhibition and playground), where children can have their photograph taken on an ostrich egg! Agios Giannis Malountas, about 25 minutes from Nicosia. Open Wed 3–8pm, Sat and Sun 10am–8pm.

Culture

Music, Theatre and Dance

The main location for cultural events such as art exhibitions, classical music concerts, ballet, opera and theatre is Nicosia (the one city with the venues to put on such shows regularly). Limassol, Larnaka and Pafos have their own cultural programmes and venues, with less-frequent events sprinkled through the tourist season.

For listings, the Cyprus Tourist Organisation publishes a *Diary of Events* for the year, plus a *Monthly Events* guide.

Venues

Larnaka
• Municipal Theatre, tel: (04) 665794.
• Larnaka Fort, tel: (04) 654322. Occasionally hosts concerts and theatre.
Limassol
• Municipal Theatre, tel: (05) 348783.

Youth Card

Available to anyone aged 13 to 26, the Youth Card costs the equivalent of £6 for a year and is valid in 29 countries. It entitles you to reduced prices on theatre and cinema tickets, air and taxi fares, books, clothes and sports goods. It is available from youth agencies such as Student Travel Centre, 24 Rupert Street, London W1V 7FN, tel: 0171-434 1306 or the Cyprus Youth Board, 41 Odos Themisokli, Nicosia, tel: (02) 304160-5.

• Limassol Castle, tel: (05) 330419. Occasionally hosts concerts and theatre.
• Kourion Odeon, tel: (05) 362756. A great place to see classical Greek plays, as well as Shakespeare, performed.**Nicosia**
• Municipal Theatre, Odos Mousieou, tel: (02) 781105. Classical music, dance and opera, as well as classic and modern plays in both Greek and English are performed here.
• Famagusta Gate Cultural Centre. Pyli Ammochostou, tel: (02) 430877. Art exhibitions and experimental theatre.
• British High Commission, Mousieou Street, tel: (02) 861100. Chamber music and other events are occasionally featured.
Pafos
• Municipal Theatre, tel: (06) 232571.
• Ancient Odeon, Harbour Archaeological Area, tel: (06) 232841. Classical Greek plays, as well as Shakespeare and modern opera, are occasionally performed here.
• Pafos Fort, Harbour, tel: (06) 232841. Occasionally hosts concerts and theatre.

Folk Festivals

An important part of Cyprus's cultural life is covered by festivals, some of which are island-wide and some local.

January
Epiphany: on 6 January, coastal towns hold a traditional procession, known as the Blessing of the Sea. The local bishop throws a crucifix into the water, and youngsters dive in after it.
February/March
Carnival: Monday 50 days before Orthodox Easter is "Clean Monday", the start of Lent. Carnivals are held in many towns and villages the week beforehand. The biggest and most colourful is in Limassol, where the

Carnival King's arrival is the signal for masquerades and feasting, culminating in a float procession on the final Sunday.

March/April

Orthodox Easter: this is the biggest Orthodox festival of the year, well worth witnessing. Following morning mass on Holy Thursday, it is traditional for housewives to paint eggs red. In the evening icons in the church are draped in black.

On Good Friday the sepulchre is decorated with flowers, and a procession of flower-bedecked images of Christ is carried through the streets during mass at 9pm. Parishes compete for the best-decorated sepulchre and most beautiful procession. In the village of Kathikas in Pafos, the priest walks the streets laden with a cross.

On Easter Saturday the black drapes come off the icons and the congregation rap their seats to express their joy and chase the demon of Hades away. Housewives bake Easter breads, pastries and *flaoúnes* (cheese pies). At midnight,

dressed in their Easter best, they gather for mass. Then bonfires are lit, and effigies of Judas are thrown onto them. Everyone goes home by candlelight to eat the Easter feast of traditional *avgolemono* soup (egg and lemon rice), and to crack the red eggs.

On Easter Sunday and Monday it is customary to roast lamb outdoors on the spit or in big clay ovens, and celebrations may continue all day long with games at the church yard or village square. Villages that retain these traditions include: Paralimni, Agia Napa, Deryneia (Ammochostos district), Akaki, Geri and Tseri (Nicosia area), Aradippou and Pervolia (Limassol), Neon Chorion, Geroskipou, Pegeia and Pafos.

May

Anthestiria: flower festivals are held in Pafos, Limassol and several other towns, celebrating spring's return with parades and re-enactments of the ancient Greek myths.

June

Feast of Saint Paul: on the 28th

and 29th, the Bishop leads a procession through Pafos, carrying an icon of Saint Paul.

July

Kataklysmos (Festival of the Flood): Noah's Ark and the Great Flood are recalled, especially in Larnaka and Limassol, with three days of fairs and water-throwing contests.

August

The month of the village festival, when relatives and friends get together for a drink, a dance and a song – this is a chance to get a flavour of true Cypriot life. Festivities can include folk music and dance, exhibitions of agricultural products, flowers, folk art, photography, painting, silverware and (particularly in Lefkara and Omodos) embroidery.

September

Limassol Wine Festival: the city's Municipal Gardens are filled with throngs of people drinking free wine from stalls set up by the island's many wineries. There are also folk dancing, fairground stalls, amusements and food.

Arts Festivals in Cyprus

Nicosia International Arts Festival

A two-week programme of art exhibitions, theatre, music and dance. It takes place in June at various venues in the city, particularly the Famagusta Gate Cultural Centre.

Limassol International Arts Festival

For 10 days in June and July the city's Municipal Gardens are the venue for a programme of music, song and dance by both international and local artists.

Curium Drama Festival

Throughout July and August the 2,000-year-old Theatre at Kourion stages classical and modern theatre, including Shakespeare. There is also classical and modern music,

ballet performances, and a sound-and-light show.

Musical Sundays

During March, April and May, in the morning or late-afternoon, performances of folk music, dance and classical and jazz music can be seen in Larnaka (opposite the Municipal Hall), Limassol (Municipal Gardens) and Pafos (Castle Square or Central Kiosk).

Ancient Greek Drama Festival

There's nothing quite like the spectacle and atmosphere of watching a Greek play by candlelight on a balmy summer evening in an open-air ancient theatre. A festival of popular works is staged from June to August in some of the old theatres, such as the Kourion and Pafos Ancient Odeion.

Though they are performed in the original ancient Greek, they're surprisingly easy to follow (and a précis of the plot is provided in English if you're struggling!). For exact dates and venues, see the *Monthly Events* guide available from tourist offices.

Pafos Festival

A full programme of theatre, music and dance takes place from June to September at the ancient Odeion and in the Pafos castle area.

Larnaka Festival

A month of dance, theatre and music performed by both local and international artists in the courtyard of the Larnaka Medieval Fort and Patticheion Municipal Amphitheatre takes place during July.

Shopping

Souvenirs

Typical souvenirs from Cyprus, aside from the local wine, spirits and *halloumi* cheese, include various Cypriot handicrafts such as lace, leather goods, pottery, glassware, woodcarvings and embroidery.

Many towns are known for a specific product, for example ceramics from Kornos, Koloni, Lemba and Foini; high-quality embroidered lace from Lefkara and Omodos; hand-blown glassware from Omodos; silver jewellery from Lefkara; basketry from Liopetri, Sotira and Geroskipou; woven wares and tapestry from Fyti; silk products and Cyprus (Turkish) Delight (*Loukoúmia*) from Geroskipou. Good-quality gold jewellery and leather goods can be very reasonably priced.

Two handicrafts that travelled with the Greek Cypriot refugees in their flight from the north to south after 1974 and are now produced in the south are lefkonika woven cloth (from Lefka) and the pottery cats of Lapithos.

In addition to the numerous privately operated souvenir shops, the national **Cyprus Handicraft Service** maintains branches in the old parts of Nicosia, Limassol, Larnaka and Pafos. At its workshop in Nicosia visitors can watch various craft items of a notably high quality being made. The shops open between 7.30am–2.30pm Mon–Fri, Thur 3–6pm, except June and August. The CHS has several branches that offer craftwork at fixed prices:

Nicosia
186 Leoforos Athalassis (workshop and shop), tel: (02) 305024; Laïki Geitonia, tel: (02) 303065.
Larnaka
Odos Kosma Lysioti, tel: (04) 630327.
Limassol
25 Odos Themidos, tel: (05) 330118.
Pafos
64 Leoforos Apostolou Pavlou, tel: (06) 240243.
August is a good time to pick up handicrafts in Pafos, when the Pafos Folkloric organises exhibitions of local specialities, some of which are for sale.

Monasteries and abbeys

These are also sources of souvenirs. Icons range from simple little pieces to superb works, often made with gold-leaf imbued paint, made by Father Kallinikos at Stavrovouni Monastery. Nuns at some of the convents produce and sell excellent honey.

Food

Cyprus does not go in for the huge supermarkets of central Europe, but there are many corner stores and small super-markets in main towns. Food is usually labelled in English as well as Greek.

Each town also has a central market hall, an excellent source of meat, fruit and vegetables. Once a week (for example, on Saturday in Pafos) there will also be a lively adjacent street market. Though northern shops and markets are less opulent than in the south, there are good market halls at Keryneia and north Nicosia.

Fruit is plentiful and delicious in Cyprus (in the south all of it is home grown), with many (such as strawberries and melons) appearing long before they do in central Europe.

Outdoor Activities

Bird watching

There are around 100 bird species on the island and many more on the migratory path from Europe to Africa. One of the highlights of the year is the arrival of 10,000 flamingoes, which winter on the salt lakes. Details are available from the **Cyprus Ornithological Society**, 4 Odos Kanaris, Nicosia, tel: (02) 420703.

Cycling

Given the mountainous terrain of the hinterland, a cycling holiday in Cyprus will probably only appeal to the dedicated cyclist. But for those who do not enjoy struggling up steep inclines, opportunities abound for exploring the countryside away from the main roads. In the Troodos Mountains, in particular, there are earth and sand tracks through remote, wooded areas offering shade – but do not set off without plenty of drinking water.

Cycle hire facilities exist in most tourist resorts, but more ambitious cyclists would do better to bring their own bike.

You need a good level of fitness and cycling skill before trying mountain biking seriously, but in the Troodos Mountains and Arkamas Peninsula you'll get all the action you can handle. Mountain bikes can be hired in Platres, Pafos, Polis and other resort towns.

Various non-racing activities and events, which welcome participants, are organised by the **Cyprus Cycling Federation**, PO Box 4572, 1301 Nicosia, tel: (02) 456344, fax: (02) 360150; and **Limassol Cycling Club**, tel: (05) 363787.

Fishing

Most coastal resorts have fishing boats from which you can try your hand at catching sea fish. It is also possible to go angling in some of the inland reservoirs, which stock 17 species (including trout, bass and carp). You'll need a licence from the Fisheries Department (or one of its district offices in Larnaka, Limassol and Pafos). The department sells a booklet with details of all fish found in the reservoirs: **Fisheries Department** 13 Aiolou Street, Nicosia, tel: (02) 303526, fax: (02) 365955

Golf

There are two golf courses in the Pafos area, both of them 18-hole and par 72:
• Secret Valley Golf Club, tel: (06) 642774.
• Tsada Golf Club, tel: (06) 642774.
The Elias Country Club, near Limassol, also has a golf course, as well as offering horse riding, archery and bowling.
• Elias Country Club, Pareklisia, tel: (05) 535000, fax: (05) 3200880.

Hiking

The Cypriot authorities produce two leaflets on walks and nature paths on the Akamas Peninsula and in the Troodos Mountains. As well as outlining the itinerary, they also contain information on flora to be found en route. A map of walking routes in both regions is given on the inside back cover of this book.

Akamas Peninsula
Situated in the westernmost part of Cyprus, this peninsula,

Spectator Sports

● **Cyprus Motor Rally**
This exciting annual spectacle takes place in September, following a gruelling course through much of the central and western areas of the island, including the mountains. Results count towards the European Championships. Details from The Cyprus Automobile Association, tel: (02) 313233.
● **Cycling**
The main cycling organisation holds international road racing and mountain bike contests in spring and autumn.
Cyprus Cycling Federation, tel: (02) 456344.

named after Akamas, the son of the Greek hero Theseus, offers wonderful opportunities for hiking (as well as swimming). There are two fairly well-trodden nature trails – the Aphrodite and Adonis trails – but the region is never crowded with visitors. For further information about hiking in the Akamas Peninsula, turn to the special feature on pages 218–19.

Troodos Mountains
In summer, these mountains offer active visitors many inviting hiking opportunities. Even during August, daytime temperatures do not rise above 27°C (80°F). It is possible to set off along either an undeveloped path or on one of the official trails that have been marked by the Cyprus Tourism Organisation (CTO), among which four are classified as nature trails. The point of departure for any hike is Troodos itself, where you'll find hotels, a youth hostel, restaurants and souvenir shops.
The trail named Persephone runs for about 2 miles (3 km) southeast to a scenic viewpoint; the Atalante trail runs about 6 miles (10 km) northwest, making its way past Mount

● **Football** CTO carry details of fixtures.
● **Horse racing**
Nicosia's race course holds regular meetings. Nicosia Race Club, tel: (02) 379566.
● **Kite flying at Pafos**
Every year the Pafos Municipality organises a kite flying competition in the first or second week in March. This colourful event takes place in the castle area near the harbour. Details from the Municipality, tel: (06) 232014.
● **Tennis** Nicosia hosts an international Davis Cup tournament in May.

Olympus and finally ending at an abandoned chromium mine last used in 1974. If you follow the asphalt road at the mine for about 2 miles (3 km), you'll eventually find yourself back in Troodos.
To reach the Kaledonia trail beside the Kryos Potamos (Cold River), hikers must first gain the road that leads to the summer palace of the president, located to the southwest of Troodos. From here the path follows the Cold River for about 1 mile (1½ km) downhill to the picturesque Kaledonia Waterfalls. At the Psilodendro fish restaurant, about a 45-minute walk south of the falls, you can treat yourself to fresh trout. And if you're too tired to walk the trail back to Troodos, use the restaurant's telephone to order a taxi.
Another walk, the Artemis, leads through the forest around Mount Olympus and runs for about 3 miles (5 km). It starts and finishes a short distance from the Prodromos–Mount Olympus road junction.
It is not possible to climb to the top of the mountain – at 1,951 metres (6,505 ft) the highest point on the island – as the British operate an air

surveillance radar station here.

Those planning an extended hike in the Troodos region and planning on staying overnight should bear in mind that in August, the peak holiday season for Cypriots, all accommodation is generally booked solid.

Horse Riding

There are a number of riding centres with trained instructors that offer lessons for both beginners and advanced riders. These include:
Amathus School of Riding, Pareklisia, tel: (05) 320339.
Elias Horse Riding Centre, Pareklisia, tel: (05) 325000 ext 317.
George's Ranch, near Agios Georgios, Pegeia, tel: (06) 621790.
Lapatsa Sports Centre, Nicosia, tel: (02) 621201/2/3.
Or contact the central horse riding body:
Cyprus Equestrian Federation PO Box 4860, Nicosia, tel: (02) 472515 or 349858.

Skiing

Snow falls heavily in the Troodos Mountains during winter: it is not for nothing that the nickname of Mount Olympus is *khionistra* – "chillblain".

There are three ski lifts and four runs at Mount Olympus. You can rent all the ski gear you need at the Cyprus Ski Club Hut, and also in the village of Troodos itself. For further details contact the **Cyprus Ski Club** Nicosia, tel: (02) 365340.

Watersports

Throughout the summer watersports enthusiasts will have no difficulty renting the necessary equipment (surf-boards, water-skis, pedal boats, dinghies, yachts, motor boats and so on) at any of Cyprus's more popular beaches.

Sports Information

For details of indoor and out-door sporting facilities in southern Cyprus, the Cyprus Tourism Organisation publishes a six-page leaflet.

Diving

All of the bigger resorts have diving schools with trained professional (PADI) instructors. More experienced divers can do their own thing but must have a permit. Using underwater spearguns is not permitted, nor is collecting sponges or archaeological artefacts. For more information, contact:
The Cyprus Federation of Underwater Activities PO Box 1503, 1510 Nicosia, tel: (02) 454647.

Sailing

With Cyprus's temperate climate, sailing is pleasant right into winter. Several companies offer chartered yachts for licensed sailors or skippered boats for non-sailors:
Interyachting PO Box 4292, Limassol, tel: (05) 7255533, fax: (05) 720021.
Navimed Nicosia, tel: (02) 338950, fax: (02) 338951.
The Old Salt Yachting Co PO Box 7048, Limassol, tel: (05) 337624, fax: (05) 337768.
Sail Fascination Shipping 27 Nikiforou Foka, PO Box 257, Limassol, tel: (05) 364200/ (09) 555799, fax: (05) 352657.

Swimming

There are numerous inviting beaches on Cyprus, some more frequented than others. During summer the beaches on the southern coast are busiest. Agia Napa, Protaras and Paralimni, as well as the those close to Larnaka, Pafos and Limassol, are especially crowded. The majority of tourist hotels are also concentrated in this area.

There are a number of beautiful beaches which are less developed in the area around Polis. The tavernas and pubs thereabouts are conse-quently more authentic than those at other, more developed spots and tend to offer more traditional, native cuisine (although Polis is catching up fast on the development front).

The sandy beach of Coral Bay extends from the northwest of Pafos; adjacent to this is a cliff-lined, wildly romantic stretch of shoreline called Cape Drepanon, near Agios Georgios. If you're looking for relatively untouched, rarely frequented beaches try the Chrysochou Bay between Cape Arnaoutis (at the western tip of the island) and Polis (at the centre of the bay shore).

Although nude bathing is strictly prohibited, going topless – both on the beaches and at hotel swimming pools – is tolerated. You can contrive to do nude sunbathing and swimming if you are prepared to hike into the Akamas Peninsula to get away from the maddening crowds at the pocket-handkerchief-sized beaches in this area, or if you can afford to hire a speedboat at nearby Latsi to get you there in style.

In terms of natural beauty, the beaches in the northern part of the island beat those in the south. There are splendid bays and sandy beaches around Keryneia and in the east, in close proximity to Salamis. Many of the best spots have been commandeered by hotels and provided with sanitary facilities such as showers and toilets. They charge admission onto the beach for people who are not hotel guests.

Another inside tip for those in search of unspoilt beaches is the Karpasia Peninsula, jutting out to the northeast, which is graced by many inviting coves and beaches (even if many of them have become "nesting grounds" for dumped black plastic rubbish bags and their odoriferous contents).

Language

Language Tips

In the southern part of the island the official language is Greek, although visitors should have no trouble communicating in English due to the fact that until 1960 Cyprus was a British colony and the British still maintain military bases on the island. German and French are spoken by some people in the tourist industry.

In northern Cyprus Turkish is the official language. Turkish Cypriots who have been living in the country since before 1974 can, for the most part, understand both Greek and English, while young people learn English at school. German is also spoken by some people in the tourist industry.

One of the blessings of Cyprus is you need never speak a word of anything but English. But a frustration is that if you do venture to ask for something in Greek or Turkish you're more than likely to be answered in English. English is the language of sophistication in both sectors of the island, and the route to career advancement.

If you know some Greek already, beware – Cypriot Greek can be a far cry from what is spoken on the mainland. In fact, until recently Cypriots could only hold virtually incomprehensible conversations with a man from Athens. About 15 per cent of vocabulary is unique to Cyprus, and the distinctive Cypriot accent may make it incomprehensible to anyone who has learned Greek elsewhere.

Places and Facilities

English/Greek/(Turkish)
bank/*i trápeza/(banka)*
envelope/*to fákelo/(mektup zarfi)*
letter/*to ghramma/(mektup)*
letter box/*to ghramma-tokivótio/ (posta kutusu)*
money/change/*ta leftá/ta chrímata/ta psìlá/(para/bozuk para)*
petrol station/*to pratírio venzínis/(petrol ofisi/benzin istasyonu)*
police/*i astinomía/(polis)*
post office/*to tachidhromío/ (postane)*
postcard/*i kárta/(kartpostal)*
stamps/*ta ghrammatósima/ (posta pulu)*
telephone/*to tiléfono/(telefon)*

Useful Words/Phrases

English/Greek/(Turkish)
Bon appetit/*kalí órexi /(afiyet olsun)*
Cheers!/*(stín) yá mas!/(serefe!)*
excuse me or sorry/*signómi/ (affedersiniz)*
Good evening/*kalí spéra* (from midday)/*(iyi aksamlar)*
Good morning/*kalí méra* (up to midday)/*(gün aydin)*
Good night/*kalí nihta/(iyi geceler)*
Goodbye/*adío* or *yía sas/(allaha-ismarladik)*
Hello/*kalí méra/(merhaba)*
How are you?/*ti kánete?/ (nasilsiniz?)*
...Very well/*kalá/(iyiyim)*
How much is...?/*póso káni?/(kaç para?)*
How?/*pos?/(nasil)*
I don't understand/*dhen katalavéno/(anlamiyorum)*

Pronunciation Tips

● In the south
ai = e as in egg
oi/ei/y = i as in India
ou = ou as in tour
● In the north
s = sh
ç = ch
g = y

I'd like.../*thélo/(istiyorum)*
I'd like to pay now/*thélo na pliróso/(ödemek istiyorum)*
It's cheap/*íne ftinó/(ucuz)*
It's expensive/*íne akrivó/ (pahali)*
It's good/*íne kaló/(iyi)*
It's nice/*íne oréo/(güzel)*
No/*óchi/(hayir)*
Okay/*endáxi/(tamam)*
Please/*parakaló/(lütfen)*
Thank you/*efharistó/(tesekkür ederim)*
Tomorrow/*ávrio/(yarin)*
We'd like to see some folk dances/*théloume na dhoume laikóus hórous (oyun havasi görmek istiyoruz)*
We'd like to go to a coffee house/*théloume na páme s'éna kafenío (bir kahvehane'ye gitmek istiyoruz)*
What's that?/*ti íne aftó?/(bu ne?)*
What's your name?/*pos se léne?/(adin ne?)*
When?/*póte?/(ne zaman?)*
Where can I find...?/*pou ipárchi edó...?/(burada nerededir...?)*
...Cypriot music?/*...i kypriakí mousikí?/(...kibris'den müzik?)*
Where is a beach?/*pou ipárhi paralía?/(Nerede sahil vardir?)*
Where?/*pou?/(nerede?)*
Who?/*piós?/(kim?)*
Why?/*yatí?/(niçin?)*
Yes/*né/(evet)*
Yesterday/*htes/(dün)*

Food

Fruit
apple/*to mílo/(elma)*
banana/*i banána/(muz)*
broad beans/*ta koukiá/(bakla)*
cherries/*ta kerásia/(kiraz)*
fig/*to síko/(incir)*
fruit/*ta froúta/(meyve)*
grapes/*ta stafilia/(üzüm)*
musk melon/*to pepóni/(kavun)*
orange/*to portokáli/(portakal)*
peach/*to rodhákino/(seftali)*
pear/*to achládhi/(armut)*
plums/*ta dhamáskina/(erik)*
pomegranate/*to ródhi/(nar)*
strawberries/*i fraoules/(çilek)*
watermelon/*to karpoúsi/ (karpuz)*

Vegetables

artichoke/*i anginára/(enginar)*
asparagus/*to asparagos/
(kuskonmaz)*
aubergine/*i melintsána/
(patlican)*
cabbage/*to rambi/(lahana)*
carrots/*to karóto/(havuç)*
celery/*to sélino/(kereviz)*
courgettes/*to kolokitháki/
(kabak)*
cucumber/*to angoúri/(salatalik)*
garlic/*o skórdhos/(sarmisak)*
green beans/*ta fasolákia/(taze
fasulye)*
green/red pepper/*to pipéri/
(biber)*
navy beans/*ta fasólia/(kuru
fasulye)*
olives/*i eliés/(zeytin)*
onion/*to kremídhi/(sogan)*
peas/*ta bizélia/(bezelye)*
potatoes/*i patátes/(patates)*
Romaine lettuce/*to maroúli/
(marul salatasi)*
spinach/*to spanáki/(ispanak)*
tomato/*i tomáta/(domates)*
vegetables/*ta hórta or ta
lachaniká/(sebze)*

Miscellaneous

bread/*to psomí/(ekmek)*
butter/*to voútiro/(tereyagi)*
cheese or sheep's cheese/*to
tyrí or i féta/(peynir or beyaz
peynir)*
chicken/*to kotópoulo/(pilic)*
egg/*ta avghá/(yumurta)*
fish/*to psári/(balik)*
honey/*to méli/(bal)*
hors d'oeuvre/*to orektikó/
(çerez)*
ice-cream/*to pagotó/
(dondurma)*
meat/*to kréas/(et)*
oil/*to ládhi/(yag)*
pasta/noodles/*ta makarónia/
(sehriye)*
pepper/*to pipéri/(biber)*
rice/*to rízi/(pilav)*
ripe/*órimos/(olgun)*
salad/*i saláta/(salata)*
salt/*to aláti/(tuz)*
soup/*i soúpa/(çorba)*
vinegar/*to xídhi/(sirke)*

Drinks

aniseed brandy/*i ouzó/(raki)*
beer/*i bíra/(bira)*
bottle/*i boukála/(sise)*
brandy/*to brandy/(keskin içki)*
cup/*to flintsáni/(fincan)*
glass/*to potíri/(bardak)*
juice/*o chimós/(meyva suyu)*
lemon/*to lemóni/(limon)*
milk/*to ghála/(süt)*
mineral water/*i sódha/(maden
suyu/soda)*
nescafé/*to nescafé/(nescafé)*
orangeade/*i portokaládha/
(limonata)*
refreshments/*to anapsiktikó/
(alkolsüz icki)*
sugar/*i zachari/(seker)*
without sugar/*skétos/(seker
siz)*
sweet/*glikís/(çok sekerli)*
tea/*to tsai/(çay)*
Turkish/Greek coffee/*o
ellinikós kafés/(kahve)*
water/*to neró/(su)*
wine/*to krasí /(sarap)*

Architectural Words

fresco/*i tiçoghrafía/(fresk)*
church/*i eklisía/(kilise)*
mosaic/*to psifídhoto/(mozaik)*
mosque/*to tzamí/(cami)*
temple/*o naós/(tapinak)*

Directions

right/*dhexiá/(sag)*
left/*aristerá/(sol)*
straight on/*ísia/(dogru)*
go back/*píso/(geri)*
Where does this road go?/*Pou
pái aftós o dhromos?/(Nereye
bu yol gidiyor?)*
**From where/when does the bus
go?**/*Apó pou/póte févghi to
leoforío?/(Otobüs nerede/ne
zaman gidiyor?)*
**How much is a ticket/the
entrance fee?**/*Pósa íne to
isitírio/i ísodhos?/(Bilet/giris
kaçedir?)*
**When does the archaeological
museum open?/where
is...?**/*Póte íne anihtó to
archeologhikó mousío?/Pou
ine...?/(Arkeoloji müzesi ne
zaman açik? ...nerede?)*

Numbers

1/*éna/(bir)*
2/*dhío/(iki)*
3/*tría/(üç)*
4/*téssera/(dört)*
5/*pénte/(bes)*
6/*éxi/(alti)*
7/*eftá/(yedi)*
8/*ochtó/(sekiz)*
9/*enniá/(dokuz)*
10/*dhéka/(on)*
100/*ekató/(yüz)*
1000/*chília/(bin)*

Driving Terms

petrol/*ì venzíni/(benzin)*
oil/*to ládhi/(yag)*
tyres/*to lástiho/(lastik)*
insurance/*ì asfália/(sigorta)*
Can you repair it, please?/*sas
parakaló na dhiorthósete
aftó?/(lütfen bunu tamir edin?)*
**I'd like to rent a
car/motorbike/ bicycle**/*thélo
na nikiáso éna aftokínito/mía
motosiklétta/éna podhílato/(bir
otomobil/ motosiklet/bisiklet
kiralamak istiyorum)*

General Terms

ashtray/*to tasáki/(kül tablasi)*
matches/*ta spírta/(kibrit)*
cigarettes/*ta tsigára/(sigara)*
battery/*i bataría/(pil)*
film/*to film/(filim)*
spoon/*to koutáli/(kasik)*
fork/*to piroúni/(çatal)*
knife/*to mahéri/(biçak)*
teaspoon/*to koutaláki/(çay
kasik)*
plate/*to piáto/(tabak)*
soap/*to sapoúni/(sabun)*
newspaper/*i efimerídha/
(gazete).*

Further Reading

Good Companions

Journey Into Cyprus by Colin Thubron, who trekked 600 miles through Cyprus in 1972. He said, in retrospect, "The nervous cohabitation which I witnessed in 1972 was, I now realise, the island's halcyon time – and this is the record of a country which will not return."

British Cyprus by W Hepworth Dixon. A classic travelogue first published in 1887.

Bitter Lemons by Lawrence Durrell. What Durrell called "a somewhat impressionistic study of the moods and atmosphere of Cyprus during the troubled years 1953–6." Durrell went to live in the village of Belapais to write about the island and thus complete his trilogy of Greek island books.

Cyprus by Christopher Hitchens. A political work examining the Greek/Turkish struggle on Cyprus, blaming it on policies of the British, Greek, American and Turkish governments.

Cyprus: Images of a Lifetime by Reno Wideson. 1992. In this large-format book, the author/ photographer uses several decades of his sensitively shot pictures to take a nostalgic look back at the Cyprus that has vanished. His colour photography captures a more innocent time before overdevelopment and bitter division.

Exerpta Cypria by Claude Delaval. First published in 1908, this is a fascinating series of excerpts from writers who have turned their pens – or styluses – on Cyprus from AD 23 to 1849.

The Aphrodite Plot by Michael Jansen. A factually parallel novel based around the events of 1974, and the Greek-inspired coup against President Makarios that led directly to the Turkish invasion. The author was an American correspondent who covered the crisis. Did the Americans and British give the nod to the invasion? Was the CIA behind it all?

Other Insight Guides

Other Insight Guides that cover destinations in this region include *Greece*, *Athens*, *Greek Islands*, *Crete*, *Turkey*, *Istanbul* and the *Turkish Coast*.

Insight Pocket Guide: Aegean Islands highlights the author's recommendations to help short-stay visitors make the best use of their time. It also contains a fold-out map. Other titles include *Rhodes*, *Athens*, *Crete*, *Istanbul* and *Turkish Coast*.

Insight Compact Guide: Cyprus is one of a series of nearly 100 portable, fact-packed guides intended for use on the spot. Other titles include *Greece*, *Rhodes*, *Crete*, *Turkey*, and *Turkish Coast*.

ART & PHOTO CREDITS

Cartographic Editor **Zoë Goodwin**
Production **Stuart A. Everitt**
Design Consultants **Klaus Geisler, Carlotta Junger, Graham Mitchener**
Picture Research **Hilary Genin**

Index

Numbers in italics refer to photographs

The World of Insight Guides

400 books in three complementary series cover every major destination in every continent.

Insight Guides

Alaska
Alsace
Amazon Wildlife
American Southwest
Amsterdam
Argentina
Atlanta
Athens
Australia
Austria
Bahamas
Bali
Baltic States
Bangkok
Barbados
Barcelona
Bay of Naples
Beijing
Belgium
Belize
Berlin
Bermuda
Boston
Brazil
Brittany
Brussels
Budapest
Buenos Aires
Burgundy
Burma (Myanmar)
Cairo
Calcutta
California
Canada
Caribbean
Catalonia
Channel Islands
Chicago
Chile
China
Cologne
Continental Europe
Corsica
Costa Rica
Crete
Crossing America
Cuba
Cyprus
Czech & Slovak Republics
Delhi, Jaipur, Agra
Denmark
Dresden
Dublin
Düsseldorf
East African Wildlife
East Asia
Eastern Europe
Ecuador
Edinburgh
Egypt
Finland
Florence
Florida
France
Frankfurt
French Riviera
Gambia & Senegal
Germany
Glasgow

Gran Canaria
Great Barrier Reef
Great Britain
Greece
Greek Islands
Hamburg
Hawaii
Hong Kong
Hungary
Iceland
India
India's Western Himalaya
Indian Wildlife
Indonesia
Ireland
Israel
Istanbul
Italy
Jamaica
Japan
Java
Jerusalem
Jordan
Kathmandu
Kenya
Korea
Lisbon
Loire Valley
London
Los Angeles
Madeira
Madrid
Malaysia
Mallorca & Ibiza
Malta
Marine Life in the South China Sea
Melbourne
Mexico
Mexico City
Miami
Montreal
Morocco
Moscow
Munich
Namibia
Native America
Nepal
Netherlands
New England
New Orleans
New York City
New York State
New Zealand
Nile
Normandy
Northern California
Northern Spain
Norway
Oman & the UAE
Oxford
Old South
Pacific Northwest
Pakistan
Paris
Peru
Philadelphia
Philippines
Poland
Portugal
Prague

Provence
Puerto Rico
Rajasthan
Rhine
Rio de Janeiro
Rockies
Rome
Russia
St Petersburg
San Francisco
Sardinia
Scotland
Seattle
Sicily
Singapore
South Africa
South America
South Asia
South India
South Tyrol
Southeast Asia
Southeast Asia Wildlife
Southern California
Southern Spain
Spain
Sri Lanka
Sweden
Switzerland
Sydney
Taiwan
Tenerife
Texas
Thailand
Tokyo
Trinidad & Tobago
Tunisia
Turkey
Turkish Coast
Tuscany
Umbria
US National Parks East
US National Parks West
Vancouver
Venezuela
Venice
Vienna
Vietnam
Wales
Washington DC
Waterways of Europe
Wild West
Yemen

Insight Pocket Guides

Aegean Islands★
Algarve★
Alsace
Amsterdam★
Athens★
Atlanta★
Bahamas★
Baja Peninsula★
Bali★
Bali Bird Walks
Bangkok★
Barbados★
Barcelona★
Bavaria★
Beijing★
Berlin★

Bermuda★
Bhutan★
Boston★
British Columbia★
Brittany★
Brussels★
Budapest & Surroundings★
Canton★
Chiang Mai★
Chicago★
Corsica★
Costa Blanca★
Costa Brava★
Costa del Sol/Marbella★
Costa Rica★
Côte d'Azur★
Crete★
Denmark
Fiji★
Florence★
Florida★
Florida Keys★
Gran Canaria★
Hawaii★
Hong Kong★
Hungary
Ibiza★
Ireland★
Ireland's Southwest★
Israel★
Istanbul★
Jakarta★
Jamaica★
Kathmandu Bikes & Hikes★
Kenya
Kuala Lumpur★
Lisbon★
Loire Valley★
London★
Macau★
Madrid★
Malacca
Maldives★
Mallorca★
Malta★
Mexico City★
Miami★
Milan★
Montreal★
Morocco★
Moscow
Munich★
Nepal★
New Delhi
New Orleans★
New York City★
New Zealand★
Northern California★
Oslo/Bergen★
Paris★
Penang★
Phuket★
Prague★
Provence★
Puerto Rico★
Quebec★
Rhodes★
Rome★
Sabah★

St Petersburg★
San Francisco★
Sardinia
Scotland★
Seville★
Seychelles★
Sicily★
Sikkim
Singapore★
Southeast England
Southern California★
Southern Spain★
Sri Lanka★
Sydney★
Tenerife★
Thailand★
Tibet★
Toronto★
Tunisia★
Turkish Coast★
Tuscany★
Venice★
Vienna★
Vietnam★
Yogyakarta
Yucatan Peninsula★

★ = Insight Pocket Guides with Pull out Maps

Insight Compact Guides

Algarve
Amsterdam
Bahamas
Bali
Bangkok
Barbados
Barcelona
Beijing
Belgium
Berlin
Brittany
Brussels
Budapest
Burgundy
Copenhagen
Costa Brava
Costa Rica
Crete
Cyprus
Czech Republic
Denmark
Dominican Republic
Dublin
Egypt
Finland
Florence
Gran Canaria
Greece
Holland
Hong Kong
Ireland
Israel
Italian Lakes
Italian Riviera
Jamaica
Jerusalem
Lisbon
Madeira
Mallorca
Malta

Milan
Moscow
Munich
Normandy
Norway
Paris
Poland
Portugal
Prague
Provence
Rhodes
Rome
Salzburg
St Petersburg
Singapore
Switzerland
Sydney
Tenerife
Thailand
Turkey
Turkish Coast
Tuscany
UK regional titles:
Bath & Surroundings
Cambridge & East Anglia
Cornwall
Cotswolds
Devon & Exmoor
Edinburgh
Lake District
London
New Forest
North York Moors
Northumbria
Oxford
Peak District
Scotland
Scottish Highlands
Shakespeare Country
Snowdonia
South Downs
York
Yorkshire Dales
USA regional titles:
Boston
Cape Cod
Chicago
Florida
Florida Keys
Hawaii: Maui
Hawaii: Oahu
Las Vegas
Los Angeles
Martha's Vineyard & Nantucket
New York
San Francisco
Washington D.C.
Venice
Vienna
West of Ireland